Thomas Aquinas' Trinitarian Theology

Timothy L. Smith

# Thomas Aquinas' Trinitarian Theology

A Study in Theological Method

ଶ◡

The Catholic University of America Press
Washington, D.C.

Copyright © 2003
The Catholic University of America Press
All rights reserved

LIBRARY OF CONGRESS CATALOGING-IN-PUBLICATION DATA

Smith, Timothy L. (Timothy Lee)
    Thomas Aquinas' trinitarian theology : a study in theological method / Timothy L. Smith
      p. cm.
    Includes bibliographical references and index.
    1. Thomas, Aquinas, Saint, 1225?–1274  2. Theology—Methodology.  I. Title.
ISBN 0-8132-1097-6
B765.T54 S62 2002
231'.044'092—dc21
                        2001042483

## For Diana

Why did you smile at me in the old lamplight,
And why and how did you recognize me,
Strange girl with archangelic eyelids,
With laughing, blue, sighing eyelids,
Ivy of summer night on the stony moon;
And why and how, never having known
Either my face, or my mourning, or the misery
Of my days, did you suddenly come upon me
Languid, musical, misty, pale, dear to me,
Who dies in the vast night of your eyelids?
The day weeps for the emptiness of all things.

What words, what ancient melodies
Shiver terribly over me in your unreal presence,
Somber dove of long, languid, beautiful days,
What melodies echo in sleep?
Under what foliage of aged solitude,
In what silence, what music, or in what
Voice of a sick child will I find you again, o beautiful,
O chaste, o melody heard in sleep?
The day weeps for the emptiness of all things.

—O. V de L. Milosz

# Contents

Preface, ix
Acknowledgments, xiii

Introduction     1

1. The Context of the Questions on the Trinity     12
   1.1 The Structure of the *Summa theologiae* / 13
   1.2 The Structure of the *Prima pars* / 21
   1.3 Neoscholastic Readings / 23
   1.4 Thomas' Methodology / 31
   1.5 The Source of Modern Readings: Cajetan / 39
   1.6 Conclusion / 47

2. Order and Theological Method     48
   2.1 Divine Essence and Divine Persons / 48
   2.2 The Development of a Trinitarian Grammar / 61
   2.3 Defining Trinitarian Terms / 91
   2.4 Conclusion / 107

3. Coordinating Essential and Proper Terms     109
   3.1 Defining the Problem / 109
   3.2 Comparing Augustine and Aquinas / 117
   3.3 Thomas' Trinitarian Grammar / 137
   3.4 Conclusion / 158

4. Theological Language: A Question of Context and Character     160
   4.1 The Question of Context / 161
   4.2 The Question of Character / 192
   4.3 Conclusion / 202

5. Naming God: The Heart of the Matter — 204
   5.1 The Thirteenth-Century Context / 207
   5.2 Interpreting Pseudo-Dionysius / 210
   5.3 Thomas' Argument in ST I, q. 13, a. 2 / 224
   5.4 Conclusion / 228
   5.5 Epilogue / 229

Conclusion / 231
Bibliography / 237
Index of Names / 253
Index of Topics / 256

# Preface

How do we talk about God? How can it be that God is one and yet a Trinity? And how can this mystery be discussed without sounding nonsensical? These questions press on the mind of anyone attempting to discuss the mystery of the Trinity. Fundamental questions of knowledge, language, and argumentation are inescapably present at every turn. In fact, the very idea of trying to explain what is avowedly a mystery seems to be an affront to the mystery itself. To be mysterious does not mean to be irrational, secret, or random. "Mysterious" in the theological sense means to be beyond human understanding, human comprehension. That Christ is both God and man is a mystery, yet we can talk about what that means. We talk about the fullness of Christ's humanity and divinity. We affirm without question that he was born of a woman, truly ate, drank, slept, and suffered death on a cross. We confess every day his divinity from eternity and his work of salvation for humankind. The fullness of this truth eludes our comprehension and many questions about it will remain unanswered, but our speech on this matter is not in short supply. Similarly, we confess one God in three Persons. Our confession is undisturbed until we begin to ask what the three are and how they are one. The work of the theologian is not to dissolve such mysteries but to find more meaningful ways of understanding them and to show the coherence among the truths of the Christian faith. For example, Paul calls Christ the "power and wisdom of God." Surely the Father is not powerless or ignorant. Christ himself says that he and the Father "are one." Is the wisdom of God known only in Christ or especially in Christ? The theologian's task is to explain what is meant by Christ being especially what is held in common with the Father and the Holy Spirit, bringing to bear one truth on the understanding of another. The aim is to draw out the implications of revelation, to see and to understand in what way the work of Christ, for example, is especially a work of wisdom. This is the meaning of "faith seeking understanding," the motto, as it were, of medieval theology. Of course, in such cases, one will have to make a decision regarding what is more fundamental and first in our explanations, the unity or the distinction of Persons? One quickly realizes that one's starting point greatly constrains one's method and outcome. If one begins by narrating the life of Christ in which we come to know the fact of three divine Persons, then it would appear that the divine Persons are merely functional and not eternal, simply modes in which God works and reveals Himself to us. It is not without reason then that Augustine said that nowhere is a mistake more dangerous, or the search more laborious, or the discovery more advantageous, than in seeking the unity of Father, Son, and Holy Spirit.

Thomas understood very well the principle of order and its implications. One need not read far into Thomas' *Summa theologiae* before noticing the careful attention given to the order of topics and arguments. And this order is not for its own sake. The multiplication of summas in the thirteenth century was in part an attempt to overcome the deficiencies of the textbook for systematic theology at that time, Peter the Lombard's *Sentences*. Thomas was not alone in seeing in that text problems of order, repetition, and the ill-considered connection of issues. One can find alternative approaches for systematic presentations of theology in the summas of William of Auxerre, Alexander of Hales, Bonaventure, and Albert the Great. And there is much to commend each of these works. On the issue of naming God, however, Thomas' *Summa* remains unsurpassed in clarity and insight. The way in which he deals with questions of what can and cannot be known, what can and cannot be said, what is a useful and proper argument for a theologian, and what is in fact detrimental to the faith are all points at which Thomas surpasses his contemporaries. His scholastic method of argumentation is no doubt difficult for the modern reader today, but his discussions remain stimulating and extremely insightful. In fact, he himself understood very well the problem of reading "ancient" texts. In commenting on the difficulty in reading Pseudo-Dionysius' *Divine Names*, he remarked that for the "modern" reader the style is "unfamiliar" and his vocabulary is "arcane." Thomas went on to explain in clear terms that unfamiliar and arcane text and even made great use of it. His own method may be unfamiliar to the modern reader, yet it is not something to be bypassed. We cannot understand his meaning without understanding his method. The *Summa contra Gentiles* and the *Summa theologiae* are neither uselessly repetitious nor the works of a schizophrenic theologian, but two different approaches to the same faith: one treats first all that can be known by natural reason and then proceeds to revealed truths—a presentation of the Christian faith as wisdom; the other begins in revealed truth, sacred doctrine. And this is precisely the shoal upon which many modern interpreters have foundered. It is not customary today to consider in theology minute matters of order, the relation between topics. We rush too quickly to what is central and most interesting. We are complacent in dealing with fundamental matters. Medieval theologians understood very well that theology cannot be an encyclopedia of disconnected answers—it is an organic whole. Every aspect is related with every other. Further, the theologian is himself connected with his predecessors. The theologian does not proceed from nakedness but must be clothed in the fullness of the tradition which is the Christian faith.

As Thomas worked through the problems of naming God, of making sense of our confessional language, he perceived patterns of understanding and signification in the mundane that could be applied to the sacred. We find in Scripture both metaphorical and more proper language about God. God is a rock, a lion; God alone is "good"; yet God is most properly Father, Son, and Holy Spirit. It is a fact deserving of much contemplation that God's revelation in both Testaments is of actions *and* words. Through the prophets and in the person of Jesus Christ, we hear the words spoken by God to His people. Those words are indeed in human tongues, but we are not deceived in using them. We accept such revelation for what it is: truthful. Moderns have unfortunately developed a great mistrust in words and their connection to reality. For Thomas, as for most any medieval theologian, words make sense only by virtue of their relation to reality *extra animam*. Without a fundamental belief in the intelligibility of all things, communication is impossible. Such affirmation is based not on a naïve epistemology, a mechanical one-to-one correspondence between words and things, but rather on a sophisticated psychology in which we can knowingly contemplate and discuss concrete things in an abstract way and visa versa. Moreover, the fact that our words signify things by means of our conceptions does not demand that our conceptions are perfect. There may be no end to our learning about the simple housefly, but our speech about it is no less true in signifying.

So as we come to understand more about God, we come to understand the way our words do and do not signify the truth about God. We learn not so much what God is but what God is not: not like us in emotions, in passivity, in change and development. The theologian formulates ways of signifying such differences even though "what God is" remains elusive.

Santa Paula, California
January 2001

# Acknowledgments

Words cannot capture the depth of my gratitude for all those who have made this work possible. It is not mine alone but is also the product of all who have taught me and and supported me, especially when the goal seemed unattainable. First and foremost I would like to thank my beautiful wife, Diana, whose love and patient counsel kept me going and helped me to keep a seemingly unmanageable task in manageable perspective. She has sacrificed so much in order that I may succeed. To her this work is dedicated.

I wish to thank the faculty of The University of Notre Dame's Medieval Institute for their guidance, especially Kent Emery, Jr., whose lectures and publications have proven to be a goldmine of insights into the intellectual life of the later Middle Ages. To Marina Smyth, the Medieval Institute Librarian, I am grateful for her conscientious and expert guidance at many points in my tenure there, but even more I appreciate her friendship. In particular I would like also to thank Rev. David Burrell and John O'Callaghan for reading drafts of several chapters and offering many insightful comments. Special thanks are also due to Mario Enrique Sacchi, editor of *Sapientia*, for his kind consideration of my work and for publishing previous versions of my first two chapters. Thanks are also due to *The Thomist*, which published an earlier version of my third chapter.

Permission for reprinting Kenneth Rexroth's translation of O. V. de L. Milosz's poem from the volume *Fourteen Poems*, © Copper Canyon Press, 1983, has been given by Copper Canyon Press: www.copper-canyonpress.org.

Most importantly, I wish to thank Ralph McInerny. His work has been my constant guide in understanding St. Thomas.

# Introduction

Modern theologians have almost en masse criticized Thomas' presentation of Trinitarian doctrine in his *Summa theologiae* because it appears to be a rational demonstration of the divine Persons.[1] For the past century, this work, along with Augustine's *De Trinitate*, has been read as representative of a Latin Trinitarian tradition that "begins with the one God, the one divine essence as a whole, and only afterwards does it see God as three in persons."[2] Philosophical concerns rather than the revelation of God in Christ are assumed to be the basis for the discussion of this doctrine since all divine works *ad extra* are common to the three Persons and accordingly give us no information about the Persons' proper identities. According to many contemporary theologians, the immanent life of God in this tradition is thereby separated from the rest of Christian faith and, consequently, has no relevance for the believer.

Thus, the treatise on the Trinity occupies a rather isolated position in the total dogmatic system. To put it crassly, and not without exaggeration, when the treatise is concluded, its subject is never brought up again. Its function in the whole dogmatic construction is not clearly perceived. It is as though this mystery has been revealed for its own sake, and that even after it has been made

---

1. The so-called "Trinitarian treatise" encompasses qq. 27–43 of the first part of Thomas' *Summa Theologiae*. For Aquinas' own outline of the whole *Summa* and of the first part in particular, refer to the prologue to question two.

2. Karl Rahner, *The Trinity*, trans. Joseph Donceel (New York: The Crossroad Publishing Company, 1997; reprint of the 1970 edition), p. 19. Original German text appeared in *Mysterium Salutis*, Bd. II (Zurich: Benziger Verlag, 1967).

known to us, it remains, *as a reality,* locked up within itself. We make statements about it, but as a reality it has nothing to do with us at all.³

Taking their cue from, among other things, the ordering of the *Summa theologiae,* Part I, in which the discussion of God as one (qq. 1–26) precedes the discussion of God as three (qq. 27–43), Thomas' modern critics contend that he derives the divine Persons from the essence by means of psychological speculations. By introducing the processions of divine Persons as acts of knowledge and love, Thomas appears to have pursued the same troublesome path paved by Anselm.⁴ The attempt to derive the Persons from such acts in God invariably leads to a multitude of processions, since each (resulting) Person will have his own knowledge and love. Thus, after applying such notions speculatively to the Trinity, Thomas "must admit that this application fails because he has clung to the 'essential' concept of knowledge and love."⁵ Thomas work is, therefore, condemned as a failure to appreciate the biblical, creedal, and liturgical priority of salvation history in which the three Persons play specific roles in the work of restoration and are known by such roles.

The purpose of this present study is to show the inaccuracy of this interpretation and to reveal the value of Thomas Aquinas' theological method. His method is neither speculative in the modern pejorative sense nor void of attention to salvation history. On the contrary, a study of Thomas' theological work reveals a remarkable sensitivity to the very purpose and method of theological endeavor as well as a deep understanding of the nature of theological language, both its power and limitations. The real value of Thomas for contemporary theology lies precisely in his understanding of theological method, the manner and order of pursuing one's investigations. Thomas' lasting contribution to theology, however, is at present lost in the tangle of interpretations and criticisms, most of which presume unproven and sometimes

---

3. Ibid., 14.
4. On the insoluable dilemma of multiplying divine Persons through psychological analogies, see Anselm, *Monologion,* chs. 61–63.
5. Rahner, *The Trinity,* pp. 317–404.

unreal patterns and connections among Thomas, his predecessors, and his contemporaries.

To begin with, Thomas quite explicitly denounced such demonstrations as Anselm attempted. By means of reason alone, one can know only what pertains to the oneness of God not to the Trinity of Persons. Moreover,

> he who attempts to prove the Trinity of Persons by natural reason derogates the faith in two ways: First, because it demeans the dignity of the faith that, as it pertains to invisible things, exceeds human reason.... Secondly, when someone, for purposes of evangelization, offers proofs of the faith that are not cogent, he risks being mocked for having believed on account of such reasons.[6]

Describing the real distinction and real unity of the Father, Son, and Holy Spirit, however, cannot but involve analogies. While admitting that the mystery of the Trinity is beyond the range of philosophical proof, he argues, "it is nevertheless right to try to explain it through things more plainly evident."[7] Hence, Thomas does not shy away from attempts "to make the divine Persons known by way of similitudes and dissimilitudes."[8] His presentation of the Trinity is neither a demonstration nor a systematic construction, only a manner of understanding what is beyond but not contrary to reason, an example of faith seeking understanding.

Further, it is not at all certain that there is such a Latin Trinitarian tradition as some suppose. The conception of a Latin Trinitarian tradition is not historical but heuristic. A French theologian, Théodore

---

6. "Qui autem probare nititur Trinitatem Personarum naturali ratione, fidei dupliciter derogat. Primo quidem, quantum ad dignitatem ipsius fidei, quae est ut sit de rebus invisibilibus, quae rationem humanam excedunt.... Secundo, quantum ad utilitatem trahendi alios ad fidem. Cum enim aliquis ad probandam fidem inducit rationes quae non sunt cogentes, cedit in irrisionem infidelium: credunt enim quod huiusmodi rationibus innitamur, et propter eas credamus." Thomas Aquinas, *Summa Theologiae* (Leonine edition) I, q. 32, a. 1 c. He also explicitly addresses Anselm's mistakes, at ST I, q. 34, a. 1 ad 2 & 3.

7. "[C]onvenit tamen ut per aliqua magis manifesta declaretur." ST I, q. 39, a. 7 c.

8. "[S]ed ad manifestandum Personas per viam similitudinis vel dissimilitudinis." ST I, q. 39, a. 7 ad 1.

de Régnon, proposed a Greek/Latin schema in the late nineteenth century to interpret perceived distinctions within the Trinitarian tradition, specifically between Aquinas and Bonaventure.[9] While admitting that these traditions do not corresponding to strict linguistic or geographical divisions, de Régnon delineates these "traditions" with the help of certain stylistic features.[10] He notes that certain Greek-inspired discussions of the Trinity begin with the three Persons explicitly and focus more on salvation history to elucidate the mystery (eg., Pseudo-Dionysius, Richard of St. Victor, Alexander of Hales, and Bonaventure). Other presentations began with the unity of God and then proceeded to discuss the three divine Persons in terms of intellectual nature. This group, he identified as a "Latin" tradition (eg., Augustine, Anselm, Peter the Lombard, Albert the Great, and Thomas Aquinas). Since de Régnon, such features including the starting point (the diversity of Persons for the Greeks, and the unity of nature for the Latins) and manner of argumentation (from the works of salvation history or "missions" for the Greeks, and from psychological speculations for the Latins) have become the very bases for Trinitarian discussions, both historical and systematic.

Michael Schmaus was perhaps the key figure in bringing de Régnon's schema into mainstream theological thought.[11] According to him, the focus of de Régnon's study is the way such differences between Bonaventure and Aquinas can be explained *vis-a-vis* Pseudo-Dionysius and Augustine. The result is the identification of "traditions," the boundaries of which can be used to determine the fundamental orientation and sources of other theologians.[12]

---

9. Théodore de Régnon, S.J., *Études de théologie positive sur la sainte Trinité*, vol. II (Paris: Victor Retaux, 1892–98).

10. De Régnon focused primarily on scholastic texts and on their respective origins in the Cappadocians and Augustine. De Régnon, *Études de théologie positive*, vol. II, pp. 133–43, 447–51.

11. M. Schmaus, *Der* Liber Propugnatorius *des Thomas Anglicus und die Lehruntershiede zwischen Thomas von Aquin und Duns Scotus,* vol. II, "Die Trinitarischen Lehrdifferenzen" (Münster, 1930), 574–66.

12. Schmaus, *Der* Liber, 650ff. For a recent survey of this discussion and the problems raised regarding the labeling of certain figures, see Zachary Hayes' excellent intro-

In the so-called "Greek" explanation of the Trinity, in accordance with Holy Scripture, one discusses first the three Persons in their personal properties as well as in their activity in salvation history. This tradition considers in the second place the unity of [divine] essence and the equality of Persons. [On the other hand], the so-called "western" tradition, whose main representative is Augustine, first considers the unity of [divine] essence grounded in the oneness of God and then considers the threeness of Persons.[13]

Schmaus' shorthand for these lines of division is the manner of proceeding from Persons to essence (Greek) and from essence to Persons (Latin).

With the writings of Karl Rahner, the divisions themselves became the grounds for criticizing the representatives of the Latin tradition.[14] Rahner, first in an article appearing in 1967 and again in a monograph in 1970, denounces the Latin Trinitarian tradition because of what he perceives to be the direct consequences of an unsatisfactory method. According to Rahner, the Latins speak of the "necessary metaphysical properties of God, and not very explicitly of God as experienced in salvation history."[15] The Greeks, on the other hand, "would have us start from the one unoriginate God, who is already *Father* even when nothing is known as yet about generation and spiration."[16] The Greeks then proceed according to biblical revelation and salvation history in establishing the doctrine of the Trinity, while the Latins "derive" the Persons from psychological speculations on the "One God" who is known according to certain metaphysical properties. The most severe consequence of the Latin approach, says Rahner, is the complete separation of the doctrine of the Trinity from Christian faith and experi-

---

duction to Bonaventure's *Disputed Questions on the Mystery of the Trinity*, trans. Z. Hayes (St. Bonaventure, N.Y.: The Franciscan Institute, 1979), 13–29.

13. M. Schmaus, "Das Fortwirken der augustinischen Trinitätspsychologie bis zur karolingischen Zeit," in *Vitae et Veritati*. Festgabe K. Adam (Düsseldorf, 1956), 45.

14. M. R. Barnes would argue that the debate is more defined by de Régnon than by Rahner. He is right insofar as the major lines dividing Greek from Latin presentations of Trinitarian doctrine were drawn by de Régnon, but it was only with Rahner that the battle ensued over the value and implications of each side. See M. R. Barnes, "De Régnon Reconsidered," *Augustinian Studies* 26 (1995): 51–79.

15. Rahner, *The Trinity*, 18.

16. Ibid., 17.

ence. One cannot thereby relate to or pray to the Persons separately but is limited to a relation of reason with the three. The systematic division of treatises on the One God who is Creator and on the Trinity implies, in Rahner's eyes, a discontinuity between God in Himself and God's self-revelation.[17] In a system wherein a Trinity is speculatively derived from the oneness of God, the reality of Persons "remains locked up within itself . . . [having] nothing to do with us at all."[18] The traditional Latin denial that the revelation of Christ actually tells us anything about the individual Persons means that we can have only an appropriated relation with each divine Person and not a real one. The upshot is that there is no reason for the revelation of the Trinity, since it remains an isolated mystery, and we know nothing about each Person except that they are.

Rahner's answer to these problems is his thesis that the Trinity we encounter in the economy of salvation is the Trinity in itself: "the economic trinity is the immanent trinity."[19] God in Himself is the God of our salvation. The fact that it is the Second Person of the Trinity, the Word, who becomes incarnate, tells us a great deal about that particular Person. Moreover, Rahner argues, it is important that we recognize the Persons as distinct agents of our salvation with whom we have real, distinct relations.[20] Consequently, the western Latin Trinitarian tradition needs to be seriously reexamined and rebuilt upon an ontology of the economy.

In recent years, however, the awareness of this paradigm's history has faded. De Régnon's simplistic dichotomy has become so well embedded in modern systematic theology that it is now the unseen lens through which the tradition is read. Many theologians assume the truth of the paradigm without investigating its history or demonstrat-

---

17. K. Barth noted the identity of the economic and immanent Trinity almost thirty years before Rahner's famous statement, but he did so in a less dramatic and persuasive manner. Hence, Rahner is generally credited with the statement. Cf. K. Barth, *Church Dogmatics* (Edinburgh: T&T Clark, 1963, reprint of 1936 edition), 1-1, 382.

18. Rahner, *The Trinity*, 14.   19. Ibid., 22.
20. Ibid., 80–120.

ing its accuracy. Instead, the representatives of each "side" are lined up as examples of the failures or successes of each type of theological procedure. This unreflective grouping of rather distinctive theologians is due to a "penchant for polar categories" by which modern systematic theologians seek to make comprehensive statements about our complex theological heritage.[21] The paradigm, rather than textual analysis, is then the ground for the diagnosed problems. The resulting reconstructions of the history of Trinitarian theology are held captive to what are essentially modern interpretive categories that prevent a reading of the texts outside of de Régnon's paradigm.

Most of the treatments of Trinitarian doctrine in our time take as their point of orientation Rahner's polemic. Congar, Jüngel, Kasper, Moltmann, and Simonis are just a few of the many theologians who have embraced de Régnon's categories with Rahner's diagnosis and consequently advocate a return of the "Greek" approach beginning with the "economy."[22] Those who oppose such reductive readings still find themselves having to argue according to the established lines of debate. They are constrained to "kick against the goads" as it were by taking account of Rahner's criticism and diffusing it, even though they know full well that the Greek/Latin scheme is an invention of de Régnon with limited heuristic value.[23]

---

21. M. R. Barnes, "Augustine in Contemporary Trinitarian Theology," *Theological Studies* 56 (1995): 239. Barnes notes, however, that some French scholars such as Lafont and Malet have debated the accuracy of De Régnon's paradigm. Thus, they have at least kept in mind that it is a paradigm—one that may be wrong. Barnes, "De Régnon Reconsidered," 55-56.

22. Y. Congar, *I Believe in the Holy Spirit*, 3 vols. (New York: Seabury, 1983) esp. III intro.; E. Jüngel, *The Doctrine of the Trinity: God's Being Is in Becoming* (Grand Rapids, Mich.: Eerdman's, 1976); W. Kasper, *The God of Jesus Christ*, trans. Matthew J. O'Connell (New York: Crossroad, 1984); J. Moltmann, *The Trinity and the Kingdom of God*, trans. M. Kohl (San Francisco: Harper & Row, 1981); *The Crucified God: The Cross of Christ as the Foundation and Criticism of Christian Theology*, trans. R. A. Wilson and John Bowden (New York: Harper and Row, 1974); W. Simonis, "Über das 'Werden' Gottes. Gedanken zum Begriff der ökonomischen Trinität," *Münchener Theologischen Zeitschrift* 33 (1982): 133-39.

23. M. R. Barnes, "Augustine in Contemporary Trinitarian Theology," 237-50; H. Jorissen, "Zur Struktur des Traktates *De Deo* in der *Summa theologiae* des Thomas von

We are now at the high point of this movement to bypass or correct the Latin tradition with the Greek tradition in order to develop a new grammar for speaking of God as Trinity in a meaningful way. Contemporary systematic theologians immersed in Rahner's polemic must decide to what point in the pre-Augustinian tradition we must return or how we may appropriate the Greek tradition as an avenue of circumventing our own.[24] One can find any number of theologians championing the Cappadocian formulations, proposing alternatives for the term 'person' (what is plural with respect to God),[25] redefining

---

Aquin," *Im Gespräch mit dem Dreienen Gott* (Düsseldorf: Patmos Verlag, 1985), 231–57; H. C. Schmidbaur, *Personarum Trinitas. Dei trinitarische Gotteslehre des heiligen Thomas von Aquin.* (St. Ottilien: EOS Verlag, 1992). H. C. Schmidbaur does use de Régnon's categories in the second part of his study, yet he demonstrates an ability to think outside such categories as he discusses some of Thomas' immediate predecessors according to other terms. See H. C. Schmidbaur, *Personarum Trinitas*, 194–330.

24. C. Gunton argues for a return to the Cappadocian teaching: *The Promise of Trinitarian Theology* (Edinburgh: T&T Clark, 1991), ch. 1; E. Jungel suggests a revival of Luther's passionate and suffering-filled Christology on whose basis we may be certain of God's love: *God as the Mystery of the World* (Grand Rapids, Mich.: W. B. Eerdmans, 1983), 368–76. The imprecision of Jungel's language regarding "God" and the proper names, however, muddles his discussion and gives a strong impression of modalism. For instance, he often refers to the "Incarnation of God" (pp. 320–72); W. Kasper proposes a return to the work of Tertullian and Athanasius, that is, a return to the realm of "confession" as opposed to "doctrine": *The God of Jesus Christ,* 251–63; C. LaCugna advocates a return to pre-Nicene theology. She is especially sympathetic to the views of Arius and Eunomius as well as non-Palamite Orthodox thought, which she combines together with modern personalism, feminism, and liberation theology: *God for Us: The Trinity and Christian Life* (San Francisco: Harper Collins, 1991), 30–40 and ch. 10; J. Moltmann argues for a revival of pre-Tertullian views limited to salvation history without substance metaphysics and its "dangerous" generic terms: *History and the Triune God,* trans. J. Bowden (New York: Crossroad, 1992), ch. 8.; P. Schoonenberg, like Kasper, is uncomfortable with any definite discussion of God *in se* beyond a mere discussion of God's "modes" of revelation or expression and seems therefore to long for the confessional period of pre-Tertullian theology: "Trinity—The Consummated Covenant: Theses on the Doctrine of the Trinitarian God," *Studies in Religion* 5 (1975): 111–16.

25. K. Barth proposes *"Seinsweisen"* or "modes of being" in his *Church Dogmatics* vol. 1-1, 352–62; K. Rahner follows Barth for the most part but with an eye toward avoiding suspect terms; hence, he prefers "distinct manners of subsisting": *The Trinity,* 109–15; G. W. H. Lampe with his Joachimist reading of history prefers to use the term 'Spirit,' for that is the manner of God's presence in the world: *God as Spirit* (Oxford: Clarendon Press, 1977), 206–28.

what it means for God to be relational.[26] Some have even attempted to replace creedal formulations with the more inclusive imagery of the Old Testament and certain Gnostic texts.[27]

Thomas' discussions of naming God are a refreshing counterbalance to the prevailing winds and theological fancy. In his discussion of the way we might coordinate our language about the unity of God with that of the distinctions in God, Thomas makes his most important statements about theological method. Bringing together language about the unity of God with that on the Trinity of Persons constituted perhaps the greatest difficulty in formulating a coherent system of Trinitarian grammar. Those pursuing a metaphysical investigation of the Trinity all too easily fell into the trap of dissolving the mystery, reducing the Trinity either in a monotheistic or tritheistic manner. Others tended to dissolve the truth of theological language under the guise of a radically negative critique. That is, all naming of God falls short of the mystery itself and must therefore be left behind as ultimately inadequate. Thomas' solution to this problem shows the pro-

---

26. E. Jungel argues that God is related to the world in such a way that God is constituted as "God" only in the act of creating: *God as the Mystery of the World*, 221–25; LaCugna builds upon Jungel's work, yet without the sophistication of Jungel's concept of divine freedom and creation as a "going into nothingness." In her strongly Neoplatonic system LaCugna then proposes a stronger identification of creation and relation whereby God is God by relation to the creation inasmuch as the creative act is a real procession from God. Hence, she has abolished the distinction between the absolute and the ordained power of God (possible and actual) such that God by nature creates and could not do otherwise. Lacugna, *God for Us,* 168–69, 353–56; J. Moltmann follows Barth in advocating a discussion built upon the idea of God's lordship or dominion, thus including the revelation of God before the Incarnation in his discussion of God's relatedness. Additionally, Moltmann advocates a future-oriented faith that is "liberated" from the past, that is, liberated from Church dogmas, hierarchy, and so forth, such that the Trinity becomes merely a social programme of communitarianism: Moltmann, *History and the Triune God,* introduction and ch. 8.

27. M. Daly, *Beyond God the Father. Towards a Philosophy of Women's Liberation* (Boston: Beacon Press, 1973); S. McFague, *Models of God: Theology for an Ecological, Nuclear Age* (Philadelphia: Fortress Press, 1987); R. Ruether, *Sexism and God-Talk* (Boston: Beacon Press, 1983); P. Wilson-Kastner, *Faith, Feminism and the Mutual Relation* (Washington, D.C.: University Press of America, 1981). Many of these attempts to reformulate Trinitarian language involve the resurrecting of Gnostic terms or the borrowing of Jewish ones.

fundity and originality of his method, even though much of what is said is not original at all. The clarity of his presentation goes beyond the work of other medieval theologians, particularly with respect to his consciousness of the limitations of theological knowledge and language. He opted neither for the positivist reading whereby one analyzes the language itself for insight, nor for the radical negation of such language whereby one is left with no hold on true speech about God. It is well known that Thomas distinguished between the way things are and the ways we think and speak about them. Not the fact but the import of this distinction is what remains in question. Regardless of the interpretation, the distinction is undoubtedly central.

Thomas advances the discussion of Trinitarian doctrine primarily by reorganizing and clarifying certain key issues that had been poorly addressed by his predecessors. His discussion proves to be more fruitful not only because he infuses the tradition with a powerful philosophic hermeneutic but also because he allows the tradition to interpret itself. Just as Augustine contended that Scripture is its own best interpreter, so Thomas worked with the premise that the full theological tradition provides its own interpretation. The task of the theologian is not simply to draw up a list of difficult texts for every question, as Abelard did in his *Sic et Non*. Thomas' method of organization entailed a careful consideration of the subject whereby one moves from the more evident to the less evident. By allowing the most fundamental questions to preface and order the discussion, one is prepared for the more difficult and complex questions by way of the more evident and simple. Additionally, in moving toward greater clarity, the definition of a term will be fluid as it depends upon the immediate context.

In chapter 1, we will examine the mode and order of Thomas' theological presentation in the *prima pars*. In chapter 2, we will survey his ordering and use of theological terms. In chapter 3, we will take up the question of the analogous character of theological language. In chapter 4, we will demonstrate that the guiding principle for interpreting Aquinas' teaching on analogous language cannot be read as a naïve assertion of positivist theology. Analogous naming in Thomas must be properly contextualized historically and philosophically if it is to be understood at all. Accordingly, in the fifth and final chapter, we will show that the negative character in analogous predication offers an essential correction to language and thought without undermining its truth. In fact, revelation itself makes us more aware of the distinction between creatures and God precisely so that we may understand the truth about God's action, both in creation and in redemption. For that reason, Thomas argues, we are constricted by the language of Scripture and cannot go beyond it or set it aside in our theological reflections. This order of investigation reflects our express intention to see Thomas neither as a representative of a homogenous theological tradition nor as the synthesis of traditions but only to investigate Thomas' method, sources, and interlocutors as a way of illuminating his intentions and better understanding his teaching.

# 1. The Context of the Questions on the Trinity

In the prologue to his *Summa theologiae,* Thomas states that the reason for this work is his own dissatisfaction with the available theological textbooks. These texts, he argues, including the *Sentences* of Peter the Lombard, contain numerous useless questions and arguments, neglect to treat the subject matter according to the order of teaching, and needlessly repeat themselves, all of which leads to "boredom and confusion" in the students. There was also at that time serious disagreement about the precise subject matter of theology. Some proposed that theology is a study of creation. Others said that it should be a study of Christ, both as head and body of the Church. Such things are, for Aquinas, only a part of theology and must be subsumed into the order of the whole; that is, the order of things to the primary subject, God.[1] Thomas proposes that theology or *sacra doctrina* is "principally about God" and includes the consideration of other things only as they are "referred to God as the principle and end."[2] It is not an equal treatment of God and creatures, nor is it a study of human salvation *per se.* Further, by considering all things as knowable in the "divine light," i.e., by treating all things as *revelabilia,*[3] this discipline, according to Aquinas, comprehends all the philosophical sciences, both speculative and practical. Thomas' *Summa theologiae* is his answer to the confusion on these issues.

---

1. Thomas Aquinas, *Summa theologiae* (ST) I, q. 1, a. 7 c.
2. "[S]acra doctrina non determinate de Deo et de creaturis ex aequo, sed de Deo principaliter et de creaturis secundum quod referuntur ad Deum, ut ad principium vel finem." ST I, q. 1, a. 3 ad 1.
3. ST I, q. 1, a. 3 c.

## 1.1 The Structure of the *Summa theologiae*

After defining the nature of theology in question one, Thomas describes the structure of the *Summa theologiae* in the following manner: the three parts of the work will cover (1) God, Pt. I; (2) the movement of rational creatures to God, Pt. II (I–II and II–II); and (3) Christ, who as man is the way to God, Pt. III.[4] This organization follows what Aquinas takes to be the "order of things," beginning with God in Himself as cause, followed by creation (effect), then the natural desire and motion of rational creatures to their end, and finally the way to God provided through Christ (means). On the face of it, this order seems quite rational, but upon reflection, it raises some interesting questions. For example, how can we discuss God apart from or "prior to" creation? In what way might rational creatures move toward God apart from or "prior to" Christ? More important for our study, it appears that Thomas has somewhat distorted the order of revelation by discussing the Trinity that was revealed in Christ before discussing Christ directly. This particular point of order has led some to charge Thomas with attempting to demonstrate Trinitarian doctrine by means of an investigation of the divine essence rather than through salvation history.[5] According to this view, it is a "right understanding of the [divine] essence" rather than salvation history that guides Thomas' thought on these matters.[6] The interpretation of this order is no simple matter.

In his foundational study of 1939,[7] M.-D. Chenu opened a new avenue of investigation by proposing a comprehensive schema for inter-

---

4. ST I, q. 2 prol.

5. See Introduction, pp. 1–5.

6. G. Martelet, for example, also observes that the resulting Christology in the *tertia pars* of the *Summa* is an economy of salvation stripped of its revelatory content. Cf. G. Martelet, S.J., "Theologie und Heilsökonomie in der Christologie der 'Tertia,'" in J. B. Metz et al., eds., *Gott in Welt* (Festschrift K. Rahner), Bd. II (Freiburg: Herder, 1964), 8.

7. M.-D. Chenu, "Le plan de la *Somme théologique* de S. Thomas," *Revue Thomiste* 45 (1939): 93–107. This study was later expanded and presented in Chenu's *Introduction à l'étude de S. Thomas d'Aquin* (Paris, 1950), 255–76.

preting the structure of Thomas' *Summa,* and thereupon determined the direction of that interest well into our own day. Chenu contends that for structuring his presentation of theology, Thomas had recourse to the Neoplatonic themes of emanation and return. Since theology is a science of God, one studies all things in their relation to God in their production and in their finality.

> Such is the plan of the *Summa theologiae,* and such is the movement that it treats. *Prima pars:* the emanation, God as principle; *secunda pars:* the return, God as end; and because, in fact, this return is made possible by Christ, the God-man according to the free and wholly gratuitous design of God, *tertia pars* will study the "Christian" conditions of this return.[8]

This structure arises from Thomas' effort to provide an "order of learning" for the science of theology. Drawing upon the Neoplatonic themes of emanation and return, Thomas' schema has the advantage of ordering things in relation to God while remaining open to history. This organizational plan is then not meant to jumble the biblical narrative but to put it into a macro structure that allows for the systematic treatment of doctrines within a coherent plan.

It is unclear, however, whether the emanation-return schema defines the development within the text or the nature of the structure; that is, whether it is a literary imposition on the subject matter or the actual structure of all things. If Chenu is suggesting the latter, then his reading would also have the disadvantage of making God part of the system, a being among beings, albeit the highest. At the heart of the debate over Chenu's interpretation is a disagreement over the kind of motion within the system.[9] If the scheme is read according to temporal motion, the return does not begin until the Incarnation, the *tertia*

---

8. Chenu, "Le plan de la *Somme,*" 98.

9. O. H. Pesch argues for an immobile or ontological structure in order to protect the contingency of things, "Um den Plan der *Summa Theologiae* des hl. Thomas von Aquin," *Münchener Theologische Zeitschrift* 16 (1965): 413–17; A. Patfoort, on the other hand, wants to refer to the dynamism of the *secunda pars* and the *tertia pars* in order to emphasize the connection between history and the *ordo disciplinae*. "L'unité de la Ia Pars et le mouvement interne de la *Somme Théologique* de S. Thomas d'Aquin," *Revue des sciences philosophique et théologique* 47 (1963): 513–44.

*pars*. If, on the other hand, the structure is conceived of ontologically, then the return can be said to begin with Thomas' account of the moral life in the *secunda pars*.[10] Those who read it as a chronological structure find the text distasteful and poorly organized due to the implications of such temporal motion both in the three divine Persons following from the one divine essence and in the return of creatures to God "prior to" or "without" Christ.[11] The idea of a movement of creatures back to God without Christ is repugnant to the Christian tradition. Take away the concept of temporal motion, however, and the problems begin to disappear, for the movement of rational creatures to God is not prior to Christ in time but simply abstracted from the Incarnation for purposes of systematic discussion.

We can bring some of these complex issues to light by examining the role of history in the *Summa*. Thomas' critics accuse him of subverting the historical order. Few would deny that the doctrine of the Trinity, for instance, is the last and not the first word in the order of revelation. Others defend Thomas precisely by accounting for the perceived historical "anamolies" within the text.[12] On what side of the fence one falls seems to depend on what one understands by "salvation history." Narrowly conceived as the revelation of God in Christ with the overcoming of sin on the cross, such history seems oddly decentralized and de-emphasized in the *Summa*. Broadly conceived, how-

---

10. The part of the text Thomas calls the "movement of rational creatures to God." ST I, q. 2 prol.

11. H. Schillebeeckx first noted that the idea of a return to God apart from Christ is inconceivable and makes the discussion of Christ in the *tertia pars* a mere "addition" to a text complete in itself. *De sacramentele Heilseconomie* (Anvers, 1952), 1–18.

12. F. Bourassa, "Sur le Traité de la Trinité," *Gregorianum* 47 (1966): 254–85.; G. Lafont, *Structures et méthode dans la Somme théologique de saint Thomas d'Aquin* (Paris: Cerf, 1961); A. Malet, *Personne et amour dans la théologie trinitaire de saint Thomas d'Aquin*, Bibliothèque Thomiste 32 (Paris: J. Vrin, 1956); A. Patfoort, "L'unité"; O. H. Pesch, "Um den Plan der Summa Theologiae des hl. Thomas von Aquin," *Münchener Theologische Zeitschrift* 16 (1965): 128–37; M. Seckler, *Das Heil in der Geschichte. Geschichtstheologisches Denken bei Thomas von Aquin* (Munich: Kösel Verlag, 1964); C. Sträter, "Le point de départ du traité thomiste de la Trinité," *Sciences ecclésiastiques* 14 (1962): 71–87; U. Horst, "Über die Frage einer heilsökonomischen Theologie bei Thomas von Aquin," *Münchener Theologische Zeitschrift* 12 (1961): 97–111.

ever, as God's provision for the return of creation, the transition from the *prima* and *secunda* to the *tertia pars* is from a radically contingent fundamental structure of salvation history to its soteriological dimension.[13]

The majority of interpreters would agree with Chenu's basic thesis but are generally reticent to say much more. Horst and Lafont, for instance, devote a great deal of time to considering the many evident inconsistencies and questions left unresolved by the central thesis.[14] M. Seckler, on the other hand, wants to bring together the very idea of salvation history and the structure of the *Summa*. According to Seckler, it was not merely the demands of theology's newly established scientific character that led Thomas to adopt this schema; rather, it was his own insight into the nature of salvation history.

According to God's plan and work of salvation, all things go out from the hand of God and return to Him who is the Alpha and Omega. Thus, the theologian also treats reality according to its relation to God insofar as He is the source and goal of all things. Surprisingly, we find here a narrow correspondence in the source and goal of history, the source and fulfillment of being, the first and last ground of understanding such that no only can theology become ordered to the "science" of salvation history, but salvation history bears within itself the fundamental design of theology. The theologian does not bring order to the chaos of salutary events, but the order of salvation structures theology.[15]

The principle that orders the events of salvation history and the principle by which the science is ordered for purposes of understanding are one and the same. Hence, there is only one order that is simultaneously the order of instruction and the order of things.

For Chenu, the emanation-return schema applied to the *prima* and *seconda pars*. Chenu assumed a narrow definition of salvation history being specifically Christian and accordingly explains the *tertia pars* with an additional principle of ordering: necessary-contingent. Only

---

13. Pesch, "Um den Plan," 422.
14. Horst, "Über die Frage"; Lafont, *Structures et methode*.
15. Seckler, *Das Heil in der Geschichte*, 35.

in this last part do we enter fully into the realm of history, the realm of contingent events. "The transition from the *secunda pars* to the *tertia pars* represented the passage from the necessary order to its historical realizations, from the domain of the structures to the concrete history of the gifts of God."[16] But this manner of speaking brings up the very problem of the Neoplatonic character of Chenu's schema. In Neoplatonic terms the emanation is understood as an actual procession rather than a creation *ex nihilo*. Moreover, the implication of necessity in the philosophical doctrine means that neither the emanation nor the structure of the return are contingent in the same way that the Incarnation is presumed to be. Seckler denies such conclusions and insists that the Neoplatonic context and implication of the schema are considerably faded if not lost.[17] There is then no strict division of what is necessary and what is contingent, what is of nature and what is of grace. Nature as defined by the event of creation is no less a realization of the free love of God. "Thomas has a unified conception of the works of salvation: angels and humans are from the beginning created for salvation and grace. Creation is already grounded in an historical relation of God to creatures, therefore, creation is also a contingent event. Hence, the *Summa* is throughout christologically constructed."[18]

It is a false assumption on the part of Chenu that there is, in the *Summa*, a grace separated from Christ. The discussion of Christ in *tertia pars* is not the entrance of a new radical contingency and a new form of grace. Chenu was confusing the chronology of revelation with the order of things, thereby making the interpretation of the *Summa*'s structure a problem of theological knowledge. Hence, what Seckler sees as a crucial addition to Chenu's thesis is the assertion that "Christ is primarily not the one of whom one speaks but the one who reveals the Father . . . not the goal but the way . . . not the content but the form."[19] Christ provides insight into the order of being, the order of

---

16. Chenu, *Introduction*, 270.
17. Seckler, *Das Heil in der Geschichte*, 34.
18. Ibid., 39.
19. Ibid., 40.

things, and the content of this insight is the right understanding of creation and the way of salvation, not a new kind of return. There is then no "unhistorical" material or structure in the *Summa* wherein Thomas treats the truth of God "abstractly" over against the "concrete history" of God in Christ. The *Summa* is throughout a concrete history of salvation.

This is not to deny any necessity whatsoever in that history. The necessity of things is present at least in regard to their form. According to Seckler, there is an important difference in Thomas between the structure of history and its chronological sequence. The structure of the *Summa* cannot be divided by what is abstract and what is concrete or by what is necessary and what is contingent. The emanation-return structure denotes the meaningfulness of events in relation to their source and goal who is God. Statements about the course of history are then made within "generally valid structural laws." The events of history in Thomas' theology are structured in a circular fashion: *from* the One who is source and *to* the One who is end.[20] Throughout all three parts of the *Summa*, then, the centrality of God as the "subject of events and understanding" is maintained.[21]

Seckler's correction of Chenu's interpretation, however, lacks an appreciation of the soteriological dimension of the Incarnation. It is not merely revelatory but also effective of salvation. The presence of Christ can already be seen in the teaching of the old law that convicts sin and awakens belief in a mediator through the sacrificial laws. The moral law was valid before Christ and even before Moses as "the laws written on the hearts of men," natural law. Otherwise, there would have been no conviction of sin.[22] Thomas attempted to leave the mystery of Christ in the background throughout the first two parts, yet he always expressed salvation history in its "concrete, Christian, incarnational, sacramental and ecclesial aspect without being occasioned or structured by sin."[23] The perspective of the theologian is then that of the creature who is from God, receives all things from God and returns to God. Even in the soteriological section of the *Summa*, the acts

20. Ibid., 29–30.
21. Ibid., 42.
22. Pesch, "Um den Plan," 418.
23. Ibid., 420.

of Christ, his life, death, resurrection and reign are all the works of an instrument, the "tool of the love of God."[24] The accent in this last section of the *Summa* is not upon the end of the carnal life but upon the end of salvation history. God and not Christ thereby remains throughout the theme of theology.

No one would dispute that our knowledge of the Trinity (of Persons) comes through the life and teachings of Christ. The issue is whether it makes sense to instruct persons according to an inverse order in which the Trinity or "the movement of rational creatures to God" is considered *before* Christ. On the other hand, can Christ be understood without knowing something of creation, the moral life, and the problem of sin?[25] The answer involves not only the extent of revelation prior in time to Christ but also the need to speak of God in an a-temporal way in order to insure the eternity and equality of the divine Persons and the freedom of God to act.[26] Thomas presents a study of God prior to and apart from the acts by which we know God before discussing those acts, because revelation imparts a more full

---

24. Ibid., 423.

25. J. Pieper argues at length for the extent of knowledge presupposed by revelation. The point to be remembered is that because of God's self-revelation to humans specifically, a measure of natural knowledge is prerequisite for understanding such revelation. Further, the revelation must be investigated, pondered and interpreted for understanding, for revelation is a hidden truth unlike mathematical principles which need only to be stated to be understood. Cf. Pieper, *Problems of Modern Faith* (Chicago: Franciscan Herald Press, 1985), 157–73; see also his *Guide to Thomas Aquinas* (San Francisco: Ignatius, 1986), 144–57.

26. D. Burrell notes that freedom in acting is essential to the biblical notion of Creator. It is only by the revelation of the Word that is a revealing Word that we are enabled to speak of this Creator and to adapt our language to God. The events of the life of Christ are not merely events to be interpreted providing only historical data. Christ revealed many things about God that allow us to speak of God beyond the bounds of our experience. Burrell, *Freedom and Creation in Three Traditions* (Notre Dame: University of Notre Dame Press, 1993), 161–84. Those such as M. Wiles and G. Lampe who wish to develop theological grammar on the basis of their experience of God are forgetting that revelation (in Christ) is not merely an event that changes the state of affairs that obtains on this earth (namely, by providing grace under the new Law); it provides us with articles of faith, words, to be understood. Cf. M. Wiles, *Faith and the Mystery of God* (Philadelphia: Fortress Press, 1982), and G. W. Lampe, *God as Spirit* (Oxford: Clarendon Press, 1977).

and certain knowledge of the cause, thereby allowing one to speak about the cause directly.

The theologian extends the horizon of what is understood as history by placing the temporal in an eternal context, thereby preventing the discussion from becoming a-historical as it opens itself to the systematic discussion of doctrines. In the context of eternity, it makes perfect sense to discuss God prior to or abstracted from any consideration of creation. Likewise Thomas can discuss the original state of Man with all the powers intact prior to the destructive act of original sin because revelation provides additional data concerning human nature. For instance, from revelation we know that the present existence of human beings does not correspond to the innocent condition in which the first humans were created. Human nature is not sinful *per se*, i.e., not essentially so. The purpose for discussing cause before effect, even though the reverse is the order of learning (the order of rational investigation is from effect to cause), is to separate the being from the necessity of the act and to prevent the error of reducing the being to these acts only. In other words, specific acts have a limiting power on the agent. To speak of God as Creator or Savior (only) is to reduce the possible to the actual at a specific point in time. God's power extends beyond the horizon of God's acts; hence, "God is able to do other than he does."[27] When Thomas states that a knowledge of the Trinity is needed for a correct understanding of creation and salvation, he is referring to the freedom with which those acts are done.[28]

In treating all things in relation to the primary subject, God, Thomas subordinates the history of human salvation to the eternity of God. Everything is thereby seen in its proper context, that is, as created by and ordered to God. Regardless of whether we choose to use Chenu's emanation-return terminology, we must recognize the pedagogical organization of Thomas' *Summa*. Moreover, the order in which things are best understood corresponds to the order in which they exist, the order of being: God first, as cause, and all else, in relation to God, as effects.

---

27. "Deus potest alia facere quam quae facit." ST I, q. 25, a. 5 c.
28. ST I, q. 32, a. 1 ad 3.

## 1.2 The Structure of the *Prima pars*

Thomas indicates the structure of his text in several places.[29] In the prologue to the second question, he identifies the divisions of the *prima pars* of the *Summa*:

> The consideration of God will be tripartite. First, we will consider what pertains to the divine essence (qq. 2–26); second, [we will consider] those things that pertain to the distinction of Persons (q. 27–43); third [we will consider] those things that pertain to the procession of creatures from God (q. 44).[30]

All three parts fall under the title "On God," Thomas' title for the *prima pars*. Thomas makes a notable clarification about this order at the end of the first division, question twenty-six. At the beginning and end of that question, Thomas declares that the first section of the *prima pars* concerns the unity of the divine essence.[31] It is noteworthy that Thomas uses the term 'unity' twice to define the subject of the preceding questions and once more in the prologue to part two of "On God" (q. 27). According to his *post factum* description, Thomas understood his first two sections to concern unity and distinction respectively regarding the one God who is a Trinity. By juxtaposing unity and distinction, he treats in turn two aspects of the one subject.[32] The movement from the first to the second division is not from monopersonal to tripersonal God but from a consideration of the unity of the

---

29. Much of the literature on the structure of the *Summa* does not address specifically the details of our chosen portion of the text, the so-called "Trinitarian treatise"; rather, such studies primarily focus on the relation of each book to the other two or to the particularly troublesome situation of Christ in the *tertia pars*, as mentioned above. Of the few studies that are devoted primarily to the *prima pars*, most of these focus on the unity of qq. 44–103 rather than the unity within qq. 2–43. Hence, our citation of the secondary literature in the next few pages is primarily to establish patterns and assumptions rather than to enter into direct debate.

30. "Consideratio autem de Deo tripartita erit. Primo namque considerabimus ea quae ad essentiam divinam pertinent; secundo, ea quae pertinent ad distinctionem Personarum (q. 27); tertio, ea quae pertinent ad processum creaturarum ab ipso (q. 44)." ST I, q. 2 prologue.

31. "Ultimo autem, post considerationem eorum quae ad divinae essentia unitatem pertinent." ST I, q. 26 prol; q. 26 a. 4 ad 2; and q. 27 prol.

32. ST I, q. 27 prol.

divine essence to a consideration of the distinction of the divine Persons.

Thomas' ordering principle, the order of things, however, does not entail a philosophical discussion of the doctrine of God. The unity of theology or sacred doctrine demands that all remain under the rubric of being divinely "revealable."[33] As Thomas attempts to find a rational basis for some of those beliefs, he is pursuing a deeper understanding with the belief that the object of faith is intelligible in itself, if not always to us in this life. Reasoning upon the faith will typically but not exclusively involve the manifestation of that faith where reason cannot attain of its own accord. The argument from authority never gives up its place to rational argument, though rational argument may be employed where the authority of revelation is retained.[34] In other words, one does not reason *to* the articles of faith but reasons *from* them (see below, section 1.4). As one commentator puts it, the whole of the first forty-three questions of ST I are "a single and unified treatise of revealed theology called 'On God.'"[35] The argument from authority, that is from the authority of revelation, always reigns as the more certain and complete.

The importance of these organizational comments is seen in the interpretation of individual sections. Chenu's attempt to impose an ordering principle onto the *Summa* that did not correspond to Thomas' own words cannot but impinge upon the text's explicit organization. His emanation-return scheme raises questions about particular subsections, such as the relation between the treatments of God's oneness (qq. 2–26) and God's threeness (qq. 26–43). The treat-

---

33. "Quia igitur sacra Scriptura considerat aliqua secundum quod sunt divinitus revelata, secundum quod dictum est, omnia quaecumque sunt divinitus revelabilia, communicant in una ratione formali objecti huius scientiae." ST I, q. 1, a. 3 c.

34. "Ad primum ergo dicendum quod, licet argumenta rationis humanae non habeant locum ad probandum quae fidei sunt, tamen ex articulis fidei haec doctrina ad alia argumentatur." ST I, q. 1, a. 8, ad 1.

35. H. Jorissen, "Zur Struktur des Traktates 'De Deo' in der *Summa theologiae* des Thomas von Aquin," *Im Gespräch mit dem Dreieinen Gott: Elemente einer trinitarischen Theologie*. Festschrift zum 65. Geburtstag von Wilhelm Breuning (Düsseldorf: Patmos Verlag, 1985), 237.

ment of the divine nature (oneness) before Person, under Chenu's rubric, implies a derivation of the latter from the former as effects from a cause. We do not, however, lay the blame at Chenu's doorstep, for his terminology is only a short formula for the neoscholastic reading of the *Summa*. The late-nineteenth-century scholastic commentators commonly identified the first two sections of the *prima pars* with the titles "On the One God" and "On the Triune God". The corresponding philosophical interpretation presumes a demonstrative procedure in the text whereby the relative attributes of God are derived from the absolute ones.[36] The incredible inertia of these durable terms has unfortunately led to the assumption that they are indeed in the text and accurately reflect its structure. Many modern theologians simply refer to the text in these terms with little or no notation of Thomas' own divisions in the prologues to questions 2 and 27.[37] Moreover, the presumed demonstrative procedure associated with the movement from the absolute to the relative with respect to God colors every aspect of Thomas' work, and not to its benefit. In fact, the prevalence of this philosophical reading of the *prima pars* is the root cause for Thomas no less than Augustine being a favorite whipping-boy of post-Vatican II Trinitarian theology. Hence, in order to view the *Summa* as a theological rather than a metaphysical work and to understand the implications of that procedure, we must first extricate Thomas from the tangled web of Trinitarian criticism and historiography.

## 1.3 Neoscholastic Readings

The view that the neoscholastic interpretation with its anachronistic titles have contributed to the misreading of Thomas is not a new

---

36. C. LaCugna, "The Relational God: Aquinas and Beyond," *Theological Studies* 46 (1985): 650–54; J. Moltmann, *Trinität*, ch. 1; W. Willis, Jr., *Theism, Atheism and the Doctrine of the Trinity* (Atlanta: Scholars Press, 1987), 21–26.

37. See the following for traditional uses of these divisions with both negative and positive evaluations: Y. Congar, "Le sense de l'économie salutaire dans la 'Théologie' de saint Thomas d'Aquin (Somme théologique)," in *Glaube und Geschichte*, Festgabe Joseph Lortz, vol. II (Baden-Baden: B. Grimm, 1957), 73–122; Kasper, *The God of Jesus Christ*, 290ff.; Lafont, *Structures et méthode*; Pesch, "Um den Plan," 128–37; Rahner, *The Trinity* ch. 5; Malet, *Personne et amour*, ch. 1.

one. In the last thirty years, a few theologians have taken issue with such neoscholastic terms. Carl Sträter noted the absence of the terms "On the One God" and "On the Triune God" as well as of the implication of an absolute subsistent divine nature in the *Summa*.[38] He argues that the word 'one' is limited to being a predicate adjective, meaning that Thomas never speaks of "[The] One God" but of God who is "one."[39] Sträter also observed that the object of the beatific vision discussed in q. 12 cannot be an abstraction or a singular reality apart from the Persons but must be the whole reality of the Trinity. He proposes therefore a twofold definition of "divine essence" in which it refers to the divine totality in qq. 2–26 and to the common essence in qq. 27–43. The intuitive character of the beatific vision implies that what is seen or known will not be distinguished one part from another by an act of reason. Moreover, this beatified knowing cannot involve less than what we know by faith in this life. "The supernatural knowledge of God which we have in this earthly life is, due to its obscurity, inferior to the heavenly vision. It is, however, much superior to a natural knowledge of God because by faith we already know God to be one and three."[40] The structural transition in the prologue to q. 27 then does not begin the discussion of a new topic but rather is a shift from the discussion of unity to one of distinction within the same divine reality.[41] The subject of qq. 2–26 is, according to Sträter, the 'total divine reality' that is one according to essence and therefore can be signified by "divine essence."[42] In qq. 27–43 the essence is qualified as the absolute perfection distinguished from the relations by a

38. Sträter, "Le point de départ," 71–87.
39. Cf. ST I, q. 11.
40. Sträter, "Le point de départ," 83.
41. "Consideratis autem his quae ad divinae essentiae unitatem pertinent, restat consideratio de his quae pertinent ad trinitatem personarum in divinis." ST I, q. 27 prol.
42. Sträter, "Le point de départ," 83. Indeed, the adjective "total" may seem unnecessary to one who understands the trajectory of the *Summa*, yet the great confusion on this matter more than warrants such a corrective emphasis. Thomas' later insistence that the divine essence is signified only abstractly while the Persons are signified concretely seems to reinforce the notion that the contrast is between unity and distinction.

distinction of reason.⁴³ By defining "divine essence" as the total divine reality in qq. 2–26, Sträter makes two problems disappear: the problem of a supposed derivation of persons from essence in q. 27, and the apparent accidental character of the relations with respect to an "absolute essence." The criticisms often leveled at Thomas simply do not apply, because qq. 27–43 do not represent the introduction of new realities but only the identification of distinctions within the reality already introduced. This position also has the advantage of squaring with Thomas' own language of unity and distinction in his outline of the text in q. 2.⁴⁴

The second feature that undermines popular criticism of Thomas' work is more difficult to define. It concerns the centrality of the questions on the divine persons.⁴⁵ To say that the doctrine of the Trinity is

---

43. Ibid., 85.
44. Unfortunately, Sträter's work has received little attention. The few authors who discuss his argument do not see its importance beyond clarifying particular details of the text. H. Jorissen believes that it was unnecessary for Sträter to posit differences in Thomas' use of '*divina essentia.*' According to Jorissen, Sträter's twofold definition fails to accomplish its goal, namely, protecting Thomas from the charge of "monopersonalism," or an absolute subsistence, in qq. 2–26. Jorissen prefers to interpret the 'divine essence' of qq. 2–26 consistently with the 'divine essence' of qq. 27–43, that is, as the "one essence of three Persons." The divine essence is at no time in the *Summa* an "a-Trinitarian" essence, but is consistently the common essence that "exists in" the Persons undifferentiated. Hence, there is no need to posit any differences in the way in which Thomas uses 'divine essence' in various parts of the *Summa*. Cf. H. Jorissen, "Zur Struktur des Traktates 'De Deo' in der Summa Theologiae des Thomas von Aquin," in *Im Gespräch mit dem Dreieinen Gott: Elemente einer trinitarischen Theologie. Festschrift zum 65. Geburtstag von Wilhelm Breuning* (Düsseldorf: Patmos Verlag, 1985), 231–57. When Jorissen attempts to justify the order of Thomas' discussion in terms of the *opera ad extra*, he finds himself in a corner. The subject of qq. 2–26 must be the agent for *opera ad extra*, but Jorissen had previously excluded personal subsistence from the first section, making the "essence" an abstract term. He instinctually suggests that perhaps the Person of the Father could be the implied subject in the creative and providential acts, yet this puzzling move to fill out the "non-subsisting essence" with an underlying or implied Personhood reveals the problem with a univocal use of the term.
45. There have been several attempts to make Thomas more useful for modern theology precisely by calling attention to his Trinitarian doctrine's exceptional "personalism." The primacy of person over nature is then shown to preclude the kind of problems occurring in an essentialist portrait whereby the Persons issue forth from the one essence as perfections and, consequently, appear to be accessible to natural rea-

central to Christian theology today seems to imply a discernible threeness in things or in the acts of God whereby we could say the Father did this and the Son did that or was responsible for that, etc. We do not find such assertions in Thomas. Rather the centrality of the Trinity means that what is said about this doctrine impacts the whole of theology. We can clarify this statement by looking at the freedom of God with respect to creation and the salvation of human beings. Thomas states that blessedness is the perfect good of intellectual nature.[46] In God, to be is not other than to understand, and to understand is not other than to will and love; hence, God enjoys perfect beatitude. God knows His very being, and the divine will finds repose in this knowledge. Thomas distinguishes the perfect divine life from any act of creation by contending that beatitude does not consist in the willful apprehension of a good, i.e., in an act of the will tending toward the good.[47] Perfect goodness is realized in the notional acts or processions of knowing and willing that are the Persons of the Son and Holy Spirit.[48] The divine intellect is perfect apart from creation. Hence, creation adds nothing to God, nor does it complete God in any way. God's knowledge is then not altered or increased in any way by creation, because creation is not a good desired; rather, it is a good caused by the divine knowledge and will.[49]

This point introduces a crucial problem for modern theology that at the same time raises questions about the value of Thomas' theology. The question of God's relation to creation concerns God's knowledge and love of creatures. In order for God to love each one of us in a particular manner requires that God know each of us in a particular manner, according to our individuality. For scholastics, the question

---

son. Cf. Malet, *Personne et amour*; P. Vanier, *Théologie trinitaire chez Saint Thomas d'Aquin. Evolution du concept d'action notionelle* (Paris-Montréal, 1953); more recently, Schmidbaur, *Personarum Trinitas*.

46. ST I, q. 26 a. 1 c.      47. ST I, q. 28, a. 1, ad 3.

48. ST I, q. 27, a. 5 ad 2.

49. We should note the difference between "knowing" creatures in the modern sense and "causing" creatures in the Scholastic sense. For Thomas, "Deus est causa rerum per suum intellectum et voluntatem . . . et secundum hoc processiones Personarum sunt rationes productionis creaturarum." ST I, q. 45, a. 7 c.

was whether God possessed knowledge of all future contingents. Their affirmative answer complicated the truth of human freedom. For moderns, the question is the manner of God's knowledge of individuals. How can it be that God knows me, and yet God is not changed in any way by the existence of me? Introducing a concept of eternity does not exactly solve the problem but only makes the impact of creatures on God immediate and unified.[50] God would then see and know all in a moment. The answer is unsatisfactory, for it still implies an effect on God, an increase in God's knowledge by the fact of creation. The crux of the problem is then twofold: the manner of God's knowing (and loving) and the true contingency of human action. If God is perfect and immutable (remaining unaffected by creation) and we are truly free to do this or that, thereby becoming and changing ourselves, then it would seem that there really is no present connection between God and creatures. The distinction is absolute and prevents even a communication of knowledge. To say otherwise impinges upon divine perfection or upon human freedom. We cannot, of course, go into the details of Thomas' solution to this tangle of issues. What is important for this study is the way Thomas provides the principles for their solution in his discussion of God in the early questions of the *prima pars*. These principles include Thomas' contention that the basis of creation resides in the processions of knowledge and love, i.e., the procession of divine Persons, and that divine works *ad extra* are one by reason of one eternal cause, the unity of the divine nature.[51] For us, knowing and loving are two distinct acts with the former having both active and passive elements. God's knowing and loving of us, however, is one act, and this one act has no passive elements.

Thomas' incorporation of the Augustinian argument for the unity

---

50. Cf., e.g., Boethius, *The Consolation of Philosophy*, trans. Richard Green (New York: MacMillan, 1962), ch. 5.

51. Cf. G. Emery, *La Trinité créatrice: Trinité et création dans les commentaires aux Sentences de Thomas d'Aquin et de ses précurseurs Albert le Grand et Bonaventure* (Paris: J. Vrin, 1995). The relation between the inner and outer processions is one of cause to effect such that the efficient causality and exemplarity of creation is linked inextricably with the generation of the Son and the procession of the Holy Spirit. Cf. Thomas, ST I, q. 14, a. 8; q. 19, a. 4; q. 45, a. 6.

of divine work *ad extra* serves to connect the Trinity and creation intimately without imputing mutability to the divine Persons. If, in fact, it was the Father alone who created or the Son alone, then our knowledge would be limited to this or that Person, because our knowledge of causes is only by way of effect. If only one Person were the cause of creation, we would know only that one Person by means of the effects in creation. The point is more subtle than at first glance. When we say that the goodness or power of God is evident in creation, such goodness and power would be that of only one divine Person. There would be no basis for asserting these attributes on the part of the other two. We could in that case suppose that each divine Person possessed a different character, much as some ancient gnostics believed that the God of Jesus Christ who redeems humankind is not the same as the Creator God who is responsible for the material world. Thus, the autonomous activity of one divine Person would call into question not only the unity of God but also the very nature of the divine Persons who in that case are not acting in creation. On the other hand, to affirm that the creative power is common to the whole Trinity means that the goodness that is the creative power is common to the three divine Persons, that the Father and Son and Holy Spirit are one cause, a knowing and loving cause. The whole divinity must be the cause of all in order that we may have a basis for meaningful theological speech and are not speaking about only one Person or "part" of the divine nature, leaving the goodness of the rest in doubt.[52] That is, because all three Persons are involved in creation, whatever is evident of the divine nature through creation pertains to all three. The attributes of God are made evident in the things of this world (Rom. 1:20). This point applies to all three divine Persons. Moreover, there is a need here to balance the willful act of a loving God with the perfect beatitude of that same God. By God's knowledge and love of the divine being, God's love of his own goodness overflows into a free creative act. Herein is what is meant by the centrality of Trinitarian doctrine: the procession of knowledge and love, the procession of the Son and the

---

52. ST I, q. 45, a. 6 sc.

Holy Spirit are the very basis or principles of creation.[53] Most importantly, only through this doctrine can we understand creation to be a free act, not a necessary procession or a perfection of the divine nature. Each of the three Persons retains a causality of their own, but the creative power is one inasmuch as the one divine essence is the truth known and the good loved.[54]

This point can be made in another way. If, as some would argue, the creative power was limited to one or two persons, then it would follow that other powers might also be proper to only one Person. Such a distinction according to diverse powers would imply on our part a natural knowledge of the distinction between Persons by way of a natural knowledge of distinct powers. As a consequence, the unity and equality of the Persons would dissolve. Moreover, such knowledge on our part of what distinguishes the divine Persons would mean that the Trinity as such is no longer a mystery but three according to powers. This consequence is unacceptable, because the Trinity of Persons is "maximally one,"[55] and their distinctions cannot be known apart from revelation.[56] There is neither a multiplicity of divine natures nor a hierarchy within that divine nature. Hence, any perceived distinction (of powers) must be according to our understanding only.[57] We can employ the multiplicity of essential attributes to manifest and discuss the distinctions of Persons, yet we must remember that such distinctions of powers do not pertain to the Persons properly. The Persons are equal in every way except according to relations of opposition.

The doctrine of the Trinity is not found in creation; rather, it provides the interpretive framework for understanding all other doctrines.

---

53. ST I, q. 44.
54. ST I, q. 32, a. 1 c. Also, ST I, q. 39, a. 6 c and a. 1 c.
55. ST I, q. 11, a. 4.
56. ST I, q. 32, a. 1; q. 12, a. 13.
57. Thomas accordingly carefully contextualizes the troublesome issue of appropriating specific powers or attributes to each Person. Such appropriations are intended only to illuminate their distinctions, not to constitute these distinctions. Cf. ST I, q. 39, a. 8.

The knowledge of the divine Persons was necessary for two reasons: first, for understanding the creation of things rightly. Indeed, by saying that God created all things by his Word, we exclude the error of presuming that God produced things from a natural necessity. And by positing a procession of love within God, it is shown that God did not produce creatures on account of some need, nor on account of some extrinsic cause, but on account of the love of His own goodness.[58]

Concerning creation, Thomas insists that the overflowing goodness in divine life existed prior to or apart from creation; therefore, creation is a superabundance of a good freely given. God is not and need not be in a real relation for His own sake. It is a higher form of love to act for the sake of a creation that adds nothing to the divine life. Likewise, concerning the works of restoration, we must remember that human nature was "in" God prior to the Incarnation insofar as God is the principle and end of all things. The Second Person of the Trinity took up human nature in a visible manner *for our sakes,* for it was already present in a higher and more perfect way in the Godhead.[59]

Thus, to say that the question of distinction of Persons in the one divine essence is at the heart of the *Summa* is to affirm something important about the nature of God that cannot be forgotten as one reads the remaining questions. We must affirm a unity of Persons in divine works in the world in order to ground our knowledge of God as cause. The doctrine of the Trinity reveals a dynamic perfection of divine life that is free to overflow into a creative act for our sakes. The doctrines of soteriology and Christology grow out of this same idea of divine life. It is for our sakes alone that God provides a way by which rational creatures may attain to God. The inner divine life is the basis of that restoring act, because all divine acts in the world are based upon the inner divine (notional) acts.

---

58. "[Q]uod cognitio divinarum Personarum fuit necessaria nobis dupliciter. Uno modo, ad recte sentiendum de creatione rerum. Per hoc enim quod dicimus Deum omnia fecisse Verbo suo, excluditur error ponentium Deum produxisse res ex necessitate naturae. Per hoc autem quod ponimus in eo processionem amoris, ostenditur quod Deus non propter aliquam indigentiam creaturas produxit, neque propter aliquam aliam causiam extrinsecam; sed propter amorem suae bonitatis." ST I, q. 32, a. 1 ad 3.

59. ST III, q. 2, a. 7 c; ST III, q. 4, a. 3 c.

But nevertheless the divine Persons have a causality with respect to the creation of things according to the *ratio* of their processions.... God is the cause of things through His intellect and will, just as a maker of artificial things [acts through his intellect and will].[60]

Thomas demonstrates that God is a knowing and willing cause as opposed to a cause that knows and wills. That is, God knows and wills the divine nature, and such knowing and willing are the causes *(rationes)* for divine works (e.g., creation and salvation). Thomas is therein careful to protect God's freedom, immutability, goodness, unity, etc. An error with regard to the doctrine of the Trinity is most dangerous in Thomas' mind because what is established there informs and can possibly distort other doctrines.

## 1.4 Thomas' Methodology

Having discussed the centrality of the doctrine of the Trinity in the *Summa* and the consistency of the subject treated in the first two sections of the text (qq. 2–26 and 27–43), we move on to discuss Thomas' methodology particularly with respect to the use of philosophical argument. It cannot be the case that he has, in fact, done what he denounced—namely, attempted to prove the Trinity by arguments from reason. Attempts to prove the Trinity and divine Persons actually discredit the faith. Because the faith concerns things which exceed human reason, it offends the dignity of the faith to treat them as though they do not. Also, if one tries to prove the faith with reasons that are not cogent, one brings the faith into derision.[61] Yet Thomas offered proofs of God's existence as well as of certain essential attributes.[62] The question arises then of how we might characterize Thomas' methodology as he

---

60. "Sed tamen divinae Personae secundum rationem suae processionis habent causalitatem respectu creationis rerum.... Deus est causa rerum per suum intellectum et voluntatem, sicut artifex rerum artificiatarum. Artifex autem per verbum in intellectu conceptum, et per amorem suae voluntatis ad aliquid relatum, operatur. Unde et Deus Pater operatus est creaturam per suum Verbum, quod est Filius; et per suum Amorem, qui est Spiritus Sancuts." ST I, q. 45, a. 6 c.
61. ST I, q. 32, a. 1 c.
62. Cf. ST I, qq. 2–11.

moves from a discussion of truths accessible to natural reason to a discussion of those things wholly beyond (but not against) reason and knowable by revelation alone. In other words, what is the methodological relation between rational arguments in these two sections? Natural reason can attain to a knowledge of the existence of God and certain divine attributes. Thomas calls these demonstrable things the "preambles" to the articles of faith. These preambles concern the knowledge of God from His effects, for the effects themselves take the place of a definition of the cause.[63] Hence, the knowledge of God's existence as well as the causal nature of his Being are knowable through His effects by means of natural reason.[64]

Natural reason cannot, however, attain to a knowledge of the distinction of Persons.[65] Doctrines such as this one are knowable by revelation alone and are called "articles of faith." What pertains to the articles of faith can be known and proven only by way of authority. These truths are intelligible in themselves but not to us in this life. The distinction between preambles and articles of faith is then not whether a truth is intelligible, but whether it is accessible in this life. The preambles of faith, such as God's existence, eternity, and goodness, can be known by natural reason and yet are part of the deposit of faith. Thomas' famous "five ways" are examples of arguments whose conclusions correspond to the truths of the faith.[66] Such demonstrations, however, may be seen only by a few persons with sufficient knowledge of natural things, sufficient leisure, and a high degree of moral virtue. It is evidence of the mercy of God that these rationally accessible truths are revealed in addition to the mysteries; namely, so that all may know what is necessary for salvation.[67] All of these truths are part of the matter of theology. Thus, regarding theological doctrines in general, what is believed and not yet understood by human reason may

---

63. ST I, q. 2, a. 2 ad 2.
64. For much of this section, I am dependent upon R. McInerny's discussion in his work *St. Thomas Aquinas* (Notre Dame: University of Notre Dame Press, 1977), ch. 5.
65. ST I, q. 32, a. 1 c.
66. ST I, q. 2, a. 3 c.
67. ST I, q. 1, a. 1 c; also *Summa contra Gentiles* I, ch. 4.

possibly be understood with the aid of the right philosophical proof, and certainly in the next life by means of the light of glory.[68] Properly understood, the preambles are not prior to faith but presupposed. They are believed on the basis of revelation and even assumed in beliefs about Christ, for example, but can also be (in theory) known on the basis of philosophical truths.[69]

For most theologians, the truths concerning the Trinity, the Incarnation and the forgiveness of sins can be believed but not known demonstrably in this life and are, therefore, classified as "articles of faith."[70] The role of philosophical argument in discussing these doctrines is limited to clarifying the mysteries by way of analogies or similitudes and refuting objections brought against these doctrines. That is, having posited a particular doctrine, one can show its inner coherence (or logic) and that it is congruent with other known truths.[71] If one does not allow such an authority or the statement of such doctrine, no arguments can be adduced for proving the doctrine. Further, to attempt such proofs for what are specifically mysteries is for Thomas a derogation of the faith.

The relation between the preambles and the articles is especially

---

68. For a discussion of the *lumen gloriae,* see ST I, q. 12, a. 5.

69. It is also important to note that knowing cannot coincide with believing in the same person at the same time. One believes a given truth until it is known, and then one is said to "know" that it is true. McInerny, *St. Thomas Aquinas,* 159–61.

70. Anselm and the fourteenth-century nominalists, on the other hand, represent the extremes beyond this normative listing as found in Thomas. One may read Anselm's arguments of suitability to imply a stronger assertion about what is rationally accessible or demonstrable since he did, in fact, attempt to show by reason the truth of the Incarnation and Trinity. That is, one may read his arguments about the being of God *(Monologion)* in the same way one reads his argument for the existence of God *(Proslogion).* Ockham and later nominalists represented a much more conservative view of the ability of human reason. For them, very little of the Christian faith could be known by reason alone, because the way in which we know things is determined by our intellective acts, not by the objects known. Hence, reasoning has more to do with the workings of our minds and linguistics than with the objects of our knowledge. Cf. Ockham, *Summa Logicae* 50–52.

71. "Alio modo inducitur ratio, non quae sufficienter probet radicem, sed quae radici iam positae ostendat congruere sconsequentes effectus. . . . quia scilicet, Trinitate posita, congruunt huiusmodi rationes." ST I, q. 32, a. 1 ad 2.

problematic in discussions of the Trinity. Though this doctrine is itself an article of faith, its discussion spans the distinction between preambles and articles. Anselm, Peter the Lombard, and others attempted to bridge the two categories (or actually blur the distinction between them) by means of the divine attributes and various analogies between Creator and created. In order to protect the dignity of the faith, Thomas, however, demarcated the mysteries of the faith as articles not subject to human understanding. He wanted neither to exalt human reason beyond its capabilities nor to humble the wisdom of God by suggesting that it can be plumbed without the light of glory that is nothing less than the presence of God in the mind.[72] We will discuss in detail Thomas' treatment of these problems of Trinitarian discussion in chapter 3. For now, it is important only to note that arguments from natural reason have different import and roles in Thomas' *Summa* depending upon whether the topic is an article or preamble of the faith.

It would be simplistic, however, to see the division between ST I, qq. 2–26 and ST I, qq. 27–43 as a division between arguments from reason and those from authority. Arguments from authority do not assume center stage only in the second section; they are present throughout. Thomas states that the theologian uses the philosophical sciences "for the greater manifestation of those things treated in this science [theology]."[73] Further, "those things" referred to here are the principles of theology which are revealed by God directly or immediately. The argumentation proceeds from that which is revealed, and in cases where the revealed coincides with what is naturally attainable, i.e., the existence of God, the argument proceeds upon the more certain: the revealed truth.[74] This is not to say that Thomas limits himself

---

72. "[I]ta divina essentia unitur intellectui creato ut intellectum in actu, per seipsam faciens intellectum in actu." ST I, q. 12, a. 2 ad 3.

73. "Ad secundum dicendum quod haec scientia accipere potest aliquid a philosophicis disciplinis . . . ad majorem manifestationem eorum quae in hac scientia traduntur." ST I, q. 1 a. 5 ad 2.

74. "[I]sta scientia est principaliter de his quae sua altitudine ratione transcendunt; aliae vero scientiae considerant ea tantum quae ratione subduntur." ST I, q. 1, a. 5 c.

to arguments from authority, for he does use arguments about human knowing and willing to elucidate the mystery of the Trinity.

Thomas posits an analogy between human psychology and divine life as he proceeds in his discussion from intellectual subsistence to knowing and willing, to processions of word and love, and the subsistent character of that word and love. Yet this elucidation by means of philosophical argument does not imply a procedure in which Thomas would presume to push the analogy as far as possible in order to reveal a threeness (in oneness) in God. Augustine's attempt to do just this failed (without surprise to him) because each Person understands and loves, so that there are three Persons understanding and loving.[75] Moreover, our knowing and willing are distorted and unbalanced by sin. Psychological analogies actually reveal more about the differences between the divine Persons and human persons.[76] More importantly, for Augustine, the analogy reveals the damage done to the human person by sin and our consequent need for Christ to reform the image in which we are created so that it may rightfully assume its epistemological role.[77]

In the *Summa* the argument from psychology is actually begun with the propositions of the faith defining the reality of processions and Persons. Thomas outlines the truths of the doctrine before he introduces the argument from psychology; hence, any philosophical investigation of these truths can only be characterized as "elucidation" and not as demonstration.[78] It is also important to remember that

---

75. Augustine, *De Trinitate* XV.12, 42. On Augustine's intentional failure, see J. Cavadini, "Augustine's *De Trinitate*," *Augustinian Studies* 23 (1992): 97–128.

76. *De Trinitate* XV.21–26.

77. *De Trinitate* XIV.23–24. We must be careful, however, not to suppose that even Augustine's argument was without foundation in revelation. He says himself in *De Trinitate* XV.39 that he has been discussing the Holy Spirit according to the Scriptures. Hence, even in that heavily "philosophical" discussion of Books VIII–XV, Augustine sees himself arguing on the basis of Scripture, not on reason alone—that is, using a reasoning illumined by faith, not working toward faith. In Thomas' terms, then, Augustine's work was simply the application of psychology for elucidating an article of faith while at the same time affirming a kind of knowledge by conformity in the next life.

78. Cf. ST I, q. 1, a. 5; q. 32.

Thomas does not introduce the concept of the "image of God" until q. 93, some fifty questions after the discussion of the Trinity. He could hardly prove much analogously without having first established and defined the basis of the analogy. One must conclude that Thomas proceeds on the basis of an idea of intellectual subsistence stripped of the imperfections of the composition of body and soul and finite existence, while being imbued with all possible perfections of unity, eternity, goodness, infinity, immutability, . . . etc.

If, on the other hand, Thomas had derived the Persons from the essence by philosophical argument involving the divine attributes, the connection between essential attributes and the persons would certainly be more important to the text. The introduction of word and love or of the many Augustinian triads would have fit in quite well after q. 20, by which time Thomas had discussed the knowledge and will of God. The fact that Thomas waits until after he has already discussed the divine attributes and divine Persons separately before he broaches the way attributes (e.g., power, wisdom, love) can be used to reveal something about the distinction of Persons shows that it was not a central argument.[79] Most every aspect of Trinitarian doctrine is expounded before the discussion of the appropriation of essential attributes to specific Persons. The coordination of essential and proper terms then comes at the end of the exercise of "faith seeking understanding." That is to say, qualified and corrected theological language is the product, not the subject, of theological endeavor. More about this subject in chapter 4.

Hence, if one asks whether the ordering of topics in Aquinas' *Summa theologiae* represents the best or even a good ordering of philosophical arguments demonstrating the Trinity, the answer is, "No." Arguments from psychology or from the divine attributes would in a philosophical work precede and inform the discussion of the Persons. In the *Summa*, quite the contrary is true. Questions 27–43 contain not rational demonstrations but illustrative arguments of the articles of faith, which are themselves determined and shaped by the content of revelation.

79. Cf. ST I, q. 39.

If Thomas does not use philosophical arguments to demonstrate the Trinity, it is still unclear what the transition from q. 26 to q. 27 involves. What type of move is involved when discussion turns from the unity of the divine essence to the distinction of Persons? It seems to Thomas' critics that he sets aside revelation until q. 27 as he works with rationally attainable doctrines in the first set of questions. Because of this apparent methodological shift, many theologians have taken issue with Thomas and argued that the two sections do not share the same subject.[80] The suspicion is that Thomas is using rational speculation to introduce his doctrine of God and that this doctrine, in the early questions, does not correspond to the Christian Trinitarian doctrine that is introduced in q. 27. This suspicion is not unfounded. The idea that Thomas divided his text into philosophical and theological arguments or that he reversed the traditional relation of faith and knowledge comes directly from some of Thomas' best-known commentators.[81] Neoscholastics such as Billot, Garrigou-Lagrange, Maritain, and others used the terms "On the One God" and "On the Triune God," as well as the absolute/relative dichotomy in their reading of Thomas' *Summa*. In fact this particular reading of Thomas dates back to his late medieval commentators, John of St. Thomas and Cardinal Cajetan. According to the former,

The treatise On God contains two parts. First, it treats God as an entity with absolute attributes and in act (up to q. 27). Second, it treats God as He is relative, namely, the mystery of the Trinity (from q. 27 to q. 44).[82]

---

80. One could argue, however, that even if the *prima pars* is only a natural theology, the God of the philosopher and the God of Christian believers must be the same, though not with respect to all descriptions. Cf. McInerny, *St. Thomas Aquinas*, 158–60.

81. A related issue that underlies modern suspicions of Thomas' method is the rejection, or at least misconception, of the scientific status of theology. Cf. ST I, q. 1. For an excellent analysis of this first question of the *Summa*, see V. White, O.P., *Holy Teaching: The Idea of Theology according to St. Thomas Aquinas* (London: Blackfriars, 1958).

82. "Et tractatus de deo secundum se continet duas partes. Prima est de Deo quoad entitatem, et attributa absoluta, sive in operando a quaestione secunda usque ad XXVII. Secunda agit de Deo quoad relativa, seu mysterium Trinitatis a quaestione XXVII, usque ad XLIV." John of St. Thomas, *Cursus theologicus*, t. 1 (Paris: Ludovicus Vives, 1883), 191.

Cajetan further solidified this identification of the subject of qq. 2–26 as an absolute when he developed his notion of "this God."

> In the title an ambiguity occurs immediately. For what does 'God' supposit in this question, "Whether God is the same as His essence"? In God the individual instance of the nature is distinguished from the concrete instance [of the nature]; that is, we distinguish "this God" from the divine supposits, Father, Son, and Holy Spirit.[83]

Subsequent commentaries on the *Summa* or scholastic presentations of theology formalized this absolute/relative reading by labeling the respective parts "On the One God" and "On the Triune God." Billot, Daffara, and Dalmau are just a few of the many neoscholastics who took up these divisions in their own work.[84] There are some exceptions to this trend such as Billuart and Farrell, yet Billot's popularity among neoscholastics, together with the presence of Cajetan's commentary in the Leonine edition, overshadowed other trends of commentary and nomenclature.[85] The upshot is that the modern distaste for what seems to be overly speculative or, in a pejorative sense, "philosophical" in Thomas is more aptly leveled at Cajetan, Billot, and the neoscholastics who were responsible for characterizing ST I, qq. 1–43 as a philosophical rather than a theological work.[86] Because of

---

83. "In titulo statim occurit ambiguitas, pro quo supponit Deus in hoc quaesito, uturm Deus sit idem quod sua essentia.... In deo... distinguitur individuum naturae in concreto, idest hic Deus, a supposito divino, idest Patre et Filio et Spiritu Sancto." Cardinal Cajetan, *In Summa Theologiae* I, q. 3 a. 3, nn. I-II.

84. L. Billot, *De Deo Uno et Trino: commentarius in primam partem S. Thomae* (Rome: S.C. de propaganda Fide, 1897); M. Daffara, O.P., *De Deo Uno et Trino* (Rome: Maretti, 1945); I. Dalmau, S.J., "De Deo Uno et Trino," in *Sacrae Theologiae Summa*, II (Matriti, 1953). For these references, I am indebted to C. Sträter, "Le point de départ," 71–87.

85. F. C.-R. Billuart, *Summa Sancti Thomae hodiernis academiarum moribus accommodata* (Paris: Victorem Palme, 1867); W. Farrell, *A Companion to the Summa* (New York: Sheed & Ward, 1941).

86. The nineteenth-century Neoscholastic movement was defined by its philosophical interests and readings, giving the texts themselves a noticeable philosophical color (and in this case, a specifically metaphysical one). The theological discussions of these texts followed, yet noticeably later; hence, the philosophical issues held center stage throughout. Cf. O. Pesch, *Thomas Von Aquin* (Mainz: Matthias-Grünewald-Verlag, 1988), 29f.

Cajetan's extensive influence on modern readings of Thomas' *Summa*, we must of course go beyond a mere mention.

## 1.5 The Source of Modern Readings: Cajetan

Cajetan[87] for the most part did his work very well as he unraveled the complexities of the *Summa*, providing useful formulae for comprehension and highlighting important connections and references within the text.[88] Unfortunately, he also obscured the text at crucial points. In regard to the structure of the first book, he missed the mark by a rather wide margin.[89] Cajetan ignored the organizational comments in ST I, qq. 2, 26, and 27, as well as the divisions to which they correspond. He also broached the subject of distinguishing Person and essence thirty-six questions earlier than Thomas does. In q. 39 Thomas enunciates a number of principles by which we might understand the distinction between Persons and essence and between the Persons themselves and communicate such distinctions in meaningful speech. Cajetan, however, introduces these distinctions in q. 3 with unfortunate consequences. The resultant terminology suggests that the divine nature has an existence apart from the Persons. Thus, by introducing a precision that is not needed in q. 3, he unknowingly turns this theological text into a metaphysics. By this I mean both that he re-

---

87. Though it would be a difficult case to demonstrate, we would like to assert here that the popularity among Neoscholastics of Cajetan as a commentator on Thomas, the heavy citation of his commentaries by such great Thomists as Billot, Garrigou-Lagrange, and Maritain, and the inclusion of his commentary in the Leonine edition of the *Summa* all indicate the dominating presence of Cajetan in Thomistic studies throughout most of the last century. Cf. Patfoort, "L'unité," 513–44; Sträter, "Le point de départ," 72ff.

88. On the life and works of Cajetan, the following works may be consulted: I. Congar, O.P., "Bio-bibliographie de Cajétan," *Revue Thomiste* 17 (1934), 3–49; M. Grabmann, "Die Stellung des Kardinal Cajetan in der Geschichte des Thomismus," *Angelicum* II (1934): 547–60. For the most recent bibliography, see A. Krause, *Zur Analogie bei Cajetan und Thomas von Aquin* (Halle/Saale: Hallescher Verlag, 1999). Cajetan is most known for his commentaries on Thomas' *De ente et essentia* and *Summa Theologiae*, but he also commented upon most of Aristotle's logical works, especially in the early part of his career (1494–99).

89. On other errors of Cajetan, see R. McInerny's *Aquinas and Analogy* (Washington, D.C.: The Catholic University of America Press, 1996).

verses the movement of faith to understanding and that he defines the oneness and threeness in God as metaphysically distinct, whereas Thomas would say that they are the same except in our manner of speaking (q. 28, a. 1). That is to say, the God of revelation—the God who is Three Persons discussed as a unity in the early questions—becomes for Cajetan an absolute, concrete subject with its own subsistence (not identical with the subsistence of the three Persons). Thus, we have the three Persons, the divine essence and "this God," i.e., the individual divine nature.[90]

In order to draw out the impact of Cajetan's remarks, we will first outline two of Thomas' discussions of the name 'God;' that of qq. 3 and 39. First, in q. 3, a. 3 the matter of the question is "whether God is the same as His essence or nature."[91] In distinguishing the significate of 'humanity' and that of 'deity,' he states that those things that are not composed of matter and form are individuated *per se*. They are subsistent supposits or instances, and no difference exists between the instance (suppositum) and the nature.[92] It is evident from his response that Thomas answers the question for spiritual beings in general. The comparison then is between what is composed and what is not composed. God is one because God is not composed of parts, namely, of form and matter.

Compare this response with that of the later discussion in q. 39, which asks, "whether concrete essential names may supposit for persons."[93] The essential term 'God' can be said to supposit (or "stand for") essence insofar as it signifies the divine essence by which the divine Persons are God. Yet because we have asserted that divinity is simple (q. 3), the one having divinity (the divine person) and the

---

90. Cajetan, *In Summa Theologiae* I, q. 39, a. 8. As stated above, this first section is not a treatise "De Deo Uno." It concerns the *una divina essentia trium personarum*. Thomas' heavy use of philosophical argumentation gives the appearance at times of a metaphysical demonstration, but it is purely a theological study moving from faith to understanding, not the reverse.

91. "[U]trum sit idem Deus quod sua essentia vel natura." ST I, q. 3, a. 3.

92. ST I, q. 3, a. 3 c.

93. "[U]trum nomina essentialia concreta possint supponere pro persona." ST I, q. 39, a. 4.

thing had (the divinity itself) must be the same. 'God' signifies both the one having divinity and the divinity itself.[94] Thomas goes on to clarify this manner of signification by noting the different ways in which 'man' and 'God' supposit for person, the one having such nature. The form signified by 'man' is really divided among the many individuals of the species and is one only according to our consideration. 'Man' supposits for 'persons' properly and *per se*. 'God', however, signifies a form that is one and, therefore, supposits *per se* for the [divine] nature. Yet according to its manner of signifying, 'God' supposits for the divine Persons, since the divine nature is not other than the divine Persons being found only in them.[95] For Thomas, the unity of the nature is caused by, or consists in, the unity of the Persons (in the act of being). For this reason, 'man' and 'God' supposit in very much the same way. The difference is in the unity of the nature signified.

The level of precision and clarity in the discussion is markedly different in these two articles. Only in q. 39 does Thomas refer to notional acts, the *divina supposita*, and the different modes of signification. All that is known in q. 3 is that God is one due to the identity of form and supposit in spiritual beings. Hence, 'God' is not other than divine essence. Thomas makes this same point in q. 39, with an important clarification. There, Thomas equates divine supposita and divine nature in personal terms because the discussion concerns God particularly and not as a type of spiritual being.

Cajetan, however, does not interpret these two questions according to different manners of signification. In q. 3, a. 3, he understands 'God' to refer to an absolute or "concrete individual" more properly signified by "this God."[96] Commenting on the question, "whether God is the same as His essence," Cajetan focuses on the signification of the

---

94. "Et haec opinio processisse videtur ex consideratione divinae simplicitatis, quae requirit quod in Deo idem sit habens et quod habetur." ST I, q. 39, a. 4 c.

95. "[A]lii melius dixerunt quod hoc nomen *Deus* ex modo significandi habet ut proprie possit supponere pro persona, sicut et hoc nomen *homo*." ST I, q. 39, a. 4 c. Consequently, Thomas argues that 'Deus' cannot be a proper name, that is, one signifying a nature, because God's nature is inaccessible to us. It is a name of operation, for we understand God by way of His effects. See ST I, q. 13, a. 8.

96. Cajetan, *In Summa Theologiae* I, q. 3, a. 3, nn. I and II.

name 'God.' It becomes clear that Cajetan has raised a question that is not in the text; namely, whether divinity has a concrete existence or subsistence apart from the Persons. Cajetan's affirmative answer is troubling. He argues that the name 'God' cannot signify a specific suppositum ("one having deity") because this name signifies something common to the three. It also cannot signify the Persons because no mention is made of Person. Hence, it cannot be suppositing for Person, Persons, or personal suppositum. Cajetan then opts for another possibility, that of a non-personal suppositum. "God" he says, "signifies a concrete individual of divine nature," not the Person of the Father, the Son, or the Holy Spirit, but "this God" who is the subsisting divine nature. Of course, one would be rightly hesitant to accuse the commentator of suggesting a "fourth thing" in God.[97] Unfortunately, as he has allowed grammatical considerations to rule his discussion, he has fallen into a predicament very similar to that of Gilbert of Poitiers. The most telling evidence that Cajetan has indeed found himself in a corner is his rejection of the Augustinian axiom concerning the unity of works *ad extra* in favor of a divine nature that acts.[98] For Cajetan, it is "this God" who possesses creative power and performs all divine works *ad extra*. Having defined a concrete, subsistent "God" distinct from the Persons, Cajetan has unwittingly argued for an absolute divinity that could easily be seen as the basis for the modern charge of "monopersonalism" in the *Summa*.

At first glance it may seem that Cajetan is using the same distinction of reason that Thomas later uses, one that does not call into question the real identity of Person and essence. Cajetan, however, assumes that Thomas' later distinction supports a discussion of essence sepa-

---

97. "... [S]ignificat concretum individuale naturae divinae, idest hunc habentem deitatem, seu *hunc Deum;* sicut *homo* potest supponere pro hoc homine." Note that "this man" as Cajetan uses it is opposed to one having such nature, "Socrates." The nature then can be or not be a person.

98. "Auctor intelligat de essentia in concreto; cum dicit quod in ista, "Deus creat," ly 'Deus' supponit pro natura . . . Nec est verum quod actiones sint suppositorum, universaliter; sed singularium subsistentium, quale est 'hic Deus.'" Cajetan, *In Summa Theologiae* I, q. 39, a. 4, n. X. Compare Thomas: "Virtus autem creativa Dei est sommunis toti Trinitati." ST I, q. 32, a. 1 c.

rated from Persons. Cajetan suggests that in a similar way we can speak of "God" to indicate the divine Persons and "this God" to indicate the "individual" divine nature; that is, he makes a distinction between signifying the divine Persons and signifying the divine nature which is, unlike human nature, really one. The consequence is that divine Persons and divine nature are not identical in existence. Cajetan's third term, "This God," then indicates the divine nature as existing.[99] One might ask, however, whether this semantic distinction is helpful or not, especially as it limits the suppositional breadth of 'God.' According to Aquinas, 'man' and 'God' both properly signify the one or ones having such nature, even though the divine nature is a real unity and not merely a mental one. That is, the unity and existence of the divine nature is not found outside the divine Persons. As Aquinas said in his *Summa*, "among all things that are said to be one, the unity of the divine Trinity holds the highest place."[100] For Thomas, essence is signified "as in the one having [it]";[101] that is, not apart from Person, for the divine nature subsists only in the Persons. The distinction of reason between essence and Person that allows for a plurality of manners of signifying is logical only and is not a real distinction according to acts or existence. The identity of essence and supposita in God means that there is nothing other than the Persons in God.[102] For that reason, Thomas argues that while 'God' naturally signifies the divine nature and therefore stands for the nature, it properly supposits for the Persons.[103] The real unity of the divine nature is found in the real unity and existence of the divine Persons.

---

99. For the roots of modern existential Thomism, one need look no further. Cf. E. Gilson, *Being and Some Philosophers* (Toronto, 1949). For an excellent rebuttal, see R. McInerny, *Being and Predication: Thomistic Interpretations*, Studies in Philosophy and the History of Philosophy, vol. 16 (Washington, D.C.: The Catholic University of America Press, 1986), chs. 12 and 13.

100. "[I]nter omnia quae unum dicuntur, arcem tenet unitas divinae Trinitatis." ST I, q. 11, a. 4 sc (quoting Bernard of Clairvaux).

101. "[U]t habente." ST I, q. 39, aa. 1 and 5.

102. "[Q]uod in Deo non sit aliud essentia quam persona secundum rem." ST I, q. 39, a. 1.

103. ST I, q. 39, a. 4 c.

Commenting on q. 39, Cajetan argues that in God what is relative differs from what is absolute and not only according to reason.[104] Cajetan agrees that essence and Person are the same thing, but they do not exactly share the same existence. While paternity and essence are not actually distinct, they are "virtually" distinct. They can be distinguished not only by our manner of understanding but also by their acts.

The effect in act has a cause in the act. But without denying the difference between communicable and incommunicable, the effect in act is distinguished before any act of the intellect. Therefore, it [effect] has a cause in the act, but its cause is a distinction. Consequently, there is a distinction [in the cause] before any act of the intellect.[105]

Cajetan contends that this distinction does not depend upon our reasoning, by which a simple thing can be referred to in multiple terms due to our inability to grasp a singular. Rather, he posits an incomplete diversity based upon diversity of action. The distinction is dependent upon an equivocal cause whose equivocity betrays a distinction "virtually" present.

Nevertheless there is one response to all these things: one can deny the universal application of the proposition, namely, that distinction alone is the cause of its [distinct] effects. For the effect can arise from a distinction as from a quasi univocal cause or from a distinction virtually contained [in it] as of an equivocal cause.[106]

The virtual distinction is not solely dependent upon the work of the intellect; nor is it the formal distinction of the Scotists. Rather, it is a distinction dependent upon its own act—upon the equivocity of the cause. The effect in act has a cause in the act either by a real distinc-

---

104. Cajetan, *In Summa Theologiae* I, q. 39, a. 1, n. VII.
105. Cajetan, *In Summa Theologiae* I, q. 39, a. 1, n. X.
106. "Unica tamen responsione ad haec omnia et similia dicitur, negando universaliter illam propositionem, scilicet quod sola distinctio est cause huius effectus. Nam isti effectus potest oriri a distinctione, ut a causa quasi univoca: et a *virtualiter continente distinctionem*, ut a causa aequivoca." Cajetan, *In Summa Theologiae* I, q. 39, a. 1, n. XII.

tion in the thing or by a virtual distinction between essence and relation in which the former causes a unity and the latter a plurality. Cajetan makes this distinction more than merely one of reason, because the unity to which he is referring here is not the unity of the Persons *per se* but the substantial unity of the divine nature with its own subsistence.

When discussing the subject of 'God creates,' Cajetan argues that it refers to the divine essence as a singular or absolute, concrete subsistence. His distinction between two kinds of concrete subsistence, absolute and personal,[107] allows him to say that the creative act can be of the divine nature yet need not be of the supposita. Thomas, on the other hand, argues that 'God' supposits for the essence by reason of the identity of Person and essence only and, therefore, includes the personal supposita as well. Thomas uses an abstraction of essence for the purposes of discussion, but this procedure is not a "separation" of essence and Person technically understood.[108] Thus, 'God creates' supposits for the Trinity of Persons who by means of their unity are one Creator. Cajetan reads the text as a metaphysician and sees a distinction between acts of Persons and acts of the divine nature.

We can make this clearer: for Thomas, there is nothing other than Persons in God.[109] Certain notional acts (begetting, spirating) are proper to one Person or to two; other acts, specifically acts in the world, are common to all three Persons, not *of* the common essence but *common to* the Trinity of Persons.[110] God is three by reason of the

---

107. Often read as "monopersonal" and "tripersonal."

108. According to Thomas, *"separatio"* is the proper mode of reasoning in metaphysics. By this term he means the intellectual act by which one may determine what is the being of the thing and what is not. For instance, one may "separate" being white from being human because whiteness is not proper to human nature. Another way of considering this operation is the "separation" of substance from accidents. The intellectual operation of abstraction then involves the whole and the part (universal from the particular) or the form and the matter (mathematics), or knowing one thing without the other even though they are one in reality. See Thomas, *Expositio super Boethii De Trinitate*, q. 5, a. 3.

109. ST I, q. 39, a. 1.

110. "[C]reare non est proprium alicui Personae, sed commune toti Trinitati." ST I, q. 45, a. 6.

distinction of Persons and one by reason of the unity of Persons. Cajetan, however, bases the unity of God on the unity of the subsistent nature, "this God" (subsistent, singular divine nature). He interprets Thomas' "God who is one" as a singular subsistent divine nature ('this God'), thereby establishing a virtual distinction between the divine essence, "this God who creates," and the personal supposita. In other words, the acts of the personal supposita are immanent and relative. Divine acts in the world proceed from the subsisting nature that is itself absolute and concrete. One can then distinguish grammatically and notionally between the 'God' who begets and the 'God' who creates. Indeed, Cajetan goes so far as to say that the "divine nature subsists from itself not deriving [literally, "begging"] its subsistence from the supposits, but on the contrary, conferring it on them."[111]

The impact of Cajetan's reading is severe. His prominence and popularity as the commentator of St. Thomas has made his commentary the lens through which Thomas has been read and taught, especially since *Aeterni Patris* and the Leonine edition of the *Summa* appeared around the turn of the century. Cajetan's metaphysical reading of Thomas has obscured the procedure of the text. Thomas treats the Godhead as a whole before treating it according to its parts using a type of abstraction. Cajetan and scholars dependent upon him failed to see what kind of science Thomas' theology is, and they have mistakenly read into the text the metaphysical procedure of separation by means of which the subsistent divine nature would be treated before and without the personal supposita. Read in this way, the *Summa* does, in fact, separate the Trinity of Persons completely from the acts of creation and salvation. Contemporary scholars have rightly bristled at the apparent non-identity between the One God and the Triune God. But it is the metaphysician Cajetan, not Thomas, who proposes a One God creating and restoring humankind.

---

111. "[D]ivina natura ex seipsa subsistit nec mendicat subsistentiam a suppositis, imo confert eam illis." Cajetan, *In Summa Theologiae* I, q. 39, a. 4, n. VIII.

## 1.6 Conclusion

In treating God in more rationally accessible terms in qq. 2–26, Thomas is not leaving aside the existence of Persons, only their distinctions. The interpretation of the divine essence in the early questions as an absolute existent distorts the entire treatise and leads to the divorce of Trinitarian doctrine from the rest of Christian theology. In order to insure that the doctrine of the Trinity is integral to the entire *Summa*, the subject of the early questions must be properly clarified to include the totality of God, encompassing what is distinct as well as what is common and one. It is the abstracted whole of the Godhead that is seen as a unity and exists, is simple, is perfect, is good, infinite, immutable, eternal, and one. Because God is nothing other than Persons,[112] the divine unity is none other than the three Persons (Father, Son, and Holy Spirit) who are supremely one.[113]

---

112. ST I, q. 39, a. 1 c.
113. ST I, q. 11, a. 4 sc.

# 2. Order and Theological Method

Thomas Aquinas' doctrine of God in the first part of his *Summa theologiae* is a carefully developed construction, and it is meant to be read according to its own development, each article contextualized within Thomas' increasingly precise terminology and distinctions. The terminology in one section, however, cannot simply be imported into another. Misplaced distinctions and an overly rigid interpretation of terms can be disastrous to one's interpretation. As we have seen in Cajetan's reading of question three, a misreading of terms and context colors his whole interpretation. There is, on the other hand, weighty evidence that Thomas is not and cannot be discussing an absolute, concrete essence in the first 26 questions of his *Summa*. The subject of the discussion is God, one and three, not separated from relations and Persons, nor absolutized as a monopersonal God. Going beyond a mere critique of Cajetan, we will in this chapter offer a constructive proposal for reading the first part of the *Summa*. We will first demonstrate the implication (presence) of divine Persons throughout the text, thereby clarifying the *point de départ* for treating the distinction of Persons (qq. 27ff.). Secondly, we will elucidate the development of Thomas' use of divine essence and why it is necessary to postpone the distinction Cajetan interpolated in q. 3. And finally we will analyze the way in which Thomas makes use of various terms as he fills out the discussion of the distinction and unity of divine Persons.

## 2.1 Divine Essence and Divine Persons (ST I, qq. 2-26)

Our case involves two avenues of demonstration: one is textual, following the development of Thomas' doctrine of God as a whole;

# Divine Essence and Divine Persons 49

the other avenue demonstrates the impossibility of the alternative, the impossibility of a discussion of an abstract essence without the reality of divine Persons. It is our intention not only to show what Thomas is doing in his ordering of topics but also to reveal why such ordering is effective in clarifying certain issues. In particular, Thomas' solution in defining the distinction and subsistence of the three Persons steers clear of "demonstrating" such things while providing rather satisfying modes[1] of explicating the doctrine.

First, the textual development: Thomas refers to the Trinity of Persons or to individual Persons at several points in the *Summa* prior to discussing the Persons *per se*. Often the reference is found in the *sed contra* where Thomas offers the principle of his response in terms of the Persons.[2] This phenomonon is most common in the articles on "the manner in which God is known by us." These references are not simply passing remarks or glimpses of what is to come in the next section. On the contrary, they betray the implicit subject of the text; that is, the whole divine essence that is God, one and three. In discussing the way in which we know God, Thomas treats first the vision of the blessed and then our vision, or knowledge. In the course of thirteen articles, Thomas explains piecemeal the means and manner of our vision of God in this life and the next as well as the theoretical limit of any intellectual being's vision of God.

He begins his argument with the text of 1 John 3:2, "we will see Him as He is."[3] God is most knowable in Himself, but not to any created intellect. As a night creature could not bear to look upon the sun,

---

1. By 'modes' I mean to imply that Thomas does not offer definitive answers to the great questions of Trinitarian doctrine. Rather, he approaches such questions from different points of view in order to clarify what is meant by particular expressions. Hence, he defines *divina essentia* in three very different contexts (ST I, qq. 3, 12, 39). The statements from each one of these particular discussions cannot be joined to statements from other discussions without qualification. The 'essence', for example, described in q. 39 is perhaps more intelligible to the Aristotelian, while the 'essence' of q. 3 that is one with being lies more in the domain of the theologian. On the other hand, between q. 3 and q. 39, Thomas develops a theory of naming that alters the import of the Aristotelian language to suit the theological demands.

2. Cf. ST I, q. 3, a. 3; q. 10, a. 2; q. 11, a. 4.

3. ST I, q. 12, a. 1 sc.

so our human intellects cannot "look" upon God because of the excess of His intelligibility. The highest desire and operation of our being—in which beatitude consists—must consist in a vision of the First Cause if this desire is not in vain; hence, we must affirm that the blessed see the essence of God.

Thomas implies that the beatific vision does attain to the Persons in some way. Divine revelation reveals to us God's more excellent effects so that we may be able "to attribute [to God] that which natural reason cannot attain."[4] The blessed's vision of God is distinguished from the comprehension one divine Person has of another,[5] for God is beyond every existent and, therefore, exceeds every creaturely cognition of Him.[6] Creaturely beatitude lies somewhere between a vision of an undivided One and a comprehension of the three Persons in their proper identity, equality, and unity. To clarify the nature of this vision Thomas makes an important distinction between seeing and knowing (*videre* and *cognoscere*). What is perfectly seen is perfectly understood, but what is imperfectly understood is still seen *totaliter*, albeit imperfectly.[7] In other words, to say that God is incomprehensible to any created intellect (with or without the aid of an uncreated light) is not to say that something of God is not seen. God is seen as He is but not known as He is, because our manner of knowing is finite and God is infinite.[8] The beatific vision involves more than a philosophic knowledge; hence, it includes the unity of God as well as the plurality of Persons. Our assurance on this point is seen in that we can in this life

---

4. "[I]nquantum plures et excellentiores effectus eius nobis demonstrantur; et inquantum ei aliqua attribuimus ex revelatione divina, ad quae ratio naturalis non pertingit, ut Deum esse trinum et unum." ST I, q. 12, a. 13 ad 1.

5. "[V]isionem hic dicit certissimam Patris considerationem et comprehensionem, tantam quantam Pater habet de Filio." ST I, q. 12, a. 1 ad 1.

6. "Unde ex hoc non sequitur quod nullo modo possit cognosci, sed quod omnem cognitionem excedat: quod est ipsum non comprehendi." ST I, q. 12, a. 1 ad 3.

7. "[Q]uod non propter hoc Deus incomprehensibilis dicitur, quasi aliquid eius sit quod non videatur: sed quia non ita perfecte videtur, sicut visibilis est." ST I, q. 12, a. 7 ad 2.

8. "[Q]uod totaliter dicit modum objecti: non quidem ita quod totus modus objecti non cadat sub cognitione; sed quia modus objecti non est modus cognoscentis." ST I, q. 12, a. 7 ad 3.

know more than is available through natural reason alone; namely, that God is one and three. Through the Incarnation, both in the events and in the teachings of Christ, we can know something of the Trinity. Prior to blessedness, our understanding is guided by revelation toward the vision for which we long.

If, on the other hand, in the beatific vision we do not know anything of the distinction of Persons, then one of two conclusions must be drawn. Either we will know less in that vision than we do now, or the Persons really are only modes of divine being. Both of these conclusions must be denied categorically. Against the Albigensians and Joachim of Fiore, the Fourth Lateran Council declared:

> We firmly believe and simply confess that there is only one true God, eternal, without measure, incomprehensible, omnipotent and ineffable, the Father and the Son and the Holy Spirit: three Persons but one essence . . . and according to the personal properties discreet.[9]

The divine Persons are really distinct. These three are eternal, not temporal manifestations of a single divinity. They are the eternal Persons who are God and are revealed to us in this life through sensible things, in prophetic visions, as well as in the words of Christ.[10]

It is one of Thomas' most famous yet fiercely contested points that there is a continuity in the manner of knowing between this life and the next, through phantasms or intelligible species formed in the agent intellect. In the next life the intelligible species formed in our intellect will be replaced with the intelligible form known as the "light of glory," the medium under which God is seen.[11] The intellect will not simply have possession of a better similitude but will in fact be a "glorified faculty," made more "potent" for seeing the divine essence.[12] This intel-

---

9. "Firmiter credimus et simpliciter confitemur, quod unus solus est verus Deus, aeternus, immensus et incommutabilis, incomprehensibilis, omnipotense et ineffabilis, Pater et Filius et Spiritus Sanctus: tres quidem personae, sed una essentia. . . . secundum personales proprietates discreta. Denzinger, *Enchiridion Symbolorum* #428.

10. Cf. ST I, q. 10. a. 2 sc; q. 12, a. 13 c.

11. ST I, q. 12, a. 5 c; a. 6 ad 3. Cf. J.-P. Torrell, "La vision de Dieu *per essentiam* selon saint Thomas d'Aquin," *Micrologus* 5 (1997): 43–68.

12. "[Q]uod diversitas videndi non erit ex parte objecti . . . sed erit per diversam facultatem intellectus non quidem naturalem, sed gloriosam." ST I, q. 12, a. 6 ad 3.

ligible form will not be derived from a sensible thing representing God, but will be the very being of God signifying itself to the soul. One must be careful, however, not to suppose that this form is some similitude or perfect image, for it is a "perfection of the intellect conforming it to see God."[13] The Condemnations at Paris in 1241 affirmed the unmediated vision of God's essence by the blessed and the angels.[14] Thomas certainly had these condemnations in mind as he discussed the beatific vision in his *Sentences* commentary.[15] There he attempted to reconcile the apophaticism of John of Damascus and Ps.Dionysius with the scriptural affirmation by defining the former as the vision of *viatores* and the latter as that of the blessed. According to the Condemnations of 1241, visions of God by the blessed and the angels must be immediate although there may be gradations among them. That is, some will have a greater participation in the light of glory than others, merited by the created grace of charity.[16] We can then agree with Ps.Dionysius' statements insofar as they can be understood in accordance with the vision of God in this life, which cannot attain to what God is. In the next life one will be "deiformed" by the light of glory so that the intellect itself becomes capable of seeing God as He is. The object of vision in the next life will indeed be the essence of God, rather than merely sensible things representing or signifying God. On this point Thomas disagrees with his teacher Albert, who argues that the blessed will not see the divine essence but "theophanies," i.e., certain effects of God signifying his attributes. More about this in chapter 5.

On the other hand, as C. Trottmann argues, Thomas retains the negative statements of Ps.Dionysius in defining the vision of God. The blessed's vision of God may be complete in some sense, but it is not

---

13. "[Q]uod lumen istud non requiritur ad videndum Dei essentiam quasi similitudo in qua Deus vidatur; sed quasi perfectio quaedam intellectus, confortans ipsum ad videndum Deum." ST I, q. 12, a. 5 ad 2.

14. For a good discussion of these condemnations and the relevant literature, see C. Trottmann, *La Vision Béatifique. Des Disputes Scolastiques à sa Définition par Benoit XII* (Ecole Française de Rome, 1995), 115–208.

15. Thomas, *Scriptum super Sententiarum* IV, d. 42, q. 2, a. 1.

16. ST I, q. 12, a. 6 c.

"exhaustive."[17] Citing the words of Chrysostom, Thomas defines the comprehension of a divine Person as "what can be had only by another divine Person."[18] The blessed's vision of God must fall short of that measure of comprehension, but in what way and to what degree? Thomas describes this incomplete comprehension in several ways: as an inability to see (around) the limits or ends of a thing; as the difference remaining between seer and seen (finite and infinite); and as the consequent finitude of the form (light of glory) insofar as it is the act of a limited subject.[19]

Having said that, we are immediately confronted with the twofold problem of Persons in God, for God is not a singular quiddity but a Trinity. In this life we know through revelation that God is a Trinity, and our vision of God in the next must be richer without negating what is known in this life. The twofold problem is this: (1) How does Thomas account for the Trinity in discussing an incomplete or imperfect comprehension of God in the next life; that is, will the divinity we see by means of the light of glory be triune? (2) How does Thomas account for our knowledge of the Trinity in this life if our knowledge is here limited to "what God is not"? We can perhaps begin to answer the first question by dealing with the second.

In the last article of the question on the vision of God, Thomas affirms a knowledge of the Persons by way of effects. Revelation imparts to us other and more excellent effects by which we may know that God is Triune. Within the category of "effects" Thomas includes the words of revelation, those of the Son and the Father speaking to or about one another.[20] Hence, here in the *Summa* he goes beyond the corresponding discussions in the *Sentences* commentary by pointing out the positive knowledge gained through revelation.[21] The philosopher can demonstrate something of God as cause but is limited to the effects of creation. Revelation imparts other effects that demonstrate

17. Trottmann, *La Vision Béatifique*, 195.
18. Thomas, *Super Sent.* IV, d. 42, q. 2, a. 1 ad 1; ST I, q. 12, a. 1 ad 1.
19. Thomas, *Super Sent.* IV, d. 42, q. 2 a. 3.
20. E.g., Matthew 3:17; 17:5; Mark 1:11; John 11:41ff.; 15:16ff.; 16 etc.
21. Cf. Thomas, *Super Sent.* IV, d. 27, q. 3, a. 1 and IV Sent c. 49, q. 2, a. 7 ad 11.

additional information about the cause; namely, that the First Cause is a Trinity. Thomas thereby defined an important dichotomy in the viator's knowing, between what is known by natural reason alone and what is known by means of grace (revelation). Later, Thomas defines the gradation of knowing from the philosopher's knowledge of God to the divine Persons' vision of one another by formulating a way of knowing that proceeds by negation and affirmation. That is, we can know what God is not, and we can know God through revelation. A solely negative portrait of knowing in this life, such as that of Maimonides, is entirely inadequate because it denies the validity of the substance of revelation.

Knowledge of the divine Persons is beyond the reach of natural reason yet is attainable with the aid of revelation. For example, we know the divine Persons through particular or additional effects such as a descending dove, a voice from heaven, or a prophetic vision. "We know more fully," Thomas contends, "insofar as additional and more excellent effects are demonstrated to us and insofar as we attribute some of them to God as from divine revelation without which we would not know such things as that God is one and three."[22]

One could object that the bulk of the discussion in the *prima pars*, qq. 2–26 is primarily philosophical, a natural theology not involving the Persons. Some scholars have argued accordingly that these references to the plurality of Persons in God are mere "interruptions."[23] Such interruptions could also be reminders that this essence is an abstracted, common nature of the three Persons. Thomas does not refer to the Persons only when the topic or argument demands it. The mention of Persons is necessary in discussing the grades of knowing in this life and in the next.[24] But the many other occasions where Thomas refers to the Persons do not demand such complications at all. For in-

---

22. "[T]amen plenius ipsum cognoscimus, inquantum plures et excellentiores effectus eius nobis demonstrantur; et inquantum ei aliqua attribuimus ex revelatione divina, ad quae ratio naturalis non pertingit, ut Deum esse trinum et unum." ST I, q. 12, a. 13 ad 1.

23. Jorissen, "Struktur des Traktates," 245.

24. See ST I, q. 12, a. 13.

stance, in the question on the eternity of God, Thomas cites an authority whose terms do not appear to correspond to the question. Against the objections that eternity is something created and that God is before and after it, Thomas cites the Athanasian creed: "Eternal Father, eternal Son, eternal Holy Spirit."[25] The entire response as well as the objections refers to 'God' not to the Persons *per se*. The question then arises of the way in which the authority answers the objections. If 'God' refers to an abstracted essence, the question of eternity is not pertinent because it is not subsistent. If 'God' refers to an absolute essence ("this God"), then we must clarify and distinguish the way in which eternity is predicated of the Persons from the manner in which it refers to the essence, since the identity of essence and Person has not been established. One of the errors associated with the twelfth-century theologian Gilbert of Poitiers was the argument for the eternity of the nature alone. Thomas later explicitly distances himself from other Porretan errors.[26] Hence, he could have the same intention here as he affirms eternity on the level of Persons rather than on the level of nature.

This last reference to the divine Persons indicates that Thomas has at this point in the text yet to make any explicit distinction between essence and Person in God. Hence, it is not surprising that if one has in mind the rules of predication found in q. 39, the argument in this early question could appear muddled. This problem is present, however, only if we assume a distinction in the text that in fact is left unclarified, that is, a distinction between 'God' and 'Person'. By assuming on the other hand, that the proper names and 'God' signify the same "thing," the problem disappears. Far from clouding the issue of distinction, Thomas' use of this authority makes a statement about the equality of the Persons as well as the identity of divine Persons and divine essence on the most fundamental level. Hence, it is only the importing from a later question of the sophisticated distinction of reason between essence and Person that makes this authority puzzling.

---

25. "Aeternus Pater, aeternus Filius, aeternus Spiritus Sanctus." ST I, q. 10, a. 2 sc.
26. See ST I q. 28, a. 2, and q. 34, a. 2.

Thomas has merely chosen an authority that uses the personal terms instead of 'God.' The upshot is that the three Persons noted in the *sed contra* are strongly identified with the 'God' of the response. Hence, the eternal Father, eternal Son, and eternal Holy Spirit of the *sed contra* together are (the) God who is eternal and is His eternity and reigns forever.[27]

An example from the question on the unity of God further substantiates Thomas' implicit identification of divine Persons with divine essence in these early questions. Thomas cites Deuteronomy 6:4, "Hear, O Israel, the Lord your God is one."[28] God's simplicity and infinite perfection, among other attributes already defined in earlier questions, demand that there is only one God. Thomas, however, asks a further question at this point regarding the unity of the one God, that is, whether God is maximally one, unique and lacking composition. A text from Bernard of Clairvaux provides the answer: "Among all things that are said to be one, the unity of the divine Trinity holds the highest place."[29] The acknowledgment of Persons in God does not detract from God's unity but moves it to a higher level. The implication is that Christian belief affirms a more perfect unity than the Jews could proclaim.

It is noteworthy that Thomas would use a twelfth-century authority to augment the traditional discussion and affirmation of God's unity based upon the Deuteronomy text. Once again Thomas' method could be explained by an intention to avoid the kind of accusations leveled at Peter the Lombard and Gilbert of Poitiers by the great protector of orthodoxy in the twelfth century, Bernard himself. By including Bernard's own insistent words, Thomas accomplishes two objectives: (1) he clearly identifies the Trinity of Persons as what are

---

27. It is worth noting that in a similar discussion in *De potentia* q. 3, a. 17 ad 23, Thomas uses an authority shared with Anselm, "Dominus regnavit saeculum saeculis." Thomas, then, certainly knew and had even used another authority for this very question. Hence, the intentionality of his choice of this text over others here is apparent.

28. "Audi, Israel, Dominus Deus tuus unus est." ST I, q. 11, a. 3 sc.

29. "[I]nter omnia quae unum dicuntur, arcem tenet unitas divinae Trinitatis." ST I, q. 11, a. 4 sc.

maximally one and are the same as the essence; and (2) he clarifies the subject of this and other questions as the Trinity of Persons with respect to their unity. There is no reference to a fourth thing in God (Bernard's accusation against Lombard) and the Persons are not in any way inhering or added to the essence (Bernard's accusation against Gilbert of Poitiers). Consequently, any supposed problem of how the Persons can be "derived from" the essence or introduced into the discussion of essence is dissipated, because the Persons are the implicit subject throughout. The citation of Bernard here must be an attempt on Thomas' part to forestall criticism based upon a too simplistic reading of his organization. The 'God' or divine essence of which he speaks in q. 2–26 is the unity of the Father, Son, and Holy Spirit. Moreover, these Three are maximally one.[30]

Some scholars, however, have argued that such references to the Trinity before q. 27 do not break into, let alone constitute a part of, the flow of argumentation but are merely glimpses of what is to come.[31] They assume that the distinction of reason between essence and person, as well as the rules for their different manner of signifying, is in place throughout the *Summa*. Jorissen and Schmidbaur insist that Thomas uses the distinction before he discusses it and, thereby, clarifies what he has been doing only after the fact. Drawing upon the material in q. 39 where the term 'God' supposits *per se* or "in a strong sense" for the "one essence of three Persons," Jorissen and Schmidbaur counter the phantom assumption of a monopersonal God in the early questions by insisting on the abstract character of the divine essence.[32] That is, they stave off the imputation of a portrait of God in qq. 2–26 as a non- or pre-Christian God by insisting that the subject that is one by nature is the divine essence abstracted from the three Persons.

---

30. The note in q. 39, a. 1, that there is nothing other than Person in God, is then merely a recollection of this article in q. 11.

31. Ulrich Horst, "Über die Frage einer heilsökonomischen Theologie," *Münchener Theologische Zeitschrift* 12 (1961) 109; Jorissen, "Struktur des Traktates," 245–46; Schmidbaur, *Personarum Trinitas*, 28–34.

32. Jorissen, "Struktur des Traktates," 247; Schmidbaur, *Personarum Trinitas*, 456–58.

None of these scholars, however, would argue that the divine essence subsists apart from the divine Persons. Yet their insistence that 'essence' consistently signifies an abstraction leads them to posit one of the Persons as the referent at points where a subsistence of some sort is demanded, such as in the questions on knowledge (14), will (19), providence (22), and power (25).[33] This argument is particularly problematic insofar as it entails a direct knowledge of the Trinitarian relations. To propose that the Father is known first (before the Incarnation) is to propose that the Father is known distinctly. The Person of the Father is the subsistent relation of Paternity, which Paternity cannot be understood without the other two or at least without the Son. Christ did not reveal two *more* Persons but the very *fact* of personhood or relationality in God. Simply put: the Father is known only when revealed by the Son.[34]

To discuss the Father first because the Father is the unoriginate source of divinity may be a characteristically "Greek" way of proceeding and therefore a procedure Jorissen would want to point out in Thomas as a way of rescuing him from Rahner's criticism.[35] Jorissen, however, unknowingly subverts Thomas' teaching about Persons and relations by reading him as a Greek. Defining the divine Persons as subsistent relations is to say that the being of God has a particular "respect to another" that constitutes it. It is not merely according to our understanding or a failure of our understanding that we say the three are one in works in the world. They really are one *ad extra* because

---

33. Jorissen, "Struktur des Traktates," 254–56.
34. In criticizing Jorissen's position, the importance of the late entry of the appropriations in the *Summa* becomes apparent. The appropriation of essential attributes to refer to the distinct divine Persons cannot be done without the revealed knowledge of the Persons. The Father can be called "unity" only in a context where the other two Persons are also named by means of essential attributes. Affirming that a knowledge of God as a unity is a knowledge of the Father (à la Jorissen) is a great leap beyond the affirmations Thomas makes concerning the appropriation of certain essential attributes to the divine Persons. Thomas' presentation in q. 39 is a further elucidation of the doctrine of the Trinity, not a precursor to it.
35. Rahner criticized Thomas as a representative of the Latin Trinitarian tradition as opposed to a Greek tradition. Jorissen attempts to refute Rahner simply by pointing out "Greek" elements in Thomas.

they are perfectly one in knowledge and love. Whatever acts proceed from that knowledge and love will also be one. Hence, the unity in act of the Persons is a correlate of their very being.

The movement of Thomas' discussion throughout qq. 2–43 concerns first the way in which God is one and then the way in which God is three. The progression in the text is from unity to distinction, not from essence to supposita. Jorissen and Schmidbaur both use the adjective "common" to identify the divine essence that is the subject of the first section; they thus risk excluding what is proper. In other words, the distinction of reason between essence and person (supposit and form) is not the same distinction of reason as that between the "(unity of) divine essence" (qq. 2–26) and the "Trinity of Persons" (qq. 27–43). The latter is an abstraction of the whole from the parts even though the "parts" are not each less than the whole in God nor are the "parts" existent or really separable from what is the whole. To say "God is one and three" (q. 12, a. 13 ad 1) is to say that God who is Father, Son, and Holy Spirit is one and three—one nature (or essence) *in* three Persons, for the one nature is not other than the three Persons. Hence, the divine essence is not concretized except in the Persons.[36] It is only the different modes of signification that allow us to use these common and proper terms in speech about God.

36. An alternative explanation can be found in G. Emery, "Essentialisme ou personnalisme dans le traité de Dieu chez saint Thomas d'Aquin?" *Revue Thomiste* 98 (1998): 5–38. Emery claims that the division concerns two different points of view: God is then considered in the two parts "sous l'aspect de l'essence et sous l'aspect de la distinction" (p. 13). Thus, with Jorissen, Emery prefers the terminology of "common" and "proper" to define the two sections in question. However, the presence of Persons in what is billed as "common" argues against such terminology. The problem is where one begins—from the perspective of the overtly Trinitarian section, the terminology is sufficient to integrate what is gained in the first part. What is said about the divine nature in qq. 2–26 is not left behind in the later questions. But from the perspective of the early questions, the problem is one of fullness. Is what is said later of the divine Persons implicit in the early questions? Are the personal processions which are themselves the cause of the external procession of creatures contained within the unity of divinity known through creation? If in fact the Persons are not perfections of the essence and therefore not essential "processions," then the Persons also cannot be an addition to the essence, cannot be other than the essence. This is the mystery posed so acutely by Augustine: "deus pater, deus filius, deus spiritus sanctus . . . nec tamen tres dii aut tres

It is, consequently, not surprising that Thomas' preferred term in these early questions is 'God' rather than 'divine essence.' Apart from the organizational comments in the prologues to q. 2 and q. 26, the term 'divine essence' is used only in q. 12.[37] In q. 12 it is interchangeable with 'essence of God' and not used with great precision.[38] Thomas suggests a distinction within q. 12 whereby 'God' refers to what we mean by the term (from the proofs of God's existence in q. 2) while 'essence' signifies God *in se* as the object of the beatific vision. Thus, when Thomas discusses our natural knowledge or "vision" of God in this life, he consistently uses the term 'God' and not 'essence.'[39] The first ten articles of q. 12, which concern the vision of God by the blessed or the angels, refer to 'essence' in various phraseology. In the last three articles, which concern our knowledge or vision of God in this life, on the other hand, Thomas prefers the term 'God.'[40] What we know about God in this life does not attain to the 'essence of God,' to the very being of God, *quid est*.[41] This essence, which the blessed see by the light of glory, is the essence that is being itself, *ipsum esse*.[42] This definition of

---

boni aut tres omnipotentes, sed unus deus, bonus, omnipotens, ipsa trinitas. . . . Hoc enim secundum essentiam dicuntur." Augustine, *De Trinitate* VIII, prooemium. Hence, in face of the misunderstandings that have arisen on this issue, it seems imperative to align ourselves more closely with Thomas' own terminology and to use the term unity (or totality) when referring to the divine essence in qq. 2–27.

37. In q. 28 and beyond, *'divina essentia'* becomes standard and *'essentia Dei'* is completely gone as well as *'ejus essentia'*.

38. "Non autem per aliquam similitudinem creatam Dei essentia videri potest, quae ipsam divinam essentiam repraesentet ut in se est." ST I, q. 12, a. 2 c. "Manifestum est autem quod per naturas rerum materialium divina essentia cognosci non potest. . . . Unde impossibile est animae hominis secundum hanc vitam viventis, essentiam Dei videre." ST I, q. 12, a. 11 c. As the term *'Deus'* is clarified in qq. 27–43, it becomes no longer possible to speak of the *'essentia Dei'* in a meaningful way. Hence, the term *'divina essentia,'* as the more precise term, takes over completely.

39. ST I, q. 12, aa. 11 and 12.

40. "Sic autem Deus est in anima beatorum, non autem in anima nostra." ST I, q. 12, a. 11 ad 4.

41. "[I]n hac vita non cognoscamus de Deo *quid est*." ST I, q. 12, a. 13 ad 1. "Sed quia nos non scimus de Deo quid est, non est nobis per se nota." ST I, q. 2, a. 1 c.

42. For a detailed discussion of Thomas' position on the *lumen gloriae* as well as the disputes his position sparked, see Trottmann, *La Vision Béatifique*, 312–20. See also ST I, q. 3, aa. 3 and 4.

'essence' is somewhat different from the (abstract) form of divine nature as it is defined in q. 39. Only in this much later question does Thomas actually use 'essence' to refer to the abstracted form corresponding to the divinity of each Person.[43]

## 2.2 The Development of a Trinitarian Grammar
### 2.2.1 The Semantic Distance between q. 3 and q. 39 (ST I)

If we compare Thomas' treatment of the term 'essentia' at the beginning of his discussion with his treatment at the end, we can see the way in which Thomas' notion develops. Compare for example two discussions mentioned earlier, those of qq. 3 and 39. First, q. 3:

God is indeed the same as his essence or nature. We understand this point from the fact that in material things there is a composition of matter and form, [hence] it is necessary that nature or essence differs from the suppositum.... Thus, since God is not composed of matter and form (as is shown in a. 2), it is appropriate [to say] that God is his deity, his life, and whatever else may be predicated of God.[44]

Thomas argues that God is simple because there is no composition of the creaturely type. His further remarks follow from this notion of simplicity. Later, in q. 28, he begins to discuss what can be distinguished from essence by our manner of consideration. He is still treat-

---

43. In q. 39, articles 4 and 5, Thomas defines *'essentia'* and *'persona'* in terms of the thing had and the one having. The *'essentia'* is the abstract form signified by the name *'Deus'* and is one *secundum rem*. Thus, in the third response of article 5, Thomas distinguishes 'God' and 'divine essence' by reason of differing supposition. The former retains its flexibility or elasticity with respect to the Godhead and to the Persons collectively or individually. Thomas' discussion then begins with a concept of essence as possessing neither a composition of matter and form (q. 3, a. 3) nor a composition of being and essence (q. 3, a. 4); it ends later with a concept of essence as the "thing had" in the sense of an abstract form distinguished by reason from the personal supposita (q. 39, aa. 4 and 5).

44. "Respondeo quod Deus est idem quod sua essentia vel natura. Ad cujus intellectum sciendum est, quod in rebus compositis ex materia et forma, necesse est quod differant natura vel essentia et suppositum.... Et sic cum Deus non sit compositus ex materia et forma, ut ostensum est (a. 2) oportet quod Deus sit sua deitas, sua vita, et quidquid aliud sic de Deo praedicatur." ST I, q. 3, a. 3 c. See also, ST I, q. 3, a. 4 c: "quod Deus non solum est sua essentia, ut ostensum est (a. 3), sed etiam suum esse."

ing the divine essence as what is one, and, in order to affirm that relation, insofar as it is in God, must also be of the essence, he reiterates that whatever is in God is His essence.[45] Thomas thereby upholds the notion of divine simplicity while positing another clarification of what it consists. The idea of relation allows for distinctions of mutuality without detracting from the divine simplicity and unity as far as we understand.

In the later discussion, Thomas demonstrates what is distinguishable by our reasoning. The object is to clarify theological grammar without abrogating divine simplicity as previously formulated. The following texts from q. 39 reveal this higher level of precision:

> [T]he divine simplicity requires that in God essence and supposit are the same [and] that in intellectual substances, there is nothing other than person.[46]

> Names signifying the divine essence substantively are predicated in the singular and not in the plural of the three Persons . . . for we do not say that the Father, Son, and Holy Spirit are three gods but [that they are] one God. In three supposits of human nature, there are three humanities, but in the three [divine] Persons, there is one divine essence.[47]

We have then come full circle from q. 3. Thomas first established a lack of composition understood in the Aristotelian sense, that is, in terms of substance metaphysics. He then defines in a more explicitly theological sense the character of the divine essence as the form of divinity and the concept of relation as the means of marking distinctions within that singular reality. The issue of composition thereby surfaces again. In q. 39 he must deny any composition of essence and personal

---

45. ST I, q. 28, a. 2 c.

46. "[Q]uod divina simplicitas hoc requirit, quod in Deo sit idem essentia et suppositum; quod in substantiis intellectualibus nihil est aliud quam persona." ST I, q. 39, a. 1 c.

47. "Unde nomina significantia divinam essentiam substantive, singulariter, et non pluraliter, de tribus Personis praedicantur . . . Patrem autem et Filium et Spiritum Sanctum non dicimus tres deos, sed unum Deum: quia in tribus suppositis humanae naturae sunt tres humanitates; in tribus autem Personis est una divina essentia." ST I, q. 39, a. 3 c.

supposita as he clarifies the manner of signification that alone distinguishes divine essence from divine Person.

In order to determine the truth of speech, it is necessary to consider not only the thing signified but also the manner of signifying. Although according to the thing signified God and deity may be the same, they are not signified in the same manner. This name 'God' may supposit for Person from its natural manner of signification because it signifies the divine essence in the one having it. 'Essence', however, may not naturally supposit for Person because it signifies the essence as an abstract form. Therefore, those things that are proper to the Persons, and distinguish the Persons one from another, cannot be attributed to the essence. [Such attribution] would signify a distinction in the divine essence in the same way that there are distinctions in the supposits.[48]

From these texts, it is evident that Thomas' use of 'essence' becomes quite exacting, signifying in these later passages only the abstract form of divinity that at the same time is not other than the Persons. In the earlier questions, Thomas uses 'essence of God,' 'His *(ejus)* essence,' 'God,' and 'deity' without any apparent precise rules of distinction.[49] In q. 3, 'essence' is the form which is identical to 'God'. By the time he concludes the grammatical clarification about the signification and supposita of 'God' in q. 39, however, he has moved far beyond this unity of *essentia* and *esse* (i.e., beyond the philosophical assertion). Hence, he can define precisely the way in which 'God' may signify one divine Person or all three or the unity of divinity.

[O]thers have better said that the name 'God' may supposit properly for [divine] Person according to its manner of signifying. Therefore whenever this name 'God' supposits for essence, as when it says, "God creates," this predicate

---

48. "[Q]uia ad veritatem locutionum, non solum oportet considerare res significatas, sed etiam modum significandi, ut dictum est. Licet autem secundum re, sit idem *Deus* quod *deitas*, non tamen est idem modus significandi utrobique. Nam hoc nomen *Deus*, quia significat divinam essentiam ut in habente, ex modo suae significationis naturaliter habet quod possit supponere pro persona. . . . Sed hoc nomen essentia non habet ex modo suae significationis quod supponat pro persona; quia significat essentiam ut formam abstractam. Et ideo ea quae sunt propria personarum, quibus ab invicem distinguuntur, non possunt essentiae attribui; significaretur enim quod esset distinctio in essentia divina, sicut est distinctio in suppositis." ST I, q. 39, a. 5 c.

49. Cf. ST I, qq. 3, 7, and 8 especially.

is suited to the subject by reason of the form signified—deity. Whenever it supposits for Person, either one only in the case of "God generates" or two in the case of "God spirates" or three in the case of "Kings of the ages, immortal, invisible, only God."[50]

The rules for the manner of signifying are then based upon a twofold manner of predication, the substantive (corresponding to the use in q. 3) and the adjectival.

Those things that signify the essence substantively are predicated of the three Persons in the singular only and not plural. But those things that signify the essence adjectivally are predicated of the three Persons in the plural on account of the plurality of supposita.[51]

The two modes of predicating are applied to the Persons who are the supposita of the divine essence. This essence is signified through the mode of form because God is maximally one (ST I, q. 11). Note that the "maximally one" is applied specifically to the Persons *per se*. It is on the basis of this unity *of the Persons* that we can predicate things of them substantially in the singular. God remains one because 'Person' does not delimit an essence or nature but "personality."[52] There are three personalities or personal properties, and these are the subject of predication of God in the plural.

And in case anyone is still confused on the matter, Thomas makes the point crystal-clear in the next article (ST I, q. 39, a. 4). Essential names supposit for the Persons concretely such that we can say "God begot God" or "God from God."

---

50. "[A]lii melius dixerunt quod hoc nomen *Deus* ex modo significandi habet ut proprie possit supponere pro persona, sicut et hoc nomen *homo*. Quandoque ergo hoc nomen Deus supponit pro essentia, ut cum dicitur, *Deus creat*: quia hoc praedicatum competit subjecto ratione formae significatae, quae est deitas. Quandoque vero supponit personam: vel unam tantum, ut cum dicitur *Deus generat*; vel duas, ut cum dicitur *Deus spirat*; vel tres, ut cum dicitur *Regi saeculorum, immortali, invisibilii, soli Deo*." ST I, q. 39, a. 4 c.

51. "Ea quidem quae substantive essentiam significant, praedicantur de tribus Personis singulariter tantum, et non pluraliter; quae vero adjective essentiam significant, praedicantur de tribus Personis in plurali . . . propter pluralitatem suppositorum." ST I, q. 39, a. 3 ad 1.

52. "Ad quartum dicendum quod forma significata per hoc nomen *persona*, non est essentia vel natura, sed *personalitas*." ST I, q. 39, a. 3 ad 4.

[T]he name 'God' is similar to the singular terms in that the form it signifies is not multiple. It is similar to the common terms, however, in that the form signified is present in many supposits. Thus, it is not necessary that 'God' always supposit for the essence which it signifies.[53]

The justification for this manner of supposition is the real unity and plurality in God. There are only Persons in God, yet the divine essence is truly one. That is, the unity of divine nature is more real than the unity of humanity, which is one only according to our consideration of it. To signify the common nature of humans, one must supply an adjunctive term: "man is a species." With divine nature, the opposite is true. 'God' may supposit for divine nature or divine Person, but an adjunct must be supplied in order to determine *which* Person is indicated. For example, 'God' simply stated may supposit for any one Person or all three, but in the sentence "God generates" the suppositum is clearly the Father alone. Recall here the discussion in q. 3, a. 3, where Thomas defines the unity of God against the composition of matter and form in humans. There the contrasting predication revolves around the significates of 'man' and 'humanity.' In the first term are included things which are not in the second, namely, *these* bones and *this* flesh, the matter of a human. By this measure, the terms 'God' and 'divine essence' do not signify differently. On the other hand, by this same measure, the soul separated from the body in death would not be distinguishable. The concept of personhood clarifies 'this soul' such that the individual human person can be contrasted with a divine Person even though the latter has no individuating matter.

With this point we have the basis for explaining the great distance between q. 3 and q. 39 and their respective discussions of theological predication. The arguments may appear quite similar if one assumes that 'God' is a proper name. If 'God' refers to "a Person" or "Persons *per se*" in q. 3, a. 3, then the question of simplicity concerns the unity of Persons and essence. If, on the other hand, 'God' in q. 3, a. 3 refers to

---

53. "[H]oc nomen, Deus, licet conveniat cum terminis singularibus in hoc, quod forma significata non multiplicatur; convenit tamen cum terminis communibus in hoc, quod forma significata invenitur in pluribus suppositis. Unde non oportet quod semper supponat pro essentia quam significat." ST I, q. 39, a. 4 ad 1.

the subsisting nature, it is identical to the divine essence and is not distinguished even by reason. With the introduction of the term 'Person', Thomas adds a great deal of precision to his theological language. He uses 'Person' to define the supposita of the divine nature while 'God' stands for what is maximally one and is the Father, Son, and Holy Spirit. The primary referent then in q. 39 is not 'God' but the three Persons who are God. These three Persons are the focus of his efforts there to coordinate the use of common and proper terms. By reason of differing supposition, 'God' may supposit for divine Person or divine essence. Yet the term is not indifferent to forms of speech such that one may say that the "essence begets" or "essence proceeds." Only personal supposita may be the subject of actions within God or in the world. For the same reason, it is improper to substitute essential names for 'God' or to suppose that essential names such as Wisdom and Love may supposit for essence or Person in the same way that the term 'God' does.[54]

Thomas' language becomes ever more precise in the *Summa* as he moves toward that most complex discussion of essential names in q. 39. The terms 'essence,' 'essence of God' and 'God' are used interchangeably and in the most general way in qq. 2–26. In q. 12, there is an explicit distinction made, but it is certainly not the distinction between 'essence' and 'person' but that between 'essence' and 'God'.[55] The subsequent discussions of relation and Person are built upon the affirmation that they are one with the divine essence and distinguished only according to our understanding. Hence, Thomas can strongly identify 'relation' as the being of God while affirming a real distinction of Persons.[56]

The order of Thomas' discussions of predication in ST I is not a

54. "[Q]uia ad veritatem locutionum, non solum oportet considerare res significatas, sed etiam modum significandi. . . . Licet autem, secundum rem, sit idem *Deus* quod *deitas,* non tamen est idem modus significandi utrobique. Nam hoc nomen *Deus,* quia significat divinam essentiam ut in habente, ex modo suae significationis naturaliter habet quod possit supponere pro persona." ST I, q. 39, a. 5 c.

55. In qq. 27–43, Thomas drops the use of '*essentia Dei*' in favor of '*divina essentia*' or '*essentia*' alone in the context of the explicit discussion of Persons.

56. "[Q]uidquid est in Deo, est eius essentia. Sic igitur ex ea parte qua relatio in rebus creatis habet esse accidentale in subjecto, relatio realiter existens in Deo habet esse

matter of indifference. It is of the utmost importance that the reader attend to the placement of such material. The result of combining them haphazardly as Cajetan and others have done is the introduction of an overly strict separation between the sections of this text. That is, one might suppose that Thomas treats divinity as a form without supposita before he treats the supposita of that form (the divine nature without the fact of the divine Persons). It is one thing to abstract essence from existence in a composite being, but it is quite another (and an impossible) endeavor to abstract the essence from existence in one whose essence is being itself. Divine nature is really one and identical with its supposita. Having said that, the question remains as to why Thomas did not place the more advanced discussion of predication (q. 39) before the discussion of the Persons, or at least at the point where he introduced the term into his treatise. He could have perhaps forestalled some misunderstandings by informing the reader earlier that he was making a shift in his use of certain terms. In that case, we would be able to make better sense of his treatment of the Persons. On the other hand, such conjecture supposes that one first clarifies one's speech in order to understand and communicate such understanding to others. Could it be that a precise way of speaking (theological grammar) is the result and not the basis of theological discussion? This question will remain in the background as we attempt to analyze the progression of argumentation leading to q. 39.

### 2.2.2 Order and Method

In the following section we will examine Thomas' theological method in order to shed light on its ordering principles. We will use the term "topical" as a way of distinguishing Thomas' method from a systematic one, a construction of theology from a few basic premises.[57] Thomas' order of discussion makes sense, of course, but it does not follow a logical progression of argumentation whereby each ques-

---

essentiae divinae, idem omnino ei existens. . . . Et sic manifestum est quod relatio realiter existens in Deo, est idem essentiae secundum rem." ST I, q. 28, a. 2 c.

57. Abelard was alone among medievals in thinking that theology could be systematically constructed. Such a methodological assumption is, however, quite commonplace among modern theologians. Cf. Schmidbaur, *Personarum Trinitas*, 110ff.

tion follows from its predecessor as a conclusion follows a major and minor premise.[58] The explanation of Thomas' ordering of topics will at the same time open the door for discussing the role and character of rational argument, or, in more proper terms, the character of a Thomistic argument in addressing theological issues.[59]

The schematic outline of Thomas' discussion of the Trinity found in Figure 1 is based upon the instructions Thomas gives to the reader in the prologues to several key questions.[60] Obviously, the bulk of the discussion is given over to the Persons rather than to the processions or relations. Also, it is noteworthy that the divine missions, the means by which we know the divine Persons, comes last in this ordering.

In order to clear the table of certain assumptions about Thomas' methodology, we will distinguish here Thomas' ordering from that of Augustine, the father of the so-called "Latin Trinitarian tradition" and a very important guide for Thomas. Thomas does not imitate Augustine's *De Trinitate*. There are some important and very telling differences between the two theologians. First, Thomas' sequence of topics—processions, relations, missions—is the reverse of Augustine's ordering. Second, the bulk of Augustine's text (Bks. VIII–XV) is an investigation of the processions as a way of understanding the perfect distinction, equality, and oneness of the Three.[61] Aquinas, on the other hand, is most concerned with the issue of relations, or more specifically with the use of 'person' for identifying what those relations constitute. As seen above, only the first question concerns the processions strictly speaking.[62] Admittedly, the idea that the Father, Son, and Holy

---

58. Regarding a logical progression, one might ask why Thomas does not begin the discussion of distinctions in God with the appropriations. It would seem logical to place the theory of appropriation at the transition point between what is more easily understood by natural reason (i.e., being within its grasp) and what is known only by revelation. Such would be the case if Thomas proceeded rationally, or was, in fact, attempting to demonstrate the Trinity, as Abelard had.

59. See L. Elders, "Structure et fonction de l'argument 'sed contra' dans la Somme Théologique de Saint Thomas," *Divus Thomas* 80 (1977): 245–46.

60. ST I, qq. 27, 29, 33, 39.

61. See the prologues to Bks. VIII and IX of Augustine's *De Trinitate*.

62. The issue of procession does return to the fore in q. 41 on the notional acts, but the use of the term "procession" as a way of speaking about derivative divine nature

FIGURE 1

A. Processions (q. 27)[a]
B. Relations (q. 28)
C. Persons (constituted by subsistent relations) (qq. 29–43)[b]
   1. 'person' considered absolutely (qq. 29–38)
      a. considered in common (qq. 29–32)
         —definition of 'person' (q. 29)
         —number of Persons (qq. 30–31)[c]
         —our knowledge of the Persons (q. 32)
      b. Persons considered singly (qq. 33–38)
         —Father (q. 33)
         —Son (qq. 34–35)
         —Holy Spirit (qq. 36–38)
   2. Persons considered comparatively (qq. 39–42)
      a. Persons and essence (q. 39)
      b. Persons and relations or properties (q. 40)
      c. Persons and notional acts (q. 41)
      d. Persons with one another (q. 42)
   3. Missions (q. 43)

    a. Procession in the manner of a word (a. 3); procession in the manner of love (a. 4).
    b. The nature or character of 'person' (a. 2); their distinction (a. 3); their number (a. 4).
    c. Q. 30 concerns the issue of number itself in God; q. 31 concerns the implications of such plurality.

Spirit are subsistent relations is Augustine's own contribution to Trinitarian discussions. He was unable, however, to make any fruitful use of the term 'person' due to the imprecision and improper connotations in its Greek use at that time in theater and politics. Not until Boethius wrote his theological tractates in the sixth century did the term receive a specifically Latin definition. Thomas made great use of Boethius' definition, and his own contribution lay in the focus of his discussion on the subsistent character of the Three.[63]

A third area of difference between Aquinas and Augustine is the

---

(the Father alone is unoriginate) is subordinate throughout to the conception of personal actions or "notional acts." More will be said about this later.

63. Cf. H. C. Schmidbaur, *Personorum Trinitas*, 387–447.

use of the doctrine of the divine image. This doctrine appears in the *Summa theologiae* some fifty questions after the discussion of the divine Persons (q. 93). For Augustine, this doctrine was the basis for the bulk of his work.[64] Augustine tried to locate that image in various triads in the human mind, and he eventually found the desired image of the Trinity in the mind's memory, understanding, and love, especially as such faculties are directed toward God. Augustine realized, however, that the dissimilarity between this image and the Trinity itself remained indissoluble and that the endeavor was ultimately a failure as an assent to the mystery. The issue remains whether this failure was unexpected or a point of polemics.[65] Perhaps it was Thomas' own awareness of the insurmountable divide between creatures and creator that led him to set aside this doctrine for his text. Regardless, the important point is that we cannot lump together too casually Thomas and Augustine as representing "a Latin tradition." There is no one order of topics or manner of argument in "Latin" discussions, certainly not in these two theologians.

Having made that last point, the question of Thomas' own methodology comes to the fore. That is, if he does not use the doctrine of the divine image to illustrate the way God is one and three, then what is his method? This question is inescapable precisely because Augustine's rubric is widely assumed to be *the* mode of Trinitarian discussion in the Latin West.[66] To answer this question, we will first proceed to the heart of Thomas' treatise, the question on our knowledge of the divine Persons.[67]

### 2.2.2.1 *Our Knowledge of the Trinity*

Thomas explicitly separates what can be known of God through creation from what can be known by faith.[68] The role of argument is

---

64. See Augustine, *De Trinitate* VIII–XV.
65. See J. Cavadini, "Augustine's *De Trinitate*," *Augustinian Studies* 23 (1992): 103–23.
66. Refer to "Introduction" above.
67. ST I, q. 32. a. 1.
68. Thomas is thereby categorically distinguished from those theologians who treated the doctrine of the Trinity as something knowable through the rational investi-

different in the two cases. In the latter, arguments from reason proceed from and not to affirmations of faith. Beyond merely distinguishing the categories of arguments, Thomas is also concerned about protecting the dignity of theology. Its dignity is in having God as its subject and possessing perfect certainty through divine revelation.[69] To attempt an argument from reason for the truth of any one article of faith detracts from this dignity. The proper method must move from revelation to elucidation, from the knowledge imparted through revelation to the clarification of it through careful analysis and coordination with other known truths. Misplacing arguments from reason with respect to revealed doctrines such as that of the Trinity represents a twofold danger for the faith:

> He who attempts to prove the Trinity of Persons by natural reason, denigrates the faith in two ways: (1) he harms the dignity of the faith because the faith pertains to invisible things that exceed human reason; and (2) he [endangers] the pursuit of bringing others to the faith. When someone offers reasons for proving [the truth of] the faith that are not cogent, he will be ridiculed by the unfaithful, for they believe that it is on account of these reasons that we believe.[70]

Faith is of things not seen, not irrational or unintelligible to be sure, but simply beyond the grasp of unaided reason. Where arguments cannot demonstrate a certain truth, they can provide no grounds for belief. The Christian's faith in such truths as the Incarnation or the Trinity of divine Persons rests on authority (of the entire Christian tradition), and this authority alone is the basis for any proofs.[71]

---

gation, such as Anselm and Abelard. Cf. H. Paissac, O.P., *Théologie du Verbe. Saint Augustin et saint Thomas* (Paris: Les Editions du Cerf, 1951). For an overview of the method and structuring of Trinitarian discussions of the twelfth century, see Marcia Colish's *Peter Lombard*, vol. 1 (Leiden: E. J. Brill, 1994), 227–302.

69. See ST I, q. 1, a. 1 c and *Summa contra Gentiles* I, chs. 1–9.

70. "Qui autem probare nititur Trinitatem Personarum naturali ratione, fidei dupliciter derogat. Primo quidem, quantum ad dignitatem ipsius fidei, quae est ut sit de rebus invisibilibus, quae rationem humanam excedunt. . . . Secundo, quantum ad utilitatem trahendi alios ad fidem. Cum enim aliquis ad probandam fidem inducit rationes quae non sunt cogentes, cedit in irrisionem infidelium: credunt enim quod huiusmodi rationibus innitamur, et propter eas credamus." ST I, q. 32, a. 1 c and ad 2.

71. "Quae igitur fidei sunt, non sunt tentanda probare nixi per auctoritates, his qui

Thomas makes the very same point in the very first question of the *Summa:* "Those things that are above human cognition and may not be investigated by reason are nevertheless revealed by God to be received in faith."[72]

The use of reason with regard to theological doctrine then provides two types of arguments:

> One type of argument from natural reason seeks to prove various principles. In the case of natural science, reason is sufficient for proving that the motion of the heavens is always of a uniform velocity. Regarding another type of argument, reason cannot prove the principles. With the principles already posited, however, arguments may be offered for showing that they are consistent with what follows from them.... In the first type of argument, reason may prove God to be one and the like. But in the second type, reason may lead to the manifestation of the Trinity; namely, having posited the Trinity, one may offer arguments for this doctrine's congruence with other known principles.[73]

The rational method (first mode), represented by the ancient philosophers, did not and could not attain to any knowledge of the divine Persons. Thomas is unequivocal on this matter:

> It is impossible by natural reason to attain to a knowledge of the Trinity of divine Persons... Man does not attain to a knowledge of God through natural

---

auctoritates suscipiunt." ST I, q. 32, a. 1 c. Not a few have doubted Thomas' sincerity on this point. C. Vagaggini claimed that Thomas' theory did not, in fact, cohere with his practice. Thomas had, according to Vagaggini, made extensive use of Anselmian "necessary reasons." C. Vagaggini, "La hantise des *rationes necessariae* de saint Anselme dans la théologie des processiones trinitaires de saint Thomas," in *Spicilegium Beccense,* vol. 1 (Paris: J. Vrin, 1959), 103–39. For an answer to Vagaggini, see R. Richard, *The Problem of an Apologetical Perspective in the Trinitarian Theology of St. Thomas Aquinas,* Analecta Gregoriana 131 (Rome, 1963).

72. "[E]a quae sunt altiora hominis cognitione, non sint ab homine per rationem inquirenda, sunt tamen, a Deo revelata, suscipienda per fidem." ST I, q. 1, a. 1 ad 1.

73. "Uno modo, ad probandum sufficienter aliquam radicem: sicut in sicientia naturali inducitur ratio sufficiens ad probandum quod motus caeli semper sit uniformis velocitatis. Alio modo inducitur ratio, non quae sufficienter probet radicem, sed radici iam positae ostendat congruere consequentes effectus.... Primo ergo modo potest induci ratio ad probandum Deum esse unum, et similia. Sed secundo modo se habet ratio quae inducitur ad manifestationem Trinitatis: quia scilicet, Trinitate posita, congruunt huiusmodi rationes." ST I, q. 32, a. 1 ad 2.

reason except from creatures. Creatures, however, lead to a knowledge of God as effects lead to a knowledge of a cause. Therefore, natural reason is able to know that God is the principle of all things. . . . The creative power of God, however, is common to the whole Trinity and pertains to the unity of essence and not to the distinction of Persons. Therefore, by natural reason one can know only what pertains to the unity of essence, not about those things that pertain to the distinction of Persons.[74]

Any distinctions that the philosophers posited with respect to God are necessarily false and incomplete. The philosophers' knowledge of God, or, more generally speaking, our natural knowledge of God, is limited to knowing the essential attributes. Certain Platonic philosophers may have posited that the power, wisdom, and goodness of God were three different levels of divinity. This kind of division posits false distinctions as well as inequality in God.[75] More importantly, by reasoning upon the divine attributes, the philosophers were most deficient in understanding the Holy Spirit, the third Person. Their schema of attributes led only to two levels of substance by which the Creator and the Word were distinguished. The third Person was not even posited as a substance. Platonic notions of begetting or proceeding and the related ideas of superiority and inferiority are more aptly applied to the creation of the world, not to the eternal begetting of the Son by the Father.[76]

More important for modern readers is that even as Thomas distances himself from such rational investigations of plurality in God, by similitudes or attributes or otherwise, he sees his own project as fol-

---

74. "[I]mpossibile est per rationem naturalem ad cognitionem Trinitatis divinarum Personarum pervenire. . . . homo per rationem naturalem in cognitionem Dei pervenire non potest nisi ex creaturis. Creaturae autem ducunt in Dei cognitionem, sicut effectus in causam. Hoc igitur solum ratione naturali de Deo cognosci potest, quod competere ei necesse est secundum quod est omnium entium principium. . . . Virtus autem creativa Dei est communis toti Trinitati: unde pertinet ad unitatem essentiae, non ad distinctionem Personarum. Per rationem igitur naturalem cognosci possunt de Deo ea quae pertinent ad unitatem essentiae, non autem ea quae pertinent ad distinctionem Personarum." ST I, q. 32, a. 1 c.

75. Abelard's attempt to proceed in the same manner results only in false conceptions about God, for the essential attributes are predicated in the singular and are truly one. See, e.g., Abelard *Introductio ad Theologiam* I, PL 178, 989–994.

76. ST I, q. 32, a. 1 ad 1.

lowing Augustine's. For Thomas, as for Augustine, there is no demonstration of the Trinity. Thus, we move from faith to understanding, instead of from understanding to faith.[77] Thomas boldly presents the counter-argument as the practice of Richard of St. Victor and Augustine. He is not, however, disputing the manner of argumentation presented in those texts as evidence, only the conclusion. It does not contradict Thomas' argument that "for the manifestation of the Trinity of Persons, Augustine proceeds from the procession of word and love in our minds." He merely rejects the conclusion that such procedure entails a demonstration of the Trinity.[78] The key word that distinguishes the right procedure from the wrong one is "manifest." Augustine's method as well as Thomas' own method pursues only manifestation with respect to this doctrine. The reason is this: intellect is not present univocally in us and in God, therefore, the similitude of our intellect, which Augustine uses, is "not sufficient to prove anything about God."[79] With this response Thomas set himself over against much of the early medieval tradition of reading Augustine and is distinguished from the modern readings of Augustine's *De Trinitate*.[80] The theologian can indeed reason about the Trinity using the divine attributes or

---

77. "Et inde est quod Augustinus, *Super Io.* dicit quod per fidem venitur ad cognitionem, et non e converso." ST I, q. 32, a. 1 ad 2.

78. "Augustinus vero procedit ad manifestandum Trinitatem Personarum, ex processione verbi et amoris in mente nostra: quam viam supra (q. 27, a. 1 ad 3) secuti sumus." ST I, q. 32, a. 1, obj. 2.

79. "Similitudo autem intellectus nostri non sufficienter probat aliquid de Deo, propter hoc quod intellectus non univoce invenitur in Deo et in nobis." ST I, q. 32, a. 1 ad 2. Even with such a bald statement as this, Aquinas continues to suffer from the accusation that he defines the Trinitarian mystery in rationally derived human categories. Cf. M. Corbin, *La Trinité ou l'Excès de Dieu* (Paris: Editions du Cerf, 1997). For a solid discussion of this problem and the related confusion between essential and personal properties, see G. Emery, "Essentialisme ou personnalisme?" 5–38.

80. Schmaus contends that Thomas was the first medieval theologian to understand Augustine's *De Trinitate*. Not even Albert saw the importance of the final two books and the polemic of the whole. M. Schmaus, "Die trinitarische Gottesebenbildlichkeit nach dem Sentenzenkommentar Alberts des Grossen," in *Virtus Politica* (Festschrift A. Hufnagel), ed. J. Möller (Stuttgart: Friedrich Frommann Verlag, 1974), 273–306. Anselm is then not the paradigmatic follower of Augustine, because his optimism about unaided reason is too great. This problem becomes most evident in later chapters of the *Monologion*. Anselm concludes in ch. 64 that his argument leads to

similitudes in our mind, for instance, but such work is only an aid to understanding *(eine Denkenhilfe)*. The difference between the philosopher's formulation of separated beings corresponding to the perception of identifiable attributes and the Christian's theory of appropriation (an aid in "manifestation") is that the latter alone is based upon and *proceeds from* the belief in the doctrine of the Trinity, the reality of three Persons, Father, Son, and Holy Spirit, distinct yet one in being and nature. Any findings by the philosopher can only be false and unworthy of that same Trinity.

On the other hand, the view that Thomas in some way does offer demonstrations or rational arguments for the Trinity is not entirely groundless. Thomas discusses the distinction of Persons in terms of an intellectual and willed procession much like the mental procession in our own minds. This view is generally based upon q. 27, the transition point between questions on the unity of God (qq. 2–26) and those on the Trinity of Persons per se (qq. 27–43).

> Whoever understands, there proceeds within him something from the very thing that he understands. The concept of the thing understood proceeds from knowledge of it. The voice then signifies this conception and is called a "word of the heart" signified by the word of the voice.[81]

---

positing multiple fathers and sons and processions in God. Augustine's procedure never strays into such erroneous implications because his is one of searching for an image of the Trinity whose formulation is already known and defined by revelation. Anselm set the stage for the many twelfth-century attempts to demonstrate the Trinity, which on the whole allowed the findings of image-psychology to inform the doctrine rather than the converse. Hence, it may be that Boethius is the more faithful follower of Augustine's method as he seeks to order a grammar according to the demands of the doctrine, thereby altering the nature of the language used. See his *De Trinitate*. For an examination of this kind of procedural error in Hugh of St. Victor, for example, see his *Tractatus de trinitate* edited by Roger Baron in "*Tractatus de trinitate et de reparatione hominis* du MS. Douai 365," *Mélanges de science religieuse* 18 (1961): 111–12. Also, see E. J. Fortmann, *The Triune God: A Historical Study of the Doctrine of the Trinity* (Philadelphia: Westminster Press, 1972), 173–94.

81. "Quicumque enim intelligit, ex hoc ipso quod intelligit, in eo procedit aliquid intra ipsum, quod est conceptio rei intellectae ex ejus notitia procedens. Quam quidem conceptionem vox significat; et dicitur *verbum cordis*, significatum verbo vocis." ST I, q. 27, q. 1 c.

The question for Cajetan is whether this statement (or more particularly, the "Whoever") is understood to have universal application (to creatures and to God) or to apply to creatures alone.[82] If it applies to God as well, then it seems that a procession in God can be proven, and this Cajetan denies. That is, having posited that God is a knowing being, we would know that there must be a procession within Him. Moreover, by the very perfection and simplicity of God's knowing, we could assert that the processed one (the [W]ord) must be equal to God who is knowing. We would then have two who are equal and perfect—the beginning points of a psychological proof for the Trinity. The contrary possibility is that the aforementioned statement is applicable to creatures alone and that God remains unknowable as such.

Cajetan's argument, however, is not the only way of reading Thomas' statement. Its universal validity can be affirmed without concluding that one may prove anything about such an intellectual procession in God. The applicability of the statement to God constitutes not a demonstration of procession in God but a suitable portrait of the notion of a procession remaining within the agent. As Lonergan reminds us, Thomas "regularly writes as a theologian" and therefore "simply states" what is true.[83] The fact that Thomas states "that in all intellects, there is a procession of an inner word" is not a datum of rational reflection but the truth as made known by revelation (from John 1, for instance). The central issue is not the product of this procession, the "word of the heart," but rather the fact and nature of this procession. The idea of procession is meant to be a way of understanding the relations and not a way of constituting the divine Persons.[84] But does this avenue of investigation proport to unlock the mystery of the Trinity? Did Thomas intend to use the conception of intellectual life freed from creatureliness or imperfections to tell us more about who the Father or the Son or the Holy Spirit really is?

---

82. Cajetan, *In Summa Theologiae* I, q. 27, a. 1, n. VII.
83. B. Lonergan, S.J., *Verbum: Word and Idea in Aquinas,* ed. D. B. Burrell, C.S.C. (Notre Dame: University of Notre Dame Press, 1967), 196.
84. It is no mistake then that Thomas separates the question of procession and that of the Word as a *verbum cordis* by 6 questions (q. 27 and q. 34).

For Thomas, we know causes by way of their effect, and yet God as Infinite Being exceeds our finite knowing capacity and is therefore incomprehensible to us. On the other hand, the *Summa* is not a Maimonidean lament over the impossibility of making meaningful statements about God. Nor does the doctrine of the Trinity raise the veil from the incomprehensibility of God. We must then square these two aspects of Thomas' theology with our one manner of knowing. There is a sense in which we know God as one or as three in the same way: from His effects. The effects of God in creation tell us much about God as a cause, but only as one cause. This is the rational investigation of God from creatures to Creator. Our knowledge of God as Three is also by way of effect, those of a dove, a voice from heaven, etc.—the revelation of God in Christ. Thus, to say we know something of God as three is not to say that our manner of knowing is fundamentally changed, only the manner by which those effects are made known. The effect of creation is evident to everyone always. The particular effects that make up the life, death, and resurrection of Christ as well as prophetic visions were evident to certain persons at a particular time and passed on for later generations as the Christian tradition.

What Thomas says at the beginning of his *Summa* about our knowledge of God remains true throughout.[85] Whatever we know about God, including the Trinity of Persons, is by means of particular effects.

> Through the revelation of grace in this life we do not know what God is *(quid est)*, and thus we are in a way joined to him in ignorance. Nevertheless, we know Him more fully [than through reason]: first, through the demonstration of his highest effects; second, through divine revelation we attribute something to him that natural reason cannot know, for example that God is one and three.[86]

---

85. "Ad tertium dicendum quod per effectus non proportionatos causae, non potest perfecta cognitio de causa haberi: sed tamen ex quocumque effectu potest manifeste nobis demonstrari causam esse.... Et sic ex effectibus Dei potest demonstrari Deum esse: licet per eos non perfecte possimus eum cognoscere secundum suam essentiam." ST I, q. 2, a. 2 ad 3.

86. "[L]icet per revelationem gratiae in hac vita non cognoscomus de Deo *quid est*, et sic ei quasi ignoto conjungamur; tamen plenius ipsum cognoscimus, inquantum

The incomprehensibility of God then remains a fundamental part of Thomas' theology. The insurmountable inadequacy of human knowing with respect to the essence of God is due to the infinity of God and the finitude of our minds. The road to understanding involves the increasing correspondence of the mental image to the known object, a commonplace of Thomistic epistemology. The mental image must become like the known reality. But this possibility does not entirely hold true in the case of the knowledge of God by the finite mind. The absence of this natural possibility does not, however, mean that God is for us only a vague, indefinite reality. On the contrary, "whatever is knowable is known insofar as it is in act. Thus, God, who is pure act without any mixture of potency, is maximally knowable inasmuch as He is."[87] God is not unseen or unknown but *incompletely* known, for God as an object of knowledge exceeds all created intellects. The example of an owl looking at the sun is instructive. Our blindness is produced only by the excess of light, not by its absence. The object is not elusive—our eyes are simply too weak.

On its own no created intellect can attain to a vision of God. The necessary "becoming like" is accomplished by the light of glory. This "light" makes our own intellect capable of seeing according to its own, proper habit.

A created light is necessary for seeing the essence of God, but this does not mean that the essence of God is made intelligible [for us] (the divine essence is [of course] intelligible in itself). The intellect, however, is enabled to understand.[88]

---

plures et excellentiores effectus ejus nobis demonstrantur, et inquantum ei aliqua attribuimus ex revelatione divina, ad quae ratio naturalis non pertingit, ut Deum esse trinum et unum." ST I, q. 12, a. 13 ad 1. The most telling effects of the distinction of Persons are the divine missions, which are themselves the content of revelation.

87. "[C]um unumquodque sit cognoscibile secundum quod est in actu, Deus, qui est actus purus absque omni permistione potentiae, quantum in se est, maxime cognoscibile est." ST I, q. 12, a. 1 c.

88. "[L]umen creatum est necessarium ad videndum Dei essentiam, non quod per hoc lumen Dei essentia intelligibilis fiat, quae secundum se intelligibilis est: sed ad hoc quod intellectus fiat potens ad intelligendum per modum quo potentia fit potentior ad operandum per habitum." ST I, q. 12, a. 5 ad 1.

The incomprehensibility is not eliminated, for "vision is an approach to God in his blessed, light-filled incomprehensibility."[89] The manner of human knowing is not abrogated, nor is the chasm between the infinitude of God and the finitude of our minds bridged. Rather, our minds are enabled *(disponatur)* to bear that excess of light.[90] The whole of God is seen and it is seen totally, yet such "totality" is on the part of the object, not the knowing subject.[91]

It is within this context that we must understand Thomas' statements about the processions. The intellectual justification of belief is not a proof or an attainment to such mysteries as the inner-divine processions. Rather such justification is an aid to understanding. Thomas' discussion of processions and relations, plurality in God, is built upon revealed, not naturally known, similarities. His dependence upon revelation in these arguments is seen most clearly in the way he distinguishes procession and relation in God from processions and relations in us.

### 2.2.2.2. Distinctions in God

Thomas points out that Scripture uses language pertaining to procession but not according to an outward generation. In fact, if one considers the matter carefully, it is evident that the scriptural reference to procession in God (John 8:42) is to an act remaining within God. Such action is most like, or "most evident" in, the act of understanding in the intellect of rational creatures.[92] The key to understanding this question is, however, *not* the similarity of intellectual procession in us and in God. The basis of discussion is the dissimilarity between the two, i.e., our intellect and God's being which is intellect.

---

89. Schmidbaur, *Personarum Trinitas*, 109.

90. "[O]mne quod elevatur ad aliquid quod excedit suam naturam, oportet quod disponatur aliquae dispositione quae sit supra suam naturam." ST I, q. 12, a. 5 c.

91. On the divine mode of being exceeding the human mode of knowing see W. Hoye, *Actualitas omnium actuum: Man's Beatific Vision of God as Apprehended by Thomas Aquinas* [Meisenheim (am Glan): Hain, 1975], 247–48. See also ST I, q. 12, a. 7 ad 3.

92. ST I, q. 27, a. 1 c.

In rational creatures, there are two aspects of the procession of an inner word: the productive aspect with the inner word itself, and the intelligible aspect or mental activity that is the sufficient cause of the procession. The latter aspect in us is indicative of the intelligence of the agent, since the power of understanding a thing determines the quality of the word processing or the concept of the thing. Hence, in us, there is always an imperfection or incompleteness of the concept with respect to the thing insofar as our concepts are distant from actual existent things and only intentions of them. To the objection that the implied diversity resulting from such procession negates God's simplicity, Thomas writes:

> Procession within an intelligible being need not entail diversity. On the contrary, the more perfectly something proceeds, the more it is one with the one from whom it proceeds. . . . The Divine Word is perfectly one with Him from whom He proceeds without any diversity.[93]

In God the inner word proceeds from the act of understanding alone, because intellect is the divine nature or substance. Where intellect is substance, the act of understanding is the act of existence. Consequently the Word that proceeds in Him is of the same nature and substance as its principle, His thought of Himself is Himself.

The task Thomas addresses in q. 27 is one of exegesis, however, not rational speculation. Scripture provides evidence for begetting and processing in God. The theologian must make sense of these by showing how such things cohere with what else we know about God. We know that God's being is intellect. For there to be a processing or begetting, it must be according to intellect. Such processing is a perfect and complete intellectual act which is called a generation since in God intellect and substance are identical.

---

93. "[I]d quod procedit ad intra processu intelligibili, non oportet esse diversum; imo, quanto perfectius procedit, tanto magis est unum cum eo a quo procedit. . . . verbum divinum sit perfecte unum cum eo a quo procedit, absque omni diversitate." ST I, q. 27, a. 1 ad 2.

To understand divinity is the very substance of one understanding... hence, the Word proceeding proceeds as one subsisting in its own nature. Consequently, this one is properly called 'begotten' and 'Son.'[94]

Thomas' argument in the discussion of processions is an attempt to make sense of the revelation about God by coordinating such texts with rules already established, such as the unity and simplicity of God. Thomas has available several key texts such as John 14:16, Psalm 2:7, and others, all of which indicate plurality, procession, and begetting in God.[95] To these he applies several basic principles: (I) to understand divinity is the end of perfection; (II) in God it is the same thing to understand and to be; (III) whatever is in God is God; (IV) in one simple act, God understands and wills all; (V) whatever is in God is one with the divine essence.[96] Each of these principles is the result of demonstrations in earlier questions (ST I, qq. 2–19). Thomas uses these principles to interpret and make sense of the revelation about plurality in God. The construction of Thomas' theological proposal is a careful process by which the more evident things are used to interpret and understand the less evident things. This is not to imply that Thomas' arguments become weaker and weaker as the discussion strays farther and farther from what is demonstrable. There are two different levels of meaning or kinds of meaning in the statements, "God is eternal" and "There are processions in God." The meaning of the first state-

---

94. "Sed intelligere divinum est ipsa substantia intelligentis, ut supra (q. 14, a. 4) ostensum est: unde verbum procedens procedit ut eiusdem naturae subsistens. Et propter hoc proprie dicitur genitum et Filius." ST I, q. 27, a. 2 ad 2.

95. "Ego ex Deo processi" (John 8:42); "non potest facere a se Filius quidquam" (John 5:19); "Ego hodie genui te" (Ps. 2:7); "nondum erant abyssi, et ego iam concepta eram, ante colles ego parturiebar" (Prov. 8:24); "Rogabo Patrem meum, et alium Paracletum dabit vobis" (John 14:16). These texts reveal real distinction, relations of origin as well as eternality with respect to the Three.

96. "[C]um divinum intelligere sit in fine perfectionis." ST I, q. 27, a. 1 ad 2 (I). "[I]n Deo idem est intelligere et esse." ST I, q. 27, a. 3 ad 3. Will is also identical to being and intellect. Cf. ST I, q. 19, a. 1 c (II). "[Q]uidquid est in Deo, est Deus." ST I, q. 27, a. 3 ad 2 (III). "Deus uno simplici actu omnia intelligit, et similiter omnia vult." ST I, q. 27, a. 5 ad 3 (IV). "[Q]uidquid est in divinis, est unum cum divina natura." ST I, q. 27, a. 4 ad 1 (V).

ment can be easily if not perfectly grasped. The meaning of the second statement is much more difficult to delineate.

Thomas' speech about God is guided by two fundamental beliefs: we cannot comprehend God (ST I, qq. 1–2); and we can know and name God only by means of created things (ST I, q. 13). The process of speaking about God then is essentially though not completely negative. What we mean by saying that God is eternal is that God is without beginning or end. What we mean by saying that there are processions in God is that there is an act within God dissimilar to our intellectual acts in having no beginning or end and not being other than the being and nature of God nor resulting in anything other than God—essentially a series of negations leaving us with a term defined less by its own content than by the constellation of other terms and principles that cohere with it. When Thomas reminds his reader, toward the end of the discussion of processions, that "we cannot name God except by way of creatures," his intention is to strip his terminology of all creaturely connotations. The term 'procession' may be taken from its application to creatures, but its meaning with respect to God must be determined by all the aforementioned principles which guide such removal of inappropriate meaning or connotation, the result of which is a complex concept.

Consider, for instance, the resulting distinctions and conclusions Thomas reaches in q. 27 on the processions. First, such procession is not by way of local motion, exterior or interior effect. It is most similar to intellectual emanation because intellectual substances are the highest creatures we know. Understood as a generation, it does not involve a difference in nature. This point delineates the difference between our intellectual "conceiving," whereby there proceeds in us an intellectual word that is merely similar to the thing understood, and the "generating" in God, whereby the processing and the processed are not distinct in nature or perfection.[97]

---

97. "Sed intellectu nostro utimur nomine *conceptionis,* secundum quod in verbo nostri intellectus invenitur similitudo rei intellectae, licet non inveniatur naturae identitas." ST I, q. 27, a. 2 ad 2.

By clearly distinguishing these processions from acts outside the divine nature and from those pertaining to divine power, Thomas eliminates the possibility of distinctions according to nature. In the *Summa*, he qualifies the divine processions by distinguishing its proper meaning from any outer *(ad extra)* denotation and from any causal connotation. The resulting definition is limited to acts remaining within *(ad intra)* that distinguish only the "principle" *(principium)* from the principled *(principiatum)*. Thomas aims at this last distinction in some of his earlier texts but manages only to distinguish the more general term 'principle' from the less general term 'cause' as he addressed inner and outer processions at the same time.[98] Discussing the procession of creatures and that of divine Persons together cannot but lead to complications, making creation appear necessary or the Persons contingent and temporal.

Processions within God cannot be interpreted according to cause and effect; they must therefore be distinguished from any causality or priority. Understood causally, a divine procession would result in a creature, not a divine Person—as Arius mistakenly concluded. Simi-

---

98. In the *De potentia,* Thomas discussed together divine acts *ad extra* and *ad intra* with respect to the divine wisdom and goodness. The resulting confusion of the operation of intellect and will in these acts detracted from the force of the acts *ad intra* and gave an air of plausibility to the position of Arius. The argument against the positions of Arius and Sabellius consists in showing the reality of intellectual life in God. That there are acts of understanding and willing in God demonstrates the "co-essentiality" of Father, Son and Holy Spirit. This argument, however, implicitly separates the processions *ad intra* from *ad extra*. The divine wisdom and goodness pertain to the latter while the divine intellectual life is the principle of the former. The organization of the *De potentia* is problematic for several reasons: (1) it implies that creation is a necessary act following from divine goodness and that creation is actually a perfection of God; (2) it identifies the procession of the Son with divine understanding bringing once again to center stage the problem of whether the Father understands only by means of the Son or whether the Father and the Son *each* understand; (3) it reduces the processions in God to the level of processions within our minds portraying God as "a" mind. The problem then is that the reader may not have a clear idea of whether or not Thomas understands the procession to be from the essence or within it. Although these problems do not for the most part rise to the surface of explicit presentation, the contextualization of various questions represents a danger for the careless interpreter as well as the basis for misdirected criticism. Cf. Thomas' *De potentia* q. 10, a. 1.

larly, procession cannot be understood according to what is something external. Sabellius erred by supposing that the divine processions were not within but outside the divine nature. It is for the sake of refuting more decisively these two errors that Thomas clarifies and corrects this argument from earlier texts as he attempts a better presentation in the *Summa*. Accordingly, Thomas is especially careful to restrict the discussion only to inner processions before dealing with the procession of creatures.

> Procession within should be regarded as an action that remains in the agent. This action is most clearly seen in the intellect, where its action of understanding remains in the intellect itself. . . . Procession is therefore not to be understood according to what is in bodies either as local motion or as the action of some cause leading to an exterior effect . . . but according to an intelligible emanation, just as an intelligible word proceeds from and remains in the one speaking.[99]

Thomas realized in writing the *Summa* that the key to characterizing properly the divine procession is the "remaining-within-ness" that allows no causal distinction. Having already posited the perfection of divine life in the identity of understanding and being, the subsequent discussion of a distinction or processing in that understanding does not detract from the divine unity. Moreover, he postpones the consideration of intellect and will with respect to creation until q. 43, thereby separating the necessary and perfect being of God from the free acts of creation and the contingent being of what is created. Another consequence of the clarification in the *Summa* is the elimination of the term 'natural' from the discussion of processions. To identify the intelligible or intellectual procession as "natural" implies an unnatural and even temporal act of will in every other procession, both inner and outer.[100]

---

99. "[S]ecundum actionem quae manet in ipso agente, attenditur processio quaedam ad intra. Et hoc maxime patet in intellectu, cuius actio, scilicet intelligere, manet in intelligente. . . . Non ergo accipienda est processio secundum quod est in corporalibus, vel per motum localem, vel per actionem alicuius causae in exteriorem effectum . . . sed secundum emanationem intelligibilem, utpote verbi intelligibilis a dicente, quod manet in ipso." ST I, q. 27, a. 1 c.

100. The second procession is similar to our willing love and can be considered according to the principle of the will, although not necessarily as a willful procession. Yet

The limit of two processions in God we know from revelation, however, not from an argument of reason. The evidence for the limit of two processions in God is the revelation of the two proceeding, the Son and the Holy Spirit.[101] The dissimilarity between our intellectual processions and the divine processions does not eliminate the possibility of multiple processions in God. It is merely illustrative of the limit of two processions in God. In the end, the unity and perfection of operation in God severely qualifies anything that might be gained from the creaturely analogy. That we know only two intelligible processions that remain in an agent does not in any way limit such processions remaining within the agent who is God.

One must be careful in reading these articles, to avoid confusion about what follows from revelation and what follows from analogy. The delineation of the two categories of conclusions is a way of bypassing modern assumptions about Thomas' methodology. Thomas is much more reserved in his attitude toward analogical arguments in regard to this doctrine than is usually assumed. The conclusion of the discussion is that the term 'procession' is in some way suitable for speaking about plurality with respect to God. We do not know exactly what it means for there to be a procession in God, only that it is unlike processions known to us in so many ways. One must then maintain the proper lines of the analogy between the manner of understanding

---

unlike our willed love, this second procession shares in the identity of (divine) nature; it is not distinguished from the first procession by the difference between intellect and will because the two are really one in God, nor by any proper reason because of the unity of God (aa. 3-4). The two processions are distinguished only by reason of order, not nature. Such order can be understood in terms of the order of knowing and willing in us. First there is something conceived by the intellect and then loved by the will. "Processio autem quae attenditur secundum rationem voluntatis, . . . magis secundum rationem impellentis et moventis in aliquid. Et ideo quod procedit in divinis per modum amoris, non procedit ut genitum vel ut filius, sed magis procedit ut spiritus." ST I, q. 27, a. 4 c. Note that the phrase is not "the love that proceeds" but "that which proceeds in the manner of love." Thomas' emphasis is always upon the action posited in God and found analogously in our faculties: "Huiusmodi autem processiones sunt duae tantum, . . . alia secundum actionem voluntatis, quae est processio amoris." ST I, q. 28, a. 4 c.

101. "Sed contra est quod in Deo non sunt nisi duo procedentes, scilicet Filius et Spiritus Sanctus. Ergo sunt ibi tantum duae processiones." ST I, q. 27, a. 4 sc.

and loving in us and the manner of the two processions in God. These processions are understood according to the manner of knowing and loving because these are the two processive acts (known to us) remaining in an agent, namely, the human soul. In God, however, such processions involve an identity of nature as well as an identity of act, for being and intellect are not distinct in God, nor are intellect and will.

The basis for speaking of relations with respect to God is the very relationality of the names of the divine Persons. "*Father* is not said except by means of paternity and *Son* by means of sonship."[102] The names of the Persons are indicative of relations. Moreover, such relations must be real if we affirm the reality of the Persons themselves. To question the reality of relations is to question the reality of the Father, Son, and Holy Spirit. This is not to say that we understand such relations, but only that the personal names include them. The discussion of relations in q. 28 is then a meditation of sorts upon this datum. The relevant principles of interpretation are those noted above in the discussion of processions together with the demonstrations of the absolute distinction between what is of God and what is created.

Thomas' discussion of relation is also based upon the Augustinian insight that everything that is said of God must be said substantially of God. To posit relations in God means that these relations are subsistent, not accidental (in the Aristotelian sense). The central problem is how one is to understand a plurality of subsistent relations without offending the doctrine of divine unity. Having noted in articles 2 and 3 that there are relations in God by reason of the revealed names, and that such relations must be real for Father and Son to be distinct, Thomas goes on to investigate the way in which relation multiplies or posits multiplicity in God. According to Thomas, this plurality is not said absolutely but only relatively.[103] The meaning of the term 'relation,' he states, "involves some respect of one to another according to which something is opposed relatively to another. . . . Relative opposi-

---

102. "[P]ater non dicitur nisi a paternitate, et filius a filiatione." ST I, q. 28, a. 1 sc.
103. ST I, q. 28, a. 3 c.

tion includes in its meaning distinction. Hence, there must be a real distinction in God."[104] To the objection that the identity of relation and essence precludes the possibility of distinctions between relations, Thomas again can only refer to the principles of sonship and paternity as "conveying" opposition.[105] Thomas has then not offered an answer as much as restated the previous article on predicating relation of God.[106]

He has, on the other hand, clarified some essential points left unsuitably delineated in his other discussions. In *De potentia*, Thomas allowed the implication of causality to stand. "There is a real relation in God following upon an action remaining within God."[107] Instead of considering processions alone (and only according to acts remaining within), he addressed processions and relations together, thereby implying that the divine relations are "consequent upon" the processions. The argument in *De potentia* distinguishes between the divine essence and the 'Word' processed, yet the reality of the relation seems dependent upon an action, or founded upon some action.

Thomas' attempt to coordinate the processions and relations in *De potentia* q. 8 was met with difficulty, as the many relevant distinctions clouded the issue and even unbalanced the presentation of the doctrine. This problem can be seen in the text of article 1 of q. 8, where Thomas introduces most of the distinctions he would later spread over four articles in the *Summa*.

Because the divine Persons are considered only according to a relative distinction, it is necessary to posit in God such relation as following upon [some]

---

104. "De ratione autem relationis est respectus unius ad alterum, secundum quem aliquid alteri opponitur relative. Cum igitur in Deo realiter sit relatio, ut dictum est (a.1), oportet quod realiter sit ibi oppositio. Relativa autem oppositio in sui ratione includit distinctionem. Unde oportet quod in Deo sit realis distinctio." ST I, a. 28, a. 3 c.

105. ST I, q. 28, a. 3 ad 1.

106. "[R]elatio quae est in Deo, secundum esse suum non sit idem quod divina essentia; sed quod non praedicatur secundum modum substantiae, ut existens in eo de quo dicitur, set ut ad alterum se habens." ST I, q. 28, a. 2 ad 1.

107. "Relinquitur ergo quod consequatur relatio realis in Deo actionem manentem in agente: cujusmodi actiones sunt intelligere et velle in Deo." Thomas, *De potentia* q. 8, a. 1 c.

action.... A real relation in God is consequent upon an action remaining within Him, such as the acts of understanding and willing.... If for some intellect it may be the same thing to understand and to be, it will be necessary that the word is not extrinsic to the being of the intellect itself.... Thus, there is in God a real relation both according to the word and according to the one proffering the word.[108]

The question of the reality of the relations then quickly becomes one of the reality of an act *ad intra,* a procession of a word. Taken in itself, this argument may not seem problematic, and indeed most of its individual parts are found in the *Summa* with much the same wording. The basis of the discussion, however, lies in the production of relatedness, the constitution of the Persons. The early introduction of this problem pushes the force of the arguments to the processions as the productive aspect of divine being. In the *Summa* Thomas saves this issue, the basis for real distinction in God, for a much later question in his treatise.[109] By that time, he will have carefully defined each term as well as the rules of signification and predication, in order to move from the reality of distinction to the constitution of such distinction in God. In the *Summa,* Thomas saw the extreme difficulty of denoting non-causal processions and uncaused, subsistent relations as a way of illuminating the reality of Father, Son, and Holy Spirit, One God in three Persons. He realized that the real distinction of the Persons and their constitution are two separate questions. Consequently, he left the latter, more complex problem until the end of his treatise.

Comparing Thomas' various discussions of these issues, we can see that when Thomas returns to the manner of acts *ad intra* at the end of the question on relations as a way of understanding such distinction, the nature of the argument is much clearer. Instead of using

---

108. "Relinguitur ergo quod per sola relativa distinctio in divinis personis attenditur.... oportet in eo ponere relationem actionem consequentem.... consequatur relatio realis in Deo actionem manentem in agente: cujusmodi actiones sunt intelligere et velle in Deo.... Si ergo aliquis intellectus sit cujus intelligere sit suum esse, oportebit quod illud verbum non sit extrinsecum ab esse ipsius intellectus.... Relinquitur ergo quod in divinis sit realis relatio et ex parte verbi et ex parte proferentis verbum." Thomas, *De potentia* q. 8, a. 1 c.

109. ST I, q. 40, aa. 2-3.

the analogy of intellectual subsistence to demonstrate a distinction between the principle of intelligible procession (the Father) and the processed word (the Son), Thomas uses the analogy to describe the relation between the two the way in which paternity and filiation are related by generation.

> For every procession, there are two opposing relations: one is of the one proceeding from a principle, and the other is of the principle itself. The procession of a word is called 'generation,' . . . The relation of the principle of generation in perfect living things is called 'paternity', but the relation of the one proceeding from a principle of generation is called 'filiation.'[110]

The *Summa* presentation is much clearer because of the careful and isolated exposition of each term in the discussion.

Relations can be real or merely dependent upon a reasoning mind.[111] When some respect or aspect is in the nature of the things so that it is ordered to another according to its nature, the relation is said to be real. A relational ordering to another, such as position, does not involve a thing's nature. For there to be a relation on the part of one thing, however, does not entail a relation on the part of the other. Because relation is a tendency to another and not a "thing between," the fact of a real relation of creation to God does not imply such relation from God to creation. Creation is really related to God in the sense of "being ordered to and dependent upon" God, but God is in no way defined by or ordered to creation, and thus is not related to it. The relational "respect" must be in the very nature of the thing in order to be real. Really related things are "according to their nature ordered to an-

---

110. "Secundum quamlibet autem processionem oportet duas accipere relationes oppositas, quarum una sit procedentis a principio, et alia ipsius principii. Processio autem verbi dicitur generatio, . . . Relatio autem principii generationis in viventibus perfectis dicitur paternitas: relatio vero procedentis a principio dicitur filiatio." ST I, q. 28, a. 4 c.

111. For a fuller discussion of Thomas' theory of relation, see A. Krempel, *La doctrine de la relation chez saint Thomas: Exposé historique et systématique* (Paris: J. Vrin, 1952) especially pp. 537–53 on the term's use in its Trinitarian context; H. Meyer, *Thomas von Aquin* (Paderborn, 1961), 158–64; E. Muller, S.J., "Real Relations and the Divine: Issues in Thomas' Understanding of God's Relation to the World," *Theological Studies* 56 (1995): 673–95.

other, and have such inclination to one another."[112] The Father and the Son are really (mutually) related because such ordering or inclination is a part of their identity. In fact, paternity *is* the identity of the Father as sonship *is* the identity of the Son.

With regard to things of the same nature, what proceeds and that from which it proceeds must necessarily be really related. The conceived intellectual word and the intellectual faculty are really related by the unity of their nature, the knowing mind. The being of the intellect is ordered to the word being conceived, just as the conceived word is ordered to the intellect from which it comes. The difference between the intellectual procession in our mind and the processions in God is that with God there is no causing or producing.

The divine relations and processions share the same level of distinction and are ordered to one another. Thomas' argument for the reality of distinct relations includes the argument for a real distinction of divine processions. "Father" and "Son" cannot be said except according to relations which are ordered to the processions in a real sense.[113] Yet the processions only "give evidence of" the distinct relations. They are considered neither as effects from a cause nor as a cause expressing an effect, but as a principle of proceeding who shares the very same nature with the one who proceeds.

Having shown that divine processions are really communicating one and the same nature and that relations are really ordered to the processions as that by which the nature proceeds, the identity of relation and nature must be addressed. The error Thomas wished to avoid was that of allowing processions to come between the divine nature and the divine relations. On the basis of the teaching in q. 27, it is possible to conclude that the nature processes and produces the divine Persons who are related and distinct yet one by the divine nature

---

112. "Qui quidem respectus aliquando est in ipsa natura rerum; utpote quando aliquae res secundum suam naturam sed invicem ordinatae sunt, et invicem inclinationem habent." ST I, q. 28, a. 1 c.

113. "[S]ecundum Philosophum, in V Metaphysics, relatio omnis fundatur vel suprar quantitatem, ut duplum et dimidium; vel supra actionem et passionem, ut faciens et factum, pater et filius, dominus et servus, et huiusmodi." ST I, q. 28, a. 4 c.

which is itself other than the relations.[114] This error was in Thomas' day associated with Gilbert of Poitiers, who used the terms 'assistant' and 'extrinsically affixed' to describe the ordering of relation to essence in God.[115] The simplicity of God demands that everything in God be one with the divine essence. But in what way can two things (relations), for instance, be really distinct from one another yet identical to a third (divine essence)?

## 2.3 Defining Trinitarian Terms

### 2.3.1 Relation

'Relations' are unlike other accidents. Quantity and quality, for instance, signify a measurement of the thing itself and are determined from within. A ball alone in the universe possesses the same quantity and quality as it does with a world around it. 'Relation', on the other hand, depicts a tendency to another.[116] 'Relation' signifies something in reference to another, but as an accident it also signifies an inherence in the subject. However, as Thomas points out (from Augustine and Boethius) there can be no accidental predication in God. All that God is, is of the divine essence and predicated substantially. This manner of speaking demands that the being of the relation be equated with or dependent upon the act. Thomas then accounts for the unique linguistic situation of speech about God, as well as for the complexities of relation, as a predicament which both inheres and tends to another. It is important that a father is such not by virtue of his son but by virtue of begetting. Thus we say that 'relation' signifies an inherence and that such inherence remains with the death of the other, because the relation itself is produced by the activity. The act of begetting makes a person a parent and a (new) person—a son or daughter. A mutual relation, however, cannot be understood only by means of the act linking them. This kind of strict definition denies that a foster or

---

114. "[A]liud a relationibus." ST I, q. 28, a. 4 obj. 2.
115. See ST I, q. 28, a. 2 c.
116. "Ea vero quae dicuntur ad aliquid, significant secundum propriam rationem solum respectum ad aliud." ST I, q. 28, a. 1 c.

step-father could be considered the "father" of the child. Identifying parent and child by means of the productive act that makes the two to be "related" detracts from the significance of the "being" of that relationship as it is made evident in some manner or another for the child's entire life.

What does it mean to say that "accidents" are predicated "substantially" of God? Have the terms lost their meaning as human language is stretched to the breaking point in order to accommodate the uniqueness of God? Thomas attempts an answer to this problem by examining the fundamental denotation of 'relation'. A relation has existence in a manner very different from substance. Relation has two kinds of being: *esse in* (being in) and *esse ad* (being to or being with respect to). The being of this accident is first understood as a being in the substance in which it inheres. One can say then that it does not have a being of its own but only from the substance. The other kind of being is a tendency or respect.[117] Relation refers to the host substance only but does not merely signify something about the substance in which it is. "The proper meaning of a relation is considered not according to that in which it is, but according to something outside."[118] Relation is peculiar among accidents in that it goes beyond the bearing substance and brings that one to something exterior, or at least "something else." Another way of understanding this distinction is to consider the *esse ad* as the "fundamental intelligibility of relation."[119] Relations in God then share this intelligibility with relations elsewhere. What makes the divine relations different from other relations is that the *esse in* is actually identical to the host substance, the divine essence, by reason of the divine simplicity and perfection. This "extra-mental foundation" in the divine essence is the basis for positing these relations as "real."[120]

Thomas explains the realness of the divine relations by describing their "respect," the tendency to another and the reality of such respect,

---

117. Cf. ST I, q. 28, a. 2 c. Also *De potentia*, q. 8, a. 2 c, and q. 7, a. 8.

118. "Sed ratio propria relationis non accipitur secundum comparationem ad illud in quo est, sed secundum comparationem ad aliquid extra." ST I, q. 28, a. 2 c.

119. E. Muller, "Real Relations," 675.

120. M. Henniger, S.J., *Relations: Medieval Theories 1250–1325* (Oxford: Clarendon, 1989), 17.

as opposed to the mere existence of such respect in the knowing mind. What is said in reference to another signifies something extra or outside in some way. Thomas' explanation of these terms is not exactly original. According to Schmidbaur, Thomas unabashedly borrowed from Gilbert, the supposed opponent in the discussion of relations.[121] Indeed, one familiar with Gilbert of Poitiers may well question in what way Thomas' formulation actually refutes and corrects Gilbert's "error."[122] While Gilbert referred to the divine relations as "not intrinsically affixed," Thomas chose to use "respect to the opposite."[123] Both expressions are ways of distinguishing the divine essence from the relatedness of the Persons.

Therefore, if we consider relations according to what they are in themselves, they are found to be assistant or not intrinsic to the subject itself. They signify a certain contingent respect to some related thing just as one thing tends to another. But if relation is considered as an accident, it inheres in a subject and has being accidentally in itself. But Gilbert considered relation only in the first manner.[124]

The effect of Thomas' formulation, however, is only to distinguish the divine *esse* (nature) from the *esse ad alterum* (Persons) without denying the identity of divine *esse* and relational *esse in*. Gilbert argued for no less. With both theologians, the reality of the relations cannot be other than a "being to another" *(esse ad aliquid)*. Otherwise the unity of the divine substance is endangered.[125]

---

121. Schmidbaur, *Personarum Trinitas*, 394.
122. M. E. Williams contends that Thomas and Gilbert differ very little on this issue. See his *The Teaching of Gilbert Porreta on the Trinity as Found in His Commentaries on Boethius* (Rome, 1951), 104.
123. ST I, q. 28, a. 2 c.
124. "Si igitur consideremus, etiam in rebus creatis, relationes secundum id quod relationes sunt, sic inveniuntur esse assistentes, non intrinsecus affixae; quasi significantes respectum quodammodo contingentem ipsam rem relatam, prout ab ea tendit in alterum. Si vero consideretur relatio secundum quod est accidens, sic est inhaerens subjecto, et habens esse accidentale in ipso. Sed Gilbertus Porretanus consideravit relationem primo modo tantum." ST I, q. 28, a. 2 c.
125. The proximity of these two theologians' positions can be more evidently seen in Thomas' *De potentia*, where he actually uses Gilbert's own term *"assistentes"* as well as his intended meaning. See *De potentia* q. 7.

It is evident that 'relation' is changed somewhat in its mode of signifying or use with reference to God but retains its meaning. Relation said accidentally or substantially must still be said according to an opposite. Relative opposition includes distinction; therefore the relations which are subsistent are distinct. What Thomas has been careful to do is to show how terms are to be understood with reference to God without destroying or negating the basic meaning of each term. Thus, the predication of relation in God has the same elements as in creatures, but those elements are understood in different ways corresponding to the demands of the unique linguistic situation which is speech about God. At the end of the question on relations, Thomas once again sets aside the kind of relation that is founded upon an extrinsic act. Relations in God are understood according to intrinsic acts, processions within. The beginning of the last article seems to repeat the question on processions (q. 27), but such repetition is perhaps indicative of the importance of the point, surely not the dullness of Aquinas' memory. He insists upon the unique character of relations in God. The reality of these relations consists in the identity of their nature such that the nature of one *is* the nature of the other. Their identity is then wholly ordered to one another such that the one processing and the one from whom it processes are truly within the same nature. These two are related because they are "ordered to one another" and such ordering is in the nature, namely, in the one common nature.

On the other hand, the act of being that is the subsistent divine relation is not other than the act of proceeding, by reason of the simplicity of God. Hence, Thomas can more easily describe the processions by reason of the similitude of (intellectual) processions in our intellectual nature. We are then limited to describing what relation in God is not. Procession and relation can be employed to discuss the reality of multiplicity, but such terms are limited in their epistemological value. Why? These terms seem to treat multiplicity within or in light of the whole. The problem then arises of the way in which this multiplicity is real. It is somewhat difficult to provide a sufficient answer to the twelfth-century problem of viewing the Trinity as "extrinsic," or implying that proceeding is an act of essence instead of Persons. Hence, at the end of qq. 27–28, Thomas has still not addressed the question of the constitution of the Father, Son, and Holy Spirit. The almost unavoidable implication of both questions is that two or even three are caused. On the other hand, Thomas is not here attempting an answer to how there are three but only the fact of threeness. Question 29 is then merely the beginning of the investigation of what or who are these three.

### 2.3.2 Person

The portion of our text concerning the term 'person' occupies the remaining questions (29–43) of the treatise on the Trinity. We now move into that part of the discussion in which Thomas attempts to explore more fruitful ways of discussing these Three who are subsistent relations. Thomas first defines his term and all that follows from this distinction before discussing the individual Persons and before coordinating this term with other terms already established in the text. One can surmise that the term's practical value is not due to any assumption of a subsequent epistemological treasure. Its immediate application here is to facilitate the discussion of the proper names of the Father, Son, and Holy Spirit. But what need is there for a term designating those who are better known by their proper terms? Do not the generic terms signifying God as one suffice for common and abstract words? More importantly, is it possible or even advisable to use an extra-biblical term to discuss what is known only by revelation?

Thomas makes clear, as did Augustine eight centuries before him, that 'person' is needed to give an account to heretics, or to those who ask, "three what?"

The name 'person' is not found in reference to God in the Old Testament or the New Testament; nevertheless, sacred Scripture indicates in many places what that name signifies in God, i.e., that he is supreme self-existence and that he is perfect understanding.... The use of new terms for signifying the ancient belief about God is necessary in order to dispute with heretics.[126]

---

126. "[L]icet nomen *personae* in Scriptura veteris vel novi Testamentis non inveniatur dictum de Deo, tamen id quod nomen significat, multipliciter in sacra Scriptura invenitur assertum de Deo; scilicet quod est maxime per se ens, et perfectissime intelligens.... Ad inveniendum autem nova nomina, antiquam fidem de Deo significantia, coegit necessitas disputandi cum haereticis." ST I, q. 29, a. 3 ad 1.

After all, Thomas states, if we were to limit ourselves strictly to biblical terms, as some advocated, we would, in fact, be limited to the actual Hebrew and Greek words found in the Scriptures. The very endeavor of translating the text into other languages is one of using "non-biblical" terms. Hence, his argument that 'person' signifies what is found in the Scripture is tantamount to saying that he is merely translating the text into a contemporary idiom. That God is "supreme self-existence and perfect understanding" means that God is "a person." And yet God is not "a person" but "three Persons." Hence, there is something more than mere translation present in Thomas' use of this term. Augustine pointed in this direction but was unable to make much use of the term due to its problematic connotations and its semantic proximity to substance. His primarily exegetical approach virtually precluded such redefinition of a term based on what it should mean in a theological context.[127]

Thomas' use of the terms, however, is heavily dependent upon the scholastic method of definition and distinction, specifically Boethius' definition in his *De duabus naturis*.[128] Boethius defines 'person' as "an individual substance of a rational nature."[129] 'Substance' by itself, according to Thomas, signifies something individuated by itself and is similar to 'hypostasis.' The importance of 'individual' lies in its distinguishing this substance as a subsisting particular.[130] Also, 'individual' excludes from the definition something assumable, such as human nature.[131] The adjective 'rational' defines specifically the kind of nature and excludes non-intelligent hypostases. The choice of 'nature' rather than 'essence' is due to the desire to signify a "specific differ-

---

127. See his *De Trinitate* VII.7–11. Augustine's theological method also did not extend to the kind of careful, scholastic qualification Thomas pursues.

128. Boethius' definition was formulated in reference to the explanation of the union of divine and human nature in Christ, yet Thomas finds this definition to be also the most appropriate one for Trinitarian use.

129. "Persona est rationalis naturae individua substantia." ST I, q. 29, a. 1.

130. "Et sic hoc nomen *individuum* ponitur in definitione personae, ad designandum modum subsistendi qui competit substantiis particularibus." ST I, q. 29, a. 1 ad 3.

131. ST I, q. 29, a. 1 ad 2. See Thomas' discussion of the Incarnation as the assumption of human nature on the part of a divine Person in ST III, q. 2, a. 2. This aspect of "not being assumable" indicates the dignity of having personality.

ence" denominating the thing. Essence is less formal and too common to things in general.

Besides defining the term, Thomas must also demonstrate the way in which 'person' is distinguished from other theological terms. 'Person' is needed to signify something with respect to God that 'hypostasis,' 'subsistence,' and 'essence' fail to denote with sufficient precision. Thomas for the most part affirms that 'hypostasis,' 'subsistence,' and 'person' are synonymous yet argues that only 'person' is specific to rational beings. The Greeks' use of 'hypostasis' in referring to the three is appropriate in that it signifies an individual substance. On the other hand, it is only by the habit of use that the term 'hypostasis' has come to signify an individual of a *rational* nature.[132] That is, 'hypostasis' has been employed for specifying "three what?" only through customary usage. Because of its ability to signify other things, such as non-rational substances or inanimate natures, it lacks the appropriate dignity for the unique and most excellent subject of linguistic expression, God.[133] 'Person,' on the other hand, has of itself the specificity of the highest, i.e. rational, nature.

The third possible synonym for 'person'—'essentia'—presents a different sort of problem. It signifies not an individual *per se* but by means of definition. Essence can signify the composition of matter and form as the principle of a species or of the nature of things themselves. It does not, however, connote individuality in the sense of signifying "this matter" and "this form."[134] Moreover, the implication of matter/form composition means that it is a much more general term than either 'hypostasis' or 'subsistence.' 'Person' is most appropriate because of its specific denotation of individual and, most importantly, of rational nature. Of course, the Trinitarian usage of 'person' is not its fundamental import, but the excellence and specificity of the term require that it be altered the least of these other terms in order to make it suitable for theology.

But does the term naturally or customarily, possess the dignity

132. "[S]ed ex usu loquendi habet quod sumatur pro individuo rationalis naturae, ratione suae excellentiae." ST I, q. 29, a. 2 ad 1.
133. ST I, q. 29, a. 2 c.
134. ST I, q. 29, a. 2 ad 3; see also a. 1 ad 4 on the indeterminateness of essence.

needed for Trinitarian discourse? 'Hypostasis' and 'subsistence' may lack the precision, but their specific and technical use in the sciences gives them a certain dignity. 'Person,' on the other hand, as Boethius himself pointed out in his *De duabus naturis,* was used to signify the representation of other people by an actor. The wearing of a mask to represent a public or mythic figure was signified by the word 'person'. This use in Greek drama, with the implied artifice, would seem to detract from the dignity of the word. Thomas deftly turns this potentially serious objection on its head, noting that only the most excellent and famous men were represented. The manner of signifying, by means of actors putting on masks, is not appropriate for speaking of God. On the other hand, says Thomas,

> This name 'person' is used to signify those having dignity. Hence, it is customary to call those having dignity in the Church, "persons." . . . And to subsist in a rational nature is the greatest of dignity, so every individual of a rational nature is called "person." The dignity of divine nature, however, exceeds all dignity and merits most highly being called "Person."[135]

One need only remove the distance between the mask and figure to see that 'person' was a title of great dignity. The employment of the term was due to the merit of the one signified. One could say that it was a loosening of the constraints of meaning for this term to be employed in signifying all rational creatures. We are elevated in dignity by our inclusion. Most importantly, however, 'person' is appropriate to God because of what it signifies, dignity.

In light of Thomas' organization, it is evident that he structures his discussion of the Father and Son and Holy Spirit upon this term rather than upon procession or relation *per se.*[136] He does not argue

---

135. "[I]mpositum est hoc nomen *persona* ad significandum aliquos dignitatem habentes. Unde consueverunt dici *personae* in ecclesiis, quae habent aliquam dignitatem. . . . Et quia magnae dignitatis est in rationali natura subsistere, ideo omne individuum rationalis naturae dicitur persona, ut dictum est (a. 1). Sed dignitas divinae naturae excedit omnem dignitatem: et secundum hoc maxime competit Deo nomen personae." ST I, q. 29, a. 3 ad 2.

136. The category of 'person' dominates all but the first two questions of the text in qq. 27 through 43.

from procession to relation and then to person but rather clarifies the first two before settling on the third as the more useful and fundamental. After q. 28, the term 'relation' as a basis for distinction in God is all but left behind (to be brought up again only in q. 40). Procession likewise threatened to imply a priority and succession in the divine that would destroy notions of equality and eternity. The use of 'person' is then justified by its suitability in signification and its necessity for disputation. Thomas does not make the easy argument that the term was already part of the theological tradition being used by many authoritative figures and councils. He wanted to justify the use of 'person' in the abstract without recourse to the habit of theologians. The habit itself had to be defended.

The modern assumption that Thomas' discussion was facilitated by the common currency of this term is mistaken. His work was greatly complicated by the elasticity of the term. For that reason, he had to clarify his use of 'person' against other definitions and improper connotations. One need only read the objections in qq. 29 and 30 to see the obstacles Thomas had to overcome and counter in order to clear the table for his explanation.[137] According to the scholastics, it is the theologian's task to clarify and even redirect linguistic usage. One rarely finds ready-made terms for inclusion in theological discourse. Words must be altered and reshaped to fit the demands of theological grammar; and their theological use must be clearly explained against the backdrop of inevitable changes in ordinary usage. This linguistic work is especially important in Trinitarian theology, where words are stretched to their limit. Consequently, the modern psychological and existential connotations of 'person' do not render it unusable, merely in need of clarification and correction.[138] 'Person'

---

137. Such objections include the term's implicit singularity, superficiality, artifice, inaccuracy as well as its redundancy with other theological terms.

138. There are two identifiable strains in the modern debate surrounding the use of 'person' in Trinitarian theology. First, there are those who reject the term either because of its modern connotations or because of a desire to reject the substance metaphysics of the older tradition along with its "non-biblical" terminology (Barth and Rahner); second, there are those who wish to retain the traditional terms yet adjust

can be applied to God almost as easily as the transcendental terms. Not that God is in the same way the "source" of personhood as the source of goodness, but that the Father, Son, and Holy Spirit can be called "Persons" in answer to the question, "three what?" The term applies first and foremost to the divine subsistences by reason of their most perfect being *(maxime per se ens)* and most perfect intellectual life. And regarding dignity, 'person' is "most fittingly used of God" because divine nature exceeds every dignity.[139]

In the remainder of this section (through q. 43), Thomas builds upon the material in q. 29. What it means to be person and in what way God is three Persons profoundly informs the next fourteen questions. There are two identifiable sections leading up to the focus of our study, q. 39. First Thomas discusses the nature of Person (qq. 29–32) and then the divine Persons themselves (qq. 33–38). Questions

---

their meaning to bring them in line with modern thought (Kasper and Moltmann). Following the suggestion of K. Barth (*Church Dogmatics,* I/1 408–415) that a substitution be found for the term, K. Rahner argued at length in several of his works for the use of "distinct manner of subsistence" instead of person. He believed that this formula captured the ante-Nicean understanding of the Trinity better and that it avoided the tritheistic implications of the modern sense of 'person.' He contends that 'person' and 'subject' actually refer more appropriately to the unity and oneness of God as an absolute subject in an absolute person. K. Rahner, *The Trinity,* 75. J. Moltmann, on the other hand, concerned with the unavoidable modalism of Rahner's language, prefers to retain and reinterpret traditional language. He (re)defines 'person' as an individual center of consciousness in terms of relationality. Moltmann avoids what he sees as the tritheism of intra-relatedness by turning that relationality outward. The identity of each divine Person is then defined more in terms of a relation to creation than a relation to one another. Moltmann affirms with Rahner that the immanent Trinity is the economic Trinity by subsuming the history of the world, salvation history, into the history of God, or indeed by actually equating the two. The activity of each divine Person in the world is part of that Person's identity. Hence, he agrees with Rahner that the Incarnation of the Second Person is entirely meaningful. It cannot be a matter of indifference which Person became incarnate, because that specific act is revelatory of that particular Person. We can know something not only of God in general, but also of the Second Person, the Son, the Word by this event and the acts which follow from it. The Word of God is then eternally spoken into the void, that is, as a Word directed *ad extra*. Moltmann solves the problem of oneness by preferring a perichoretic union to unity. J. Moltmann, *The Trinity and the Kingdom of God,* 22–30; 57; 95; 160–61.

139. "Sed dignitas divinae naturae excedit omnem dignitatem: et secundum hoc maxime competit Deo nomen *personae.*" ST I, q. 29, a. 3 ad 2.

30–31 represent a preliminary approach to discussing the equality of the Persons and the fullness of divinity in each. Having defined the subsistences of divine nature as 'Persons,' Thomas must immediately qualify what it means to posit a plurality of Persons in God. It cannot imply the division or multiplication of the nature, as the term 'individual' implies.[140] There are no parts of a whole, for each is no less than all. The Father is no less than the whole Trinity. This idea of equality may very well be the most difficult aspect of Trinitarian theology to explain. One can state it but not explain it except in terms of negations. One Person is not less than two or all three, yet the Father is not the Son and the Son is not the Father or the Holy Spirit. Augustine had approached the problem of equality through a discussion of essential attributes.[141] The problem was how Christ could be the wisdom and power of God yet without three wisdoms and powers. Thus, the Father is wise by his own wisdom and powerful by his own power although the wisdom of the Son is identical to the wisdom of the Father. No differences or divisions are permissible with regard to the divine nature or the absolute perfections.

Thomas recognized the extreme difficulty of explaining the equality of the divine Persons and consequently placed it at the end of his discussion of distinctions in God. In a sense, one would argue that Thomas chose not to define such terms but only their use. Also, Thomas separated the issue of equality from that of the appropriations. Hence, he treats the rules governing essential predication with respect to Persons three questions before addressing equality directly. On the other hand, as noted above, Thomas does use the fact of equality in earlier articles. Hence, the full scope of Trinitarian doctrine is in play at least implicitly from the beginning. The order of direct introduction is a matter of pedagogy not demonstration, much less derivation. Hence, it is quite appropriate that Thomas waits until q. 32, the middle of his discussion of divine Persons and their distinctions, to address the questions of how we may know these Persons.

Thomas uses the term 'person' from q. 30 onward as a short for-

---

140. ST I, q. 30, a. 1 ad 4.
141. See Augustine, *De Trinitate* V–VII.

mula for discussing the Three who are One God. The discussion is not an attempt to penetrate into the meaning of divine Persons, but to define the plurality of what we call Person in God. Hence q. 32, on "our knowledge of the divine Persons," concerns our knowledge of these Persons not by any inductive grammatical-linguistic study of the term but from what we know from revelation about these particular Persons. Hence, the investigation of 'person' as being suitable for speaking of the Father, Son, and Holy Spirit is limited to the way in which it encapsulates what is revealed of these Three. We know from revelation that these three are distinct in one divine nature. Therefore, it is neither a negation of communicability nor an intention of individuality in the same way that 'some man' signifies an instance of that nature. 'Person' signifies in God the subsisting thing in such nature.[142]

The way in which Thomas uses these terms to facilitate discussion (and not analysis) is seen in his treatment of the group of terms known as "notions" or "properties." The "notions" are abstract terms by which one may signify the relations; they correspond to the five relational aspects of God: paternity, filiation, spiration, innascibility, and procession.[143] The Father is known properly by means of innascibility and paternity. The Son is known by his filiation, or being from another by way of generation, and by common spiration with the Father. The Holy Spirit is known as the procession from the other two. Abstract and concrete terms were readily available for signifying divine unity but not the divine distinctions. These notional terms provide a way of speaking abstractly about distinctions in God, while 'Person' remains a common concrete term for these distinctions.

As Thomas stated in q. 13, we name things as we understand them. We apprehend and name simple things by means of abstract terms. Hence, we use 'Father' or 'divine Person' to signify the subsistent divine nature and 'paternity' to signify the "form" of the Father. Paternity answers the question "by what means?"

We confess the Father and the Son and the Holy Spirit to be one God and three Persons. In answer to those asking by what manner are they one God,

---

142. ST I, q. 30, a. 4 c.
143. ST I, q. 32, a. 3 c.

one may respond that they are one essence and one deity. To those asking by what manner are they three Persons, one must respond with some abstract name that distinguishes the Persons. For example, we can use the properties or notions signified abstractly such as paternity and filiation. Therefore, the essence is signified in God as "what," Person as "who," and property as "how" (by what means).[144]

And there are two reasons we must answer this question: First, to give an account to heretics, and secondly, to distinguish the two relations of the Father, one to the Son and one to the Holy Spirit. In the first case, the notions provide a way of discussing the means of distinction. The Father is the Father by means of his paternity, though the Father and Son are God by means of one divine nature. In the second case, we must find a reason for distinguishing the Spirit and Son, for if they have the same relation to the Father, then they would not be two Persons. The occasion for this second point is the importance of the *Filioque* which the Greeks rejected. The notions are a way by which the Son and Holy Spirit can be distinguished, according to the Roman Church. According to Thomas, without such teaching there is no way to distinguish these two. The relations of the Father to the Son, and the Father to the Holy Spirit, must be distinguishable in some way for the Son and Holy Spirit to be distinct. The notions of paternity and common spiration are the ways by which we can mark these distinctions. On the other hand, this formulation of the notions is not an article of faith.[145] Different opinions are permitted. What cannot be denied is the procession of the Holy Spirit from the Father and the Son. The way we express this procession and distinguish it from the generation of the Son is another matter.

We can see especially in this last question Thomas' understanding

---

144. "Cum enim confiteamur Patrem et Filium et Spiritum Sanctum esse unum Deum et tres Personas, quaerentibus *quo sunt unus Deus*, et *quo sunt tres personae*, sicut respondetur quod sunt essentia vel deitate unum, ita oportuit esse aliqua nomina abstracta, quibus responderi possit personas distingui. Et huiusmodi sunt proprietates vel notiones in abstracto significatae, ut paternitas et filiatio. Et ideo essentia significatur in divinis ut quid, persona vero ut quis, proprietas autem ut quo." ST I, q. 32, a. 2 c.

145. "Sed contra, articuli fidei non sunt de notionibus. Ergo circa notiones licet sic vel aliter opinari." ST I, q. 32, a. 4 sc.

of theological language. There are doctrines and there are ways of discussing those doctrines. A certain measure of flexibility is necessary in the latter. Given a revealed teaching, we inevitably see, further terms to speak about it both concretely and abstractly. But we should not make the mistake of positing extra-mental realities corresponding to our every manner of knowing. One of these notions, innascibility, is not a relation at all but only the denial of being from another. Also, one of these notions, common spiration, is not a property *per se*, since two Persons are signified by it. The last two notions mentioned are also not personal and, therefore, do not constitute subsistent relations.

### 2.3.3 The Divine Persons *per se*

The next section of Thomas' discussion (qq. 33–38) can be seen as the basis of Trinitarian doctrine and a bridge between Thomas' discussion of theological terms and their use. These questions are the basis for Trinitarian discussions insofar as the revelation of the Trinity consists in the revelation of the proper names. Augustine, for instance, in the first four books of his *De Trinitate*, discussed each Person in terms of its proper identity. For him, the divine missions and the proper identity of the Divine Persons were intimately related. In fact, the foundation for positing a distinction is the knowledge of the divine missions, or the "sending" of the Son and Holy Spirit. In his *Summa*, Thomas separated the issue of missions from that of the proper identity of the Persons. His reasoning will become evident later. What is evident at this point in the text is that Thomas wishes to contextualize the exposition of the proper names with more general discussions of unity and distinctions.

But one might ask, what is gained by postponing the quite biblical and more common method of discussing the distinct Persons according to their names? The proper names do not reveal the divine identities in a meaningful way. They reveal distinctions about which we can reason but not penetrate. This point may seem a bit counter-intuitive, inasmuch as the identity of the Second Person of the Trinity as the 'Son' is far more obvious than the fact that we may describe that same Person as one processing from the First Person; or that this Second

Person processes in an intellective manner such that it is more accurately called a "generation"; or that this Person is actually the subsistent relation of "filiation" or sonship. Yet we cannot describe the Son *in se* as a Son, for He is neither brought into being nor caused, but is eternal. This 'Son' is not subordinated in any way to the other Two. Nor is this one only a part of the One God, but is totally God such that this Son alone is not less than all Three together. It would be quite convenient at this point to turn to Thomas' discussion of "Son" as the proper name of the Second Person of the Trinity. Unfortunately, it is nowhere to be found. This name has virtually no epistemological value except as it is indicative of the mutual distinctions within the Trinity. Who or what this Son is, properly and distinctively, we cannot say except with reference to intra-divine distinctions, or relations and processions.

On the other hand, Thomas discusses the proper names of the Father and the Holy Spirit. Consider for a moment the way in which he treats the former:

The proper name of a person signifies that through which that person is distinguished from all other persons. . . .That through which the Person of the Father is distinguished from the others is paternity. Hence, the proper name of the Person of the Father is this name, "Father," that signifies paternity.[146]

Thomas can only repeat what he has already said in q. 28 on the mutual distinctions of relations. That is, to answer the question as to the propriety of the name "Father," Thomas turns to the relation the subsistence of which is constitutive of the First Person. Among creatures, such relations may be informative. To posit one as the mother and the other as the child is to imply, among other things, differences in age, the causal role of the first, and the subordination of the second to the first. But what does such relation mean if subordination, causality and material dependency as well as temporality are eliminated? Merely, that one is from the other without beginning or difference in na-

---

146. "[N]omen proprium cuiuslibet personae significat id per quod illa persona distinguitur ab omnibus aliis. . . . Id autem per quod distinguitur persona Patris ab omnibus aliis, est paternitas. Unde proprium nomen personae Patris est hoc nomen Pater, quod significatum paternitatem." ST I, q. 33, a. 2 c.

ture.¹⁴⁷ Augustine discovered this same limit of speech about the Persons. The quality of being "from" another without being "from" in any identifiable sense would seem to empty such statements of any epistemological value.¹⁴⁸ Consider the following argument that begins with the revealed fact of the Holy Spirit as the Third Person of the Trinity (1 John 5:7).

> This name "Holy Spirit" is not said relatively. Nevertheless, it is used relatively insofar as it is accommodated to signify a Person distinct from others only by a relation. One can indeed understand in this name some relation if Spirit is understood according to "spirated."¹⁴⁹

The argument is entirely circular. The Holy Spirit is called the "Holy Spirit" because that one is the Holy Spirit (or that one is the Third Person of the Trinity). Thomas cannot say anything about the relatedness or the proper identity, only that it is the Holy Spirit Himself. We are back to the mutual distinctions. In other words, describing who or what each one is, is the only way we can describe how the Three are mutually distinct.

On the other hand, if we remember the first twenty-six questions of the *Summa*, we can say a great deal about who each divine Person is. Yet what we say about one applies equally to all Three. We do not know "who" the Father is, beyond being fully God: eternal, simple, perfect, good, infinite, etc. What more is there to be said? Do the Father who is God and the Son who is God have different attitudes or do they differ in will or intellect or action? No, they are all one in the same divine nature; yet the Father is not the Son, because the Father is properly named by reason of paternity while the Son is properly named by reason of filiation. So when we seek further clarification of the distinction between the two, we are limited to commenting on the truthfulness or completeness of what is said above.

---

147. See ST I, qq. 27–28.
148. See Augustine, *De Trinitate* II.7–11.
149. "[L]icet hoc quod dico *Spiritus Sanctus*, relative non dicatur, tamen pro relativo ponitur, inquantum est accommodatum ad significandum personam sola relatione ab aliis distinctam. Potest tamen intelligi etiam in nomine aliqua relatio, si *Spiritus* intelligatur quasi *spiratus*." ST I, q. 36, a. 1 ad 2.

## 2.4 Conclusion

There is one more set of names that are proper, though not with a capital "P." They are proper simply by reason of being specific to one Person. Names such as 'unbegotten,' 'Word,' 'image,' 'gift,' and 'love' are in this group. 'Unbegotten' is a name of negation, signifying merely the property of "not being from another."[150] 'Image' denotes the property of being a similitude. The Son is the perfect likeness of the Father, since He proceeds from the Father by means of generation.[151] And yet are not all the Persons perfectly like one another in being divine and of the same nature? The term 'image' is used of the Son by reason of the generative procession. The Son proceeds as a generated Word who is the image of the one from whom He proceeds. We do not know anything more about the Son, or the Father, *per se*—only that the Son is the image of the Father, being the perfect similitude. To know, for instance, that Bill and Mark are twins does not involve any knowledge of Bill or Mark per se, only that they are very similar to each other in many ways. Positing a relation does not indicate identity. The term 'image' does not add to our understanding of Father or Son individually, but only of their similarity.

Likewise the names 'gift' and 'love' indicate something relational. The Holy Spirit is love because this one proceeds in the manner of love. Not that the Son and the Father love only through the Holy Spirit, but that the Holy Spirit is especially called 'love.' Such love can be essential or personal, yet only with reference to the one proceeding in the manner of love is the term personal and proper. Understood notionally, this love that is the Holy Spirit is the love by which the Father and the Son love each other. Yet because love and loving are also said essentially, this term as a proper name for the Third Person has only negligible semantic import. The name 'gift' falls into the same category insofar as it is a synonym for love. Properly speaking a gift is given without "intention of retribution," and love is the very basis for

---

150. ST I, q. 33, a. 4 c.
151. ST I, q. 35, a. 2 c.

gratuitous giving.¹⁵² Hence, love is the first gift. We have thereby plumbed the applicability of terms, not the identity of Persons.

With the term 'Word,' on the other hand, we have something verging on being meaningful in itself. This name does appear to describe the Son in some way. 'Word' renames what proceeds in the manner of intellection and pertains more to the procession than to the subsistence of the Second Person. On another level, 'Word' signifies the divine being, since "to be" and "to understand" are the same in God. When applied to a divine Person, however, 'Word' easily elides into implications of causality, production and temporality, due to the orientation to creatures it connotes.¹⁵³ This Word properly and personally is the one expressive of creatures;¹⁵⁴ that is, while creation cannot be a necessary consequence of the Word being processed, that procession is directly related to the act of creation. Thus, it has a special value as exemplar with respect to creatures. The Holy Spirit also has a special role as the love given, the gift of God's own self in the form of grace. The implication is that these acts or peculiar relations denote the Persons properly. The doctrine of the unity of divine works *(opera ad extra)* does not deny that one divine Person acts in a peculiar way. This doctrine denies that such acts are done without the other two and that they offer any insight into the proper identity of any one of the divine Persons. The Son and Holy Spirit are sent, and such sendings do seem to correspond to their proper names, Word and gift/love. But we can no more say why the Second Person was sent as Incarnate than we can say why the Second Person is called the 'Son.' We can only say that they are thus. Any argument for the appropriateness of the Son becoming incarnate cannot but fall far short of a causal explanation, because the cause sought is not a necessary one but a will, the divine will.

---

152. "[S]ciendum est quod donum proprie est *datio irredibilis,* secundum Philosophum, idest quod non datur intentione retributionis: et sic importat gratuitam donationem." ST I, q. 38, a. 2 c.

153. "Sed nomen Verbi principaliter impositum est ad significandam relationem ad dicentem: et ex consequenti ad creaturas, inquantum Deus, intelligendo se, intelligit omnem creaturam." ST I, q. 34, a. 3 ad 4.

154. ST I, q. 34, a. 3 ad 3.

# 3. Coordinating Essential and Proper Terms

In light of our consideration of the proper names in the last chapter, the discussion of the way the essential attributes can be used to reveal distinctions in God seems quite unnecessary. The distinct appropriation of essential terms to particular divine Persons seems to say less and not more than the proper names of the Trinity. The "Proper" names (Father, Son, and Holy Spirit) tell us that there are distinctions in God and that they are distinct by means of relations of origin. They do not, however, tell us about the proper identity of the Father, or of the Son, or of the Holy Spirit. The other "proper" names (small "p": word, gift/love) refer to distinct divine Persons but have more to do with the divine missions. Hence, one may ask why Thomas turns to a less informative procedure after examining the most proper manner of identifying the Persons as distinct. An even more important question for our purposes is why Thomas did not first discuss the way in which essential terms (e.g., power, wisdom, goodness) help elucidate plurality in God before discussing the processions at all.

## 3.1 Defining the Problem

What does it mean for something, some essential divine attribute, to be "appropriated"?[1] Did the Son, in becoming incarnate, "appropri-

---

1. What was among ancient and medieval theologians a discussion of illustrating the Trinity has now become a discussion of the working of the Trinity. Traditional discussions about divine acts asserted that all three Persons work together because of the unity of the divine nature and that, therefore, a given act is not absolutely proper to one only, excluding the other two, but 'appropriated' to one only, *as if* only one were responsible. The point is that the Persons are inseparable in outward acts and, conse-

ate" power and wisdom such that Christ is "the power and wisdom of God"?[2] What does it mean to describe differences by using what is common? We say that the Father is God, the Son is God, and the Holy Spirit is God; and that the Father is good, the Son is good, and the Holy Spirit is good; and that the Father is wise, the Son is wise, and the Holy Spirit is wise; yet we do not say that there are three Gods, or three good ones, but one God, good and wise: the Trinity. The attributes of goodness or wisdom or any other attribute shared by the Three do not distinguish them. Such attributes pertain to the divine nature, which is one because the Father, Son, and Holy Spirit are really one God, three Persons in one nature, one divine essence.[3] According to Thomas, appropriation is not a special divine activity or way of being but our attempt to manifest the Trinity of divine Persons by means of essential attributes.[4] Because the essential attributes are known from creation and are therefore more accessible to reason than the personal properties of the three Persons, we are more certain in our knowledge of them. Moreover, "just as we are able to use vestiges or images of the Trinity found in creation, so it seems permissible to use the essential attributes in the same way."[5] These essential attributes are not to be asserted of the divine Persons as if they were proper, but only by way of similitude or dissimilitude.[6] The intention behind such speech is primarily the removal of error in thinking about the three Persons.

---

quently, such acts give no insight into inner relations. The issue in modern theological discussions tends to center on the role of each divine Person in divine acts such as creation and incarnation. No longer is the problem one of talking meaningfully about a Trinity the inner distinctions of which are revealed only in fact and not in kind. There is an assumption that the inner life of God is not only known but intelligible to us. See, for example, P. Cary, "On Behalf of Classical Trinitarianism: A Critique of Rahner on the Trinity," *The Thomist* 56 (1992): 365–405.

2. Cf. 1 Cor. 1:24.
3. Doctrine of the Trinity formulated at the Council of Nicea. *Enchiridion Symbolorum*, 36th edition, ed. Denzinger and Schönmetzer (Barcelona: Herder, 1977).
4. ST I, q. 39, a. 7 c.
5. "Sicut igitur similitudine vestigii vel imaginis in creaturis inventa utimur ad manifestationem divinarum Personarum, ita et essentialibus attributis." ST I, q. 39, a. 7 c.
6. ST I, q. 39, a. 7 ad 1.

At first glance, Thomas' explanation of appropriations does not appear to be especially revealing or insightful. In fact, his discussion of appropriations takes only two articles in the *Summa*. Similar discussions in the texts of earlier theologians went on for pages.[7] Because of this brevity, many assume that Thomas is not as innovative in theology as he was in philosophy. His theological works are often understood to be successful only to the extent that he summarized clearly and concisely what others articulated before him. With regard to appropriation, J. Châtillon notes that

> although we do not know to what extent Thomas was able to refer to Alain de Lille, Simon de Tournai, and the porretan masters, he remains to a large extent the heir of their teaching. The porretan theologians were the first to assemble the patristic dossier that is essentially reproduced and organized into a solid structure in the *Summa Theologiae*.[8]

With these words Châtillon consigns Thomas to the status of mere heir and compiler of material that was worked out by earlier if not greater minds. Thomas' contribution is assumed to be one of putting such insights into a very concise and readable form. No doubt many eleventh, twelfth- and thirteenth-century theologians do share much in the way of detail and discussion. On the other hand, the appearance of the same words does not imply necessarily the same meaning or polemic. The way in which such words or polemical details are used is as important as the details themselves. The author quoted just above, for example, notes Thomas' distrust of deductive methods in Trinitarian theology, but he surprisingly does not bother to delineate the differences in theological method among the various theologians he considers, some of whom employ deductive arguments. What Thomas characterizes as "manifesting" the doctrine (the distinction and unity of Persons in one nature) by means of the essential divine attributes is then lumped to-

---

7. Augustine, for example, discusses the appropriation of power and wisdom to Christ for almost two entire books. Cf. *De Trinitate* VI–VII.

8. J. Châtillon, "Unitas, Aequalitas, Concordia vel Connexio," *St. Thomas Aquinas 1274–1974 Commemorative Studies*, vol. 1 (Toronto: Pontifical Institute of Medieval Studies, 1974), 375.

gether with earlier attempts to deduce the personal distinctions from these same essential attributes. Yet unlike the discussions of his twelfth- and thirteenth-century predecessors, Thomas' work is governed by a theory of naming that clearly discriminates between the mode of being in God and our mode of signifying. That is, he distinguishes and separates the mode of signifying from the thing signified in theological language in order to forestall efforts to conceptualize the Trinity. We can neither understand nor signify the Trinity accurately, because both our understanding and our naming are inescapably based upon creatures. In order to give an account of Thomas' discussion of appropriations, we must first distinguish Thomas' method from that of his ancient and medieval predecessors with whom he is all too frequently grouped and consequently silenced as a unique voice.

Because Augustine is generally considered to be the first proponent of a theory of appropriation, his work is included in most any history of the doctrine. According to Châtillon's recent study of appropriation theory, Augustine formulates his teaching on appropriations based upon a text in Romans that appears to refer to distinct divine Persons in the act of creation: "For from him and through him and for him are all things" (Rom. 11:36 [NAB]). This biblical text is for Châtillon "the point of departure" for the theological reflection that one finds in the treatise on Trinitarian appropriations.[9]

> Appropriation is then presented here as a method of research and exposition intended to place at the disposal of the theologian a language that permits one to render account of the ineffable mystery of the distinction of persons up to a point and in certain conditions.[10]

> Appropriation then involves sorting essential attributes in order to "render an account" and to provide an access to the mystery of the divine Persons.[11]

Augustine was, of course, not the first to give the Romans text a

---

9. Ibid., 340.
10. Ibid., 337.
11. In order to make his study of the theory's development more manageable, Châtillon focuses on the Augustinian triad *unitas, aequalitas, concordia*, which comes from *De doctrina Christiana*. This triad also appears in ST I, q. 39, a. 8.

Trinitarian reading. Ambrose, Hilary of Poitiers, and Eusebius of Vercelli all read the Romans text in the same way.[12] Hence, Augustine goes on to reiterate the unity and distinction of divine Persons by means of essential attributes in a straightforward way.[13] He states emphatically that the three are one and the same eternity, power, majesty, etc.; moreover, these three are one eternity and power because "these three are all one on account of the Father, equal on account of the Son, and closely united on account of the Holy Spirit."[14] Each divine Person has a role in making them One, and these three are distinct, as each one's manner of insuring oneness is distinct: the Father through unity, the Son through equality, and the Holy Spirit through concord.

Châtillon moves on to Augustine's *De Trinitate*, where he finds an extended discussion of appropriated attributes. Augustine does not, however, refer in *De Trinitate* to the triad mentioned above (unity, equality, concord). Châtillon contends that Augustine combines the teaching of Romans 1:20 (that our understanding of invisible things is had by created things) together with Romans 11:36 (from whom, through whom, and in whom all things were made) in order to justify a "method of intellectual ascension . . . to the knowledge of the mystery reflected in creation."[15] The understanding "by means of created things" is, according to Châtillon, an ascent to the mystery itself. Yet at the end of the passage taken from *De Trinitate*, Augustine goes on to say:

in bodily things down here one is not as much as three are together, and two things are something more than one thing; while in the supreme triad one is as much as three are together, and two are not more than one, and in them-

---

12. Ambrose, *De Spiritu Sancto*, ch. 9 (PL 16, cols. 731–849); Hilary of Poitiers, *De Trinitate* (CCSL 62–62A) VIII.38–39, XI.45–47; Eusebius of Vercelli, *De Trinitate* IV (Corpus Christianorum, vol. 9, pp. 3–99). Each of these references to the Romans' text takes place within a discussion of the unity of the divine nature.

13. Augustine, *De doctrina Christiana* I.5.5.

14. "In patre unitas, in filio aequalitas, in spiritu sancto unitatis aequalitatisque concordia, et tria unum omnia propter patrem, aequalia omnia propter filium, conexa omnia propter spiritum sanctum." Augustine, *De doctrina Christiana* I.5.5. The term 'conexa' in the second part of the quotation seems to be a shorthand for the more properly stated "unitatis aequalitatisque concordia."

15. Châtillon, "Unitas, Aequalitas, Concordia," 342.

selves they are infinite. So they are each in each and all in each, and each in all and all in all, and all are one. Whoever sees this even *in part*, or *in a puzzling manner in a mirror* (1 Cor 13:12), should rejoice at knowing God, and should *honor and thank him as God* (Rom 1:21).[16]

The dissimilarity between created, visible things and the Trinity is so great that even recognizing a "trace" of God in creation can lead at best only to a vision "in part" and "in a puzzling manner." According to Augustine, to see that the three-and-oneness of God is vastly different from any three-and-oneness in creation is to approach an understanding of Romans 11:36 and its Trinitarian portraits of the creative act. A rather negative or apophatic teaching, indeed: to know through created things is to understand dissimilarity with regard to the Trinity. The undeniable implication of such teaching is that through creation, by natural reason we do not know the Trinity at all; we know the Trinity by revelation. Through comparison with worldly knowing and images, we come to realize how different and unlike the Trinity is to anything we know in this world: not an understanding so much as a growing awareness of how not to understand or envision God who has revealed Himself.

So what does this criticism of Châtillon's reading of Augustine have to do with Thomas' theory of appropriations? A small error in the beginning leads to a gross error in the end. For Châtillon, as for almost any modern scholar of the history of Trinitarian theology, Augustine and Thomas are understood almost without question to be "of a piece," speaking with one voice the "Western Latin Trinitarian tradition";[17] hence, the reading of one determines the reading of the other.[18] Châtillon can use Augustine to define Thomas' work, of course, be-

---

16. Augustine, *De Trinitate* VI.12, trans. Edmund Hill, O.P., in *Works of St. Augustine*, vol. I/5 (Brooklyn: New City Press, 1991), pp. 213–14. Throughout the remainder of the book English quotations of Augustine's *De Trinitate* are taken from the Hill translation.

17. See ch. 1 for a discussion of the use of this terminology.

18. See, for example, J. Thompson, *Modern Trinitarian Perspectives* (New York: Oxford University Press, 1994); C. Gunton, *The Promise of Trinitarian Theology* (Edinburgh: T&T Clark, 1991); B. Lonergan seems also to suggest more affinity in theological method between Augustine and Thomas than is warranted by textual comparison. See Lonergan's *De Deo Trino: Pars Systematica* (Rome, 1964).

cause Augustine's teaching is the explicit source for several parts of Thomas' discussion.[19] About this there can be no dispute. Nor is there much dispute that Thomas seems to agree with Augustine in his understanding of appropriations. What difference there is primarily concerns clarity, not substance. Thomas is assumed to have given a more accurate and fuller statement about the theory taken from Augustine's writings, due in part to the work of the many gifted theologians in the intervening centuries. Yet a lack of dispute among scholars on this issue does not demonstrate accuracy.

Because of this presumed agreement, Châtillon, without explanation or apology, uses Albert the Great's definition of appropriation to define the work from Augustine to Thomas and many in between.[20] Albert defines appropriations as an *"accessus ad proprium"* (an access or approach to what is proper), apparently implying an approach to the doctrine from natural reason. Revelation supplies then the missing pieces, rather than the substance and foundation, to complete it. Nowhere in Augustine or Thomas do we find such a definition.[21] In fact, far from being an approach, the discussion of appropriations in both Thomas and Augustine comes after the treatment of divine Persons distinguished by relations and the hermeneutical principles founded therein. Arguments involving appropriated attributes would have to be at the beginning of the Trinitarian questions in order to constitute an approach. The question of context is therefore not simply an issue of rendering a fuller account; it goes to the heart of the argument's meaning, its noetic value.

One cannot make sense of the role and significance of appropriation theory without attending to larger issues of theological method.

---

19. ST I, q. 39, a. 8.
20. Châtillon, "Unitas, Aequalitas, Concordia," 338, n. 4.
21. The notable divide between Albert and Thomas on the very definition of theology almost requires that their stances on such issues as appropriations and our knowledge of God be different. What appears to be similar must be understood distinctively, because of the different assumptions and goals present in Albert's and in Thomas' theological writings. For more detailed comparison, see R. McInerny, "Albert and Thomas on Theology," in *Albert der Grosse,* ed. Albert Zimmerman, Miscellanea Mediaevalia, vol. 14, Veröffentlichungen des Thomas-Instituts der Universität zu Köln (Berlin: Walter de Gruyter, 1981), 50–60.

If one asks whether all theologians from Augustine to Thomas were doing the same thing, the answer would have to be, "No." Anselm, for instance, explicitly attempts to prove, without the benefit of revelation, the doctrine of the Trinity.[22] Abelard went so far as repeatedly to affirm the theological understanding of pagans with regard to Trinitarian doctrine. The pagans' understanding of distinct divine attributes constituted a virtual insight into Trinitarian doctrine according to Abelard. The tendency to group Augustine and Thomas so closely is due to a failure to take account of the larger methodological structures and intentions of their respective works. Châtillon, for instance, focuses on a few details while neglecting the larger and more important, if not more interesting, differences of theological method. Our purpose here is not, however, to refute Châtillon's argument, but to use it as an example of how modern scholarship often fails to do justice to the theological tradition. It is our intention to separate Thomas from his predecessors and contemporaries in order that we may hear "his voice," as moderns are wont to say. To read Thomas' *Summa theologiae* as a distinct theological work, different not only from other thirteenth-century works but also from earlier medieval and ancient works on the Trinity, is necessary if we are to understand Thomas' own method and teaching.

For Thomas there can be no approach or *accessus* to the doctrine of the Trinity apart from revelation. Arguments from natural reason have but one role: to manifest the doctrine. "Manifestation" means beginning with revealed doctrine and then providing reasons for the congruence of this doctrine with those that can be more easily known.[23] The main argument of Thomas' discussion of appropriations (ST I, q. 39, aa. 7–8) displays this procedure. Such manifestation follows rather than leads up to a clarification of the theological doctrine in question. Arguments proposing to manifest this doctrine for the faithful are first of all meant to remove errors in the understand-

22. For a detailed analysis of Anselm's procedure, cf. S. Gersh, "Anselm of Canterbury" in P. Dronke, *A History of Twelfth-Century Western Philosophy* (Cambridge: Cambridge University Press, 1988), 255–78.
23. Cf. ST I, q. 32, a. 1, and q. 39, a. 7.

ing of the faithful with regard to the articulated doctrine, i.e., errors in conceptualizing what cannot be conceptualized.

To pursue our task, we will first attend to the qualifications Augustine and Thomas place upon our knowledge of the Trinity, and second, note the purpose and place of the discussion of appropriations in the larger discussion of the Trinity. Our purpose here is to highlight the distinctive character of these theologians' discussion apart from the question of possible agreement, that is, to recover a sense of their particularity. Our procedure is not meant to replay the favorite old game of medievalists: trying to decide whether Thomas is Augustinian or not. Rather, we are acknowledging the current tendency in scholarly literature to make Augustine and Thomas agree, if not in all areas, most certainly in the doctrine of the Trinity. Hence, to take issue with this interpretation of Thomas demands that we incorporate Augustine in such investigation, if for no other reason than to make our own procedure clear and to answer the inevitable objections. Clarifying their distinctive positions will also serve to call into question modern assumptions governing intellectual history by breaking up the monolith of the "Western Latin Trinitarian tradition."

### 3.2 Comparing Augustine and Aquinas

The problem of speaking about the Trinity is complicated by the manner in which the doctrine comes to us. The doctrine of the Trinity is the result of a considered and developed reflection upon the words and person of Christ and the teaching of the apostles.[24] This doctrine, unlike that of the Incarnation, was not something to come (from the perspective of the ancient Israelites and their covenant relation with Yahweh). The Trinity is not an event of fulfillment rooted in time or space. There is no genealogy leading to or historically rooting the Trinity. In our historically oriented faith, the doctrine is decidedly un-

---

24. On the development of doctrine from the roots of Scripture to council formulations, see John Henry Cardinal Newman, *Essay on the Development of Christian Doctrine*, (London: J. Toovey, 1846), ch. 1; A. W. Wainwright, *Trinity in the New Testament* (London: SPCK, 1962), 237–67; G. L. Prestige, *God in Patristic Thought* (London: SPCK, 1952), introduction.

historical in its substance. Here we are dealing strictly with the identity of God, not the action of God. Hence, we cannot say that such doctrine can be known by effects except insofar as words (of Jesus) are posited as effects (of God, the Trinity). Who God is insofar as God is one is known by the effect of creation. Who God is as three Persons is not known by any effect but only through the revelation of God in Christ.[25] The revelation of the three Persons, Father, Son, and Holy Spirit, is incompletely or indirectly revealed in the events of salvation history. Further, the revelation of the three brings to the fore the impossibility of understanding the identity of God, God's freedom in being and in acting.[26] One finds contradictions rather than solutions. To clarify the apparent contradictions and explain the meaning of this revelation, the Church has had recourse to philosophical language[27] that serves to signify aspects of that revelation (e.g., processions, relations of origin). Philosophical language facilitates talk about the doctrine, especially in providing generic terms. For example, processions and notions signify the same realities but in different ways that together help us to grasp in some fashion the truth of divine simplicity and distinction of Persons.[28]

Not every theologian in Christian history, however, agreed that the use of philosophical language is limited to signifying variously the substance of revelation. Not a few have contended that philosophical knowledge and language itself are additional avenues for attaining to knowledge of this Trinity, perhaps even a more accurate knowledge.[29]

---

25. Cf. ST I, q. 32, a. 1.

26. Thomas, for example, argues that one of the reasons that *Qui est* is the most proper name for God is that it is the least determinative. ST I, q. 13, a. 11 c.

27. A great deal of tension in the Early Church among Latins was due to a distrust of philosophical language. The development of doctrinal expression in the East was characterized by a warm embrace and wide use of terminology coming from Greek philosophy. Cf. Prestige, *God in Patristic Thought*, 235–41.

28. ST I, q. 41.

29. For an excellent though brief investigation of the connection between grammar and theology, see M.-D. Chenu, "Grammaire et théologie," in *La théologie au douzième siècle*. Bibliothèque Thomiste 33 (Paris, 1957), 90–107; For a traditional portrait of the perils in bringing together modes of human expression and theological insight, see also Augustine's *De Trinitate* I, introduction.

Some have assumed that one could use philosophical concepts to demonstrate the Trinity in the way that one could demonstrate the existence of certain attributes of God. In this way the doctrine of appropriations would function as the entry gate into Trinitarian doctrine accessible to the philosopher as well as to the believer. Augustine and Thomas, however, insist that the Trinity is nowhere accessible to reason. The distinction and unity of Father, Son, and Holy Spirit can be known only by revelation. Yet the human desire to understand, to pursue truth and reject falsehood remains active in theological discourse. To understand what is believed and to defend such belief are both strong motivations that inevitably come to spur the explication of religious doctrine. The eminent Church historian G. L. Prestige writes:

> It appears that the long history of the evolution of Trinitarian doctrine is the record . . . of orthodox insistence on the true and full deity of the three Persons historically revealed, as against the attempts of heresy to maintain the doctrine of divine unity by misconceived and mischievous short-circuits. This orthodox insistence was based primarily on scriptural fact, but also, as comes out more and more clearly, on the philosophic sense that the being of God needs to be justified to reason alike as transcendent, as creative, and as immanent.[30]

The nature of explanation is, however, determined by motivations, and such motivations must be understood accordingly.

It is important to realize first of all that, in whatever ways Thomas and Augustine agree, their theological method is vastly different, especially in their treatment of Trinitarian doctrine. Augustine investigates the entirety of salvation history in order to ascertain when and how the doctrine of the Trinity is made known to us.[31] He discusses the major theophanies of the Old Testament as well as the speech of Christ in the Gospels. Moreover, he investigates possible natural means by which some would claim knowledge of the Trinity apart from such revelation.[32] In the later half of his book, he pursues an intellectual as-

---

30. Prestige, *God in Patristic Thought*, 300.
31. Augustine, *De Trinitate* I–IV.
32. "The reader of these reflections of mine on the Trinity should bear in mind that my pen is on the watch against the sophistries of those who scorn the starting-

cent to a knowledge of the Trinitarian mystery. The intentional and explicit failure at this ascent in the last two books does not diminish the usefulness of the endeavor as a way of revealing the limits of reason. Thomas, however, does not attempt an ascent to the mystery with or without faith. Nor for that matter does Thomas cloud his treatment of the Trinity with image-talk. He discusses the image of God in human persons only fifty questions after the treatise on the doctrine of the Trinity. For these reasons, it is somewhat difficult to compare Augustine and Thomas directly. It is also somewhat simplistic to treat them as "one voice" of a tradition, sharing a theological method and conclusions. We must not forget that the temporal distance separating Thomas from Augustine is greater than that which separates us from Thomas.[33] On the other hand, the pervasive doubt in the modern era regarding the very existence of God imposes a profound philosophical difference between this age and all preceding ages of human history, including that of the Reformation.[34] Thus, in one sense Augustine and Thomas do belong to a single era, the age of faith. We must not, however, forget the looseness of this category.

### 3.2.1 Augustine

Through the fifteen books of his *De Trinitate*, Augustine demonstrated that neither in Old Testament texts nor through philosophical investigations of the human mind could one come to such a doctrine apart from the revelation of God in Christ. One can, however, use

---

point of faith, and allow themselves to be deceived through an unseasonable and misguided love of reason." Augustine, *The Trinity*, trans. Hill, 65; Augustine then proposes to give reasons for the doctrine in order to answer the questioning of heretics, but he first insists upon establishing by the authority of Scripture whether the doctrine is true.

33. From the death of Augustine (431) to the birth of Thomas (1224) is nearly eight centuries, from the death of Thomas (1274) to the present, seven and a quarter. Moreover, it can be argued that the reintroduction of Aristotelian natural philosophy into the West, the founding of the universities and of the mendicant orders, and the professionalization of theology—all within the twelfth and early thirteenth centuries—had as much impact on theology as did the Enlightenment and the works of Kant.

34. O. Pesch, *The God Question in Thomas Aquinas and Martin Luther*, trans. Gottfried G. Krodel (Philadelphia: Fortress Press, 1972), 1–3.

non-scriptural terms to answer questions about the doctrine, to speak about what is revealed, generically.[35] Theology may employ any science and vocabulary to aid in the manifestations of the faith, but all such efforts must begin with the data of revelation, the scriptural witness.[36]

According to Augustine's letter to Aurelius, which normally prefaces his *De Trinitate*, the prologues to the first five books and the body of the last three-and-a-half books were written much later than the other parts. Augustine's methodology is most evident in these portions insofar as he clarifies the theory and character of his argument.

[W]hen we think about God the trinity we are aware that our thoughts are quite inadequate to their object, and incapable of grasping him as he is; even by men of the caliber of the apostle Paul he can only be seen, as it [Scripture] says, *like a puzzling reflection in a mirror* (1 Cor 13:12). . . . Yet . . . there is no effrontery in burning to know, out of faithful piety, the divine and inexpressible truth that is above us, provided the mind is fired by the grace of our creator and savior, and not inflated by arrogant confidence in its own powers.[37]

Book V represents the shift in Augustine's text from exegesis to systematic theology. In the first four books, he clarified his interpretation of the key New Testament and Old Testament texts that touch upon or were commonly used to determine the manner in which God revealed Himself. He concludes that all "voices or perceptible forms or likenesses" produced before the Incarnation were probably angels or created forms under their control, because the Father, Son, and Holy Spirit are manifest only in the New Testament by the "sendings" of the Son and Holy Spirit.[38] Also, Augustine formulates exegetical principles

---

35. Augustine and Thomas differ markedly in their ability and penchant for stretching language to meet the demands of theological discourse. Augustine did not see a way of getting past the material connotations of the term 'person' in order for it to be fitted for theological use. The distinction-making skill of the scholastics then can be seen as empowering for theological discourse.

36. Frequently in his *De Trinitate*, Augustine cited this text from Isaiah (7:9), "unless you believe, you will not understand," as a way of indicating the starting point for all theological reflection in the full Christian revelation as affirmed and transmitted by the Church. Augustine, *De Trinitate* VII.12 and XV.2.

37. Augustine, *De Trinitate* V, prologue, trans. Hill, p. 189.

38. Augustine, *De Trinitate* II.32–35.

by which one can understand the complex scriptural witness to the Son being "from" but not less than the Father.[39] The fact that the Son and the Holy Spirit are sent from the Father does not in any way detract from their co-eternality and co-equality with the Father.

Augustine then turns his attention in Books V, VI, and VII to refuting contemporary objections to the truth of this New Testament revelation. He focuses especially on the Arian objection to the equality of Father and Son.[40] Only in these books does Augustine discuss the appropriation of essential divine attributes to particular divine Persons.[41] The occasion for this argument is the scriptural text, "Christ, the power and wisdom of God" (1Cor. 1:24). Augustine's foremost concern is then the proper hermeneutic for this particular passage.[42] By suggesting an individual possession of essential attributes on the part of one divine Person, the Corinthians text appears at least to call into question divine equality. Augustine notes, however, that the multiplication of names for the Son, such as "power of God" and "wisdom of God," does not multiply Sons any more than such names divide the divine nature into gods. For God it is the same thing to be and to be wise or powerful or just and these things are identical.[43] Moreover, because each Person is as great as all three together, they are not three by multiplication.[44] When we say "the Father alone," we do not mean without the Son or Holy Spirit but that there are not two Fathers. Whatever we

---

39. Augustine, *De Trinitate* I.14–21.

40. Augustine, *De Trinitate* V.1–11.

41. Augustine's use of appropriations is actually a defense against the Arians. After having defined the equality and unity of divine Persons against the Arians in Book V, Augustine must answer the Arian objections concerning scriptural references to Christ being the wisdom and power of God (2 Cor 10:24). He was not using such teaching to account for the distinction of divine Persons but rather attempting to account for their unity and equality in the face of apparent difficulties in the scriptural witness. See his *De Trinitate*, Book VI.

42. Cf. Augustine, *De Trinitate*, especially VII.1–6.

43. Augustine, *De Trinitate* VI.8.

44. It is then understandable that Augustine never proposes to illumine the Trinity with any triad of attributes. As noted by Thomas' editors, the triad 'power, wisdom, and goodness' is wrongly attributed by Thomas to Augustine. Cf. ST I, q. 39, a. 8, obj. 3 note.

predicate of God in reference to divine substance must signify the Trinity and not one Person alone. The proper names are said by way of relation and can alone among theological terms signify one Person without the others. To say "Christ, the power and wisdom of God" does not eliminate the Father and Holy Spirit, as if Christ alone is power and wisdom but that Christ by reason of his divinity is power and wisdom, for to be and to be powerful is the same.

The incomprehensibility of the Trinity is due to the absolute simplicity of the divine nature. We can find all manner of examples and images within our own soul of threeness, but such triads inevitably preclude a real simplicity even within the soul itself. What one ultimately finds is "an enormous difference." For Augustine, knowing what that difference is represents a rather significant development in understanding. The direct avenue of understanding the Trinity through created things (especially our own mind) is ultimately a failed effort,[45] yet another, indirect approach to understanding is left. We may, as the apostle Paul states, see God "in a puzzling manner through a mirror." To see God in or through the image is to see the way in which the image differs from that of which it is an image. I, for instance, *am* one man and *have* the trinity of faculties I find in my own mind while the Father, Son, and Holy Spirit *are* one God and *are* three Persons.

So therefore, God the Father is wise with the wisdom by which he is his own wisdom, and the Son is wisdom from the wisdom of the Father, which is the Father from whom he is begotten as Son. The consequence is that the Father understands with the understanding by which he is his own understanding—he would not be wise unless he also understood. But the Son is understanding, begotten from the understanding of the Father, which is the Father. The same point could appropriately be made about memory. How can one who does not remember anything, or at least does not remember himself, be wise?

---

45. J. Cavadini points out that a projected ascent of the mind to God in Plotinian terms, successful or not, is nothing new. What is striking about Augustine's proposed ascent is that it is a deliberate failure. Cavadini, "Augustine's *De Trinitate*," 106. Those who see through this mirror or "in a puzzling manner," Augustine argues, are "not those who merely observe in their own minds what we have discussed and suggested, but those who see it precisely as an image, so that they can in some fashion refer what they see to that of which it is an image." *De Trinitate* XV.44, trans. Hill, 429.

It follows then that because the Father is wisdom and the Son is wisdom, the Son does his own remembering just as the Father does; and just as the Father remembers himself and the Son with his own memory not the Son's, so the Son remembers himself and the Father with his own memory not the Father's. Again, who will say that there is any wisdom where there is no love? From this we can infer that the Father is his own love just as he is his own understanding and memory.

So here we are then with these three, that is memory, understanding, love or will in that supreme and unchangeable being which God is, and they are not the Father and the Son and the Holy Spirit but the Father alone. . . . [h]e himself has these three, and he has them in such a way that he is them.[46]

Any image or triad borrowed from creation or threesome of divine attributes is inadequate for illuminating the Trinity. The mind is simply inadequate for the task of penetrating the mystery; yet in noting our manner of understanding God through created things, Augustine gives encouragement as well as a warning.

I have sufficiently warned [the reader] . . . that this image, made by the trinity and altered for the worse by its own fault, is not so to be compared to that trinity that it is reckoned similar to it in every respect. Rather, he should note how great the dissimilarity is in whatever similarity there may be.[47]

To gaze upon and grasp that holy Trinity is impossible in this life. It is only by means of an incremental reformation of our own selves, the restoration of the image, through faith, that we are prepared for such vision.[48] Until that time of vision, one can "see" God only through faith and hope. The structure of the mind of itself is useless for approaching the mystery; it is entirely dependent upon a prior understanding of the doctrine, because the image's noetic value is primarily negative, residing in dissimilarity, thus, not an *accessus*. The understanding of texts such as Romans 11:36 is then a process taking place in faith and culminating only in the next life.

---

46. Augustine, *De Trinitate* XV.12, trans. Hill, 404.
47. Augustine, *De Trinitate* XV.39, trans. Hill, 426.
48. Cf. Augustine, *De Trinitate* I.4.

### 3.2.2 Interim Developments: Abelard

Between Augustine and Thomas, theology underwent profound changes in methodology. No longer was theology primarily an exegetical pursuit; it had become one of logic as well. Beginning with Anselm's *Monologion* and *Cur Deus Homo*, one can find numerous examples of attempts to demonstrate theological truths with unaided reason.[49] Although his argument is widely understood to be one of suitability rather than demonstration, such endeavors opened wide the gates for Christian doctrine to be discussed as philosophical material. That is, instead of employing philosophical concepts and rules to understand better the truth of such doctrine, those same philosophical principles and methods were employed to arrive at such doctrines, showing their logic and even necessity.

Abelard,[50] for example, took up the task of commenting on Scripture as an exercise in logic. His bold interpretations and charismatic lectures attracted many students from all over Europe to his school where he composed one of his most controversial works, *Theologia Christiana*. This work earned him the ire of both Roscelin and Anselm of Laon,[51] and eventually the condemnation of the Council of Soissons in 1121. His second condemnation at the Council of Sens in 1140 marked the end of his public career. In both cases, the issue was

---

49. S. Gersh, however, would argue that such attempts were not wholly rational in procedure but only in their beginning. For the development of his argument, Anselm, for example, would frequently introduce evidence that is known only on the basis of revelation, not reason. These twelfth-century thinkers lacked an exact criterion for judging a given proposition as based in, and not just accessible to, reason. S. Gersh, "Anselm of Canterbury," in P. Dronke, *A History of Twelfth-Century Western Philosophy* (Cambridge: Cambridge University Press, 1988), 255–78.

50. For a general account of Abelard's life and works, see J. G. Sikes, *Peter Abailard* (Cambridge: Cambridge University Press, 1932); for a more recent assessment of the impact and importance of his teachings, see J. Marenbon, *The Philosophy of Peter Abelard* (Cambridge: Cambridge University Press, 1997).

51. Anselm himself pursued an avowedly rational method of attaining to and explaining theological doctrine for his fellow monks, but was perhaps more attune to the failings and difficulties of such methods, at least in the end. See his *Monologian*, esp. ch. 1 (his proposal) and 63 (his professed failure).

Abelard's extreme view of the power of reason to clarify matters of faith. Rather than using a knowledge of biblical languages (à la Jerome and Origen) or allowing Scripture to interpret itself, one passage throwing light on another (à la Gregory the Great and Augustine), Abelard applied logic to Scripture and to doctrine itself. Thus, to resolve difficulties in Trinitarian doctrine, he introduced a number of sophisticated analogies to illumine the truth of the mystery.

Exactly what Abelard conceived himself to be doing is a subject of heated debate even now. It is indeed likely that he was quite orthodox in his beliefs, at least he professed to be such.[52] Yet the way he explained such beliefs and resolved difficulties was not at all acceptable to his contemporaries. In his explanation of the Trinity, Abelard argued that the Father is power, the Son is wisdom and the Holy Spirit is goodness, not by way of similarity or dissimilarity but truly. He stated that the Father is specially distinguished by power because He can "accomplish anything He wills."[53] Likewise, the Son is specially wisdom, and the Holy Spirit goodness. Wisdom is, according to Abelard, a "kind" of power.[54] His contemporaries objected that such an explanation minimized or even denied the power of the Son and Holy Spirit, the wisdom of the Father and Holy Spirit and the goodness of the Father and Son.[55] The will of the Father and Son is one, as are their power and their wisdom. To say otherwise is to suppose that the Father is wise by the wisdom of the Son.[56] Moreover, we cannot say of the Son or the Holy Spirit that they do not "accomplish all they will."

---

52. The difficulty in determining Abelard's orthodoxy derives from the number of unusual statements and arguments he presents. Whether such problematic statements represent problematic beliefs or careless and unfortunate expressions only is difficult to determine. Cf. Abelard's *De Unitate* I.3 and *Theologiae Christiana* I.2. For an assessment of Abelard's influence upon theological method, see J. Cottiaux, "La conception de la théologie chez Abélard," *Revue d'histoire ecclésiastique* 28 (1932): 247–95.

53. Abelard, *Theologia Christiana* IV ("Summi boni"), PL 178, cols. 1288–1290.

54. *Introductio ad Theologiam* I, PL 178, cols. 989–994.

55. Cf. Bernard of Clairvaux, *Disputatio adversus Peterum Abaelardum*, PL 180, cols. 249–282; and Otto of Freising, *Gesta Frederici* in Monumentis Germaniae Historicis, vol. 46 (Hannover, 1912) chs. 51–54.

56. Cf. Augustine, *De Trinitate* (Books VI–VII).

We can perhaps see the reasoning in Abelard's arguments by turning to his polemical opponents. Abelard was addressing the problematic teachings of Roscelin and Gilbert of Poitiers. Because of his clumsy use of *res* (thing) for speaking about the Trinity, Roscelin's teaching on the Trinity seemed to many theologians of the time to be an unorthodox, tritheistic understanding of the three Persons.[57] Gilbert, on the other hand, was reputed by a few to have taught a quaternity by means of his efforts to draw a distinction between the personal properties and the divine nature.[58] By saying that the personal properties are logically subsistent in the sense that the Father is God and paternity, and not simply God, in order to distinguish this one from the Son who is God and sonship but not paternity, Gilbert risked incurring the charge of heresy. On the other hand, applying logic to Trinitarian language is not the same as imbuing such logically derived distinctions with metaphysical being. Gilbert explicitly avoided this dangerous leap in reasoning.[59] Nevertheless, Gilbert's teaching seemed to many, including Abelard, to posit some composition in God and even to characterize the personal properties as accidents inhering in the divine substance. We need not deal with the appropriateness of the charges at this point. It is important here only to note Abelard's intellectual concerns. For his part, Abelard turned to appropriations as a way of demonstrating that the Three are One God yet distinct Persons, hopefully without suggesting inadequate or overly strict distinctions.

Unfortunately, Abelard's effort to avoid the tritheism of Roscelin's

---

57. For a detailed discussion of these positions, confer J. G. Sikes, *Peter Abailard*, ch. VII; and J. R. McCallum, *Abelard's Christian Theology* (Oxford: Blackwell, 1948), 27–44.

58. The charge was not substantiated. At the Council of Rheims and in the presence of Pope Eugenius III, Gilbert was absolved of all culpability. Cf. N. M. Häring, S.A.C., "The Case of Gilbert de la Porrée Bishop of Poitiers (1142–1154)," *Mediaeval Studies* 13 (1951): 1–40.

59. Gilbert is throughout his work concerned with predication and the exactness of our speech about the Trinity. His distinctions between personal properties and the divine essence should be understood, therefore, in grammatical terms, not metaphysical. Cf. N. M. Häring, "A Treatise on the Trinity by Gilbert of Poitiers," *Recherches théologie ancienne et médiévale* 39 (1972): 14–50.

teaching and the inconveniences of positing a twofold being in each divine Person[60] unwittingly introduced a very problematic distinction of essential attributes. Minimally, he may be faulted for calling into question the real equality of the three Persons. Maximally, he insinuates that the revelation of God in Jesus Christ was superfluous in that one could and pagans have attained to knowledge of the Trinity by way of the naturally known essential attributes of God. By arguing that the essential attributes are present in the three Persons differently and that they distinguish the divine Persons in some way, Abelard proposed a purely logical way of knowing God both as one and as three. Abelard took great pains to show that both philosophers and the Israelite prophets and patriarchs knew of the Trinity. The Christian apologist can then interpret a key text from Romans 11 ("from him and through him, and for him are all things") in such a way that the effects of creation betray their cause as Trinitarian. Abelard reads this doctrine into Old Testament texts that refer to the action of God in terms of "in" or "through" or "for" (or "from"). He is convinced that references in the Old Testament to aspects recognizable as the Trinity of Persons must indicate knowledge of this doctrine on the part of the writer. Consequently, he argues that the author of Genesis 1 intentionally used the plural "we" for the speech of God concerning the creation of humans to indicate such plurality.[61] What is left out of his account is the basis for the initial interpretation: the revelation of Jesus Christ through whom we know that the One whom we call God is three Persons is one divine nature. That is, instead of using the New Testament text to uncover the Gospel hidden in the Old Testament, Abelard proposes to use reason alone to uncover the very same inter-

---

60. Though it is highly questionable whether Gilbert taught this twofold being when he argued that the personal properties are not the divine Persons themselves and that God is not the divine essence, his grammatical exactitude does appear to evacuate the doctrine of the Trinity of its contradictory character. That is, the result of his clarifications and proposed rules is to make the doctrine perhaps more understandable than it is. See his *Commentaria in librum de Trinitate*, PL 186 (Paris, 1895), especially col. 1268–1271. Cf. also Michael E. Williams, *The Teaching of Gilbert Porreta on the Trinity as Found in His Commentaries on Boethius* (Rome, 1951), ch. 2.

61. Abelard, *Theologia Christiana* I, cols. 1127–1136.

pretations.[62] By suggesting that some pagans knew the Trinity in part and that the Trinity of Persons was evident to the ancient Israelite prophets, Abelard makes a mess of the tradition of teaching on the unity of divine Persons, in nature and works *ad extra*. What was for Augustine a way of "manifesting" the real unity of the divine Persons in wisdom, power, will, etc. became for Abelard a way of inferring distinctions among those Persons that could be known apart from the revelation of God in Christ.

### 3.2.3 Aquinas

Contrary to Abelard, Thomas argues that the divine Persons cannot be deductively known from what we naturally know about God. Knowing that God exists and describing God by means of effects in creation allows us to know only the divine nature, not the distinction of Persons. We cannot know who or what God is because we can know God only by way of creatures (divine effects), and creation is not proper to any one divine Person.[63] The effects of God evident in creation are due to what is one in God (power, goodness, wisdom, etc.) and, therefore, do not lead to knowledge of distinctions. Neither can we nor should we purport to know the Trinity by any means other

---

62. Cf. E. F. Kearney, "Master Peter Abelard, Expositor of Sacred Scripture: An Analysis of Abelard's Approach to Biblical Exposition in Selected Writings on Scripture" (Diss. for Marquette University, 1980; University Microfilms). Augustine, on the other hand, investigated the same Old Testament texts and concluded that the identities of the Son and the Holy Spirit and the Father are made known only by the sending of the first two. For if these three are really one divine nature, one God and not three Gods, they can be known as distinct only in a very special way—that is, by self-communication. And such self-communication or revelation must take place within the substantial unity. In other words, one cannot act alone. Hence, any apparent reference in the Old Testament to a supposed particular divine Person or to a proper act of a divine Person cannot be such, or the unity is not substantial. Because the Persons are distinguished only by mutual relations within one divine nature, their proper identity can only be seen and revealed in relation to one another, not in relation to a creature. There simply are no creature-oriented acts of one divine Person only. One Person is made known to us by that one's being sent by another. The Father "sent" the Son (Gal. 4:4 and John 1). To be sent means to begin to be where one was not. The invisible Son began to be visible when He was sent into the visible world. Cf. Augustine, *De Trinitate* II.

63. ST I, q. 2, a. 1; also q. 45, a. 3.

than revelation. "Through faith one comes to cognition, not the reverse."[64]

How then does one come to know and understand distinction in God? For Augustine, one can know the Persons only through the revelation of the divine missions, the "sendings" of the Son and Holy Spirit.[65] Augustine is even quite reticent about the semantic value of non-scriptural terms such as 'person.' For Thomas, the revelation of the Trinity was given so that we might rightly understand our creation and salvation.[66] What we must know is that our salvation was not a work of necessity but due to the free love of God. That God chose freely to create and to save is seen in the revelation of the Trinity.[67] Such knowledge is a constitutive part of our salvation, for we cannot invoke one of whom we are ignorant. Our creaturely oriented way of knowing does not constitute a completely apophatic theological view. Appreciating that our understanding of God is by way of creatures allows us to talk about God in three ways: by negation, by relation, and by affirmation. By reason alone, we speak of God in terms of what He is not, i.e., by denying of God what is proper to creatures. Relational terms consider God as principle and are, therefore, more concerned with creatures than Creator. The affirmative terms are the subject of our concern here, for these terms are said of God substantially. That is, these terms signify the divine substance even though they are deficient in the manner that they represent God. The discussion of Person and essence takes place within this category of speech. The difficulty of affirmative language, however, is seen as the inevitable negative elements make themselves known. Even revealed language cannot escape

---

64. "[D]icit quod per fidem venitur ad cognitionem, et non e converso." ST I, q. 32, ad. 2. On this tenet, Augustine and Thomas wholly agree. See, for example, Augustine's introductory comments to Book I of *De Trinitate*. Moreover, the fact that Thomas quotes Augustine in the reply to the objection demonstrates that Thomas does not see himself disagreeing in any way with the great Doctor but only with certain twelfth-century or even thirteenth-century readings of Augustine.

65. Augustine, *De Trinitate* II.7–11; IV.25–32.

66. ST I, q. 1, a. 1 c.

67. ST I, q. 32, a. 1 ad 3. God's freedom as such can also be known by reason. Cf. ST I, q. 19, a. 10.

the necessity of negative elements because of our creaturely manner of knowing. Thomas demonstrates, on the other hand, how the subtle negative elements allow such language to gain a foothold on the divine reality. For if such revelation was given for the right understanding of our salvation, its truth cannot be utterly beyond us.

From q. 32 to q. 39 of his *Summa*, Thomas discusses the divine Persons individually. According to the prologue of q. 29, Thomas first treats the concept and application of 'person' in Trinitarian doctrine (qq. 29–32) and then treats the divine Persons in turn, in terms of their proper and their attributed names. Only after having discussed the distinction of Persons and the proper identity of each does Thomas turn to the complexity of speaking about the Persons and divine essence comparatively, i.e., making sense of the oneness and the threeness of God.[68] The central issue is how the divine essence and divine Persons could be the same yet differ in number. This very question caused a great deal of controversy in the twelfth century. Grammatically, distinctions must be made to preserve the meaningfulness of Trinitarian language, but such distinctions all too easily appear problematic when taken out of the strictly grammatical discussions.[69] The problem is not that this doctrine is difficult to understand but that it is impossible to understand. The theologian's task is not to "pull back

---

68. One might have the impression from a cursory reading that Thomas was referring to the divine essence as such (qq. 1–26), that by which the divine Persons are divine but not distinctly so, before discussing the relations (qq. 27–38), that by which the Persons are distinct. If this is true, qq. 1–26 would constitute a monotheistic theology, qq. 27–38 would constitute a Trinitarian theology, i.e., the specifically Christian doctrine of God. Thomas does not, however, refer to the divine essence as the abstracted "form" of divinity or as the subject of the philosopher's investigation in qq. 1–26. His favored term in those questions, *in divinis*, signifies God indistinctly. Even in the articles in which Thomas defines the term 'person' and its use with regard to Father, Son, and Holy Spirit, he does not refer to *essentia* as such. Question 39 represents the first time in the *Summa* that Thomas discusses the divine essence *per se*, that by which the divine Persons are divine but not distinctly so; or rather, that which we understand and signify in God to be form because one and simple. See ch. 1 above.

69. Gilbert of Poitiers, for example, made quite precise grammatical points that could not at all be allowed in theology if such points were to be taken *secundum rem*. Cf. Häring, "The Case of Gilbert of la Porrée," 1–40.

the curtain" in order to reveal the being of God—that experience is reserved for the blessed. The theologian's task is to interpret what comes from behind that curtain, i.e., what God reveals of Himself without revealing the divine being as such. Augustine and Thomas are in complete agreement on this point.[70]

Thomas' discussion of appropriations is an attempt to speak rightly about the Trinity within the context of the doctrine itself. Appropriation theory is not a special access to the mystery of the three Persons or an alternative approach to understanding the Trinity. It is an attempt to manifest the faith, to show the truth about the three Persons. The inner divine distinctions cannot of themselves be known. We know the personal properties only by revelation, and we know their distinction only in terms of the revealed relations. The distinction between the personal properties remains hidden. The truth about these three Persons, however, can be declared by other means; namely, by terms better known because not dependent upon revelation. The procedure itself, however, remains completely dependent upon revelation for one simple reason: the Persons can be known only by revelation. Using appropriated attributes to manifest or illumine personal identities demands that one already have knowledge of these Persons. Abelard's mistake in this matter consisted precisely in assuming that the Persons were distinct in some way other than merely through personal relations. For example, Abelard proposed that the Father actually did possess power in a way distinct from the other two and likewise the Son, wisdom. According to him pagan philosophers could know something of the Trinity insofar as they understood the function of certain divine attributes.

Thomas is insistent for his part that all things in God are one except where there is an opposition of relation. We cannot know the distinctive personal properties of the Father except as the Father of the

---

70. There is an inescapable distinction between *theologia* and *economia*. Being one in power, wisdom, and goodness, any outward act is due to the free love of God and is undetermined in its fact and manner. Accordingly, because all Persons work together in every act *ad extra*, the revealed Trinity is neither a complete nor a proper representation of the divine Persons *in se*. God *in se* cannot be known by us or conceived by us.

Son and the co-spirator of the Holy Spirit. When Thomas addresses the question of priority regarding Person and essence, he merely avoids answering the question by saying that nothing prohibits the Person being prior. Thus, while our grammar may imply a kind of accidental predication by which a divine suppositum takes on a relation, revelation disallows it.[71] The way of manifesting these Persons is then by way of similarity and dissimilarity, i.e., by using essential attributes to affirm or reiterate what is known of the Persons. Power may be appropriated to the Father in order to distinguish the divine Father from creaturely fathers who because of age lack power.[72] Likewise, wisdom may be appropriated to the Son in order to affirm that this Son is full of wisdom and unlike earthly sons who are foolish. Such affirmation in no way implies special personal properties or that one divine Person alone possesses a particular habit such as wisdom. The three Persons are entirely equal and one sharing the same wisdom and power. An attribute is asserted especially of one Person to deny any difference or inequality among the Three.

Thomas begins his analysis of various sets of appropriated terms by noting that we consider God according to the order by which we consider creatures:

First, we consider something as a thing in itself (absolute) as a certain being; second, insofar as it is one; third, according to the presence in it of power for performing an operation or causing something; and fourth, according to that one's relation to what it causes.[73]

Thomas then analyzes the various sets of appropriations according to this order. The appropriations outlined by Hilary, for example, con-

---

71. In actual fact, however, Thomas would affirm that this same point can be known on the basis of reason. The simplicity of God as a negatively defined doctrine is also the basis for Thomas' assertion of the revealed Persons being subsistent relations and their identity with the divine essence. The revelation of Persons then does not contradict the divine simplicity.

72. Cf. ST I, q. 39, a. 7.

73. "Nam primo, consideratur res ipsa absolute, inquantum est ens quoddam. Secunda autem consideratio rei est, inquantum est una. Tertia consideratio rei est, secundum quod inest ei virtus ad operandum et ad causandum. Quarta autem consideratio rei est, secundum habitudinem quam habet ad causata." ST I, q. 39, a. 8 c.

sider God as absolute. Attributing 'eternity' to the Father then is suitable insofar as the Father is without beginning and a principle without being from a principle. 'Beauty' is appropriated to the Son because He "has in Himself truly and perfectly the nature of the Father."[74] 'Use' is suited to the Holy Spirit insofar as it includes fruition by which the Father and the Son love each other by the bond that is the Holy Spirit. The second triad from Augustine is explained according to the consideration of God as One. 'Unity' is rightly attributed to the Father because it does not presuppose another. The Son is called 'equality' because this term presupposes another and a respect of equal quantity to that other. 'Connection' then is suited to the Holy Spirit in its implication of two others united together by this one. The pattern of correspondence is between the meaning *(ratio)* of the appropriated term and the meaning *(ratio)* of the divine personal name.[75]

Thomas is quite unlike his predecessors in concentrating on the divine Persons as Persons and not upon their distinction. His explanation of appropriations can be read as an attempt to forestall any efforts to reason about the Trinity in such a way as to gain a more precise knowledge of the personal distinctions. His explanations at every point serve to emphasize the *in*distinction and the equality of the divine Persons among themselves. His discussion of the attributes power, wisdom, and goodness is especially illustrative. Thomas considers these three attributes in terms of operation (causal). Power is attributed to the Father both because He is the principle of the whole divinity and also because this Father is not weak as earthly fathers are in old age. Similarly, divine operations especially defined by power are appropriated to the Father. Wisdom is well suited to the Son by corresponding to the Son's identity as the Word and proceeding according to the manner of intellection. Such appropriation also shows the difference between the divine (wise) Son and the earthly (foolish) son. On the other hand, as in the fifth objection here, it seems that the truth is not merely

---

74. "[H]abens in se vere et perfecte naturam Patris." ST I, q. 39, a. 8 c.
75. The term 'ratio' is a more complex term than any English equivalent. It may be translated as "meaning," "reason," or "account."

appropriated to the Son but proper to Him. By the reason of the Son proceeding according to intellectual procession, it seems that truth is proper to this divine Person. Truth, however, can be considered in the intellect and in the thing, both of which correspond to essence and not to personal properties. Goodness corresponds to the Holy Spirit, who is also known as love, and goodness separates this divine Holy Spirit from earthly spirits of a violent nature. Thomas is also careful here not to suggest a lack of power on the part of the Son and the Holy Spirit. They both are said to possess power insofar as they effect something. On this note Thomas appropriates the indwelling of grace to the Holy Spirit. Though the whole divine essence in three Persons is in all things through essence, power, and presence, the sanctification of creatures is appropriated to the one who is specially known as goodness itself.[76]

In discussing the operative character of the attributes power, wisdom, and goodness, Thomas reminds us that appropriations are meant to display a similarity to the properties of the divine Persons or dissimilarity with creatures. In other words, they reiterate the distinction between the divine and created orders. By determining the suitability of these appropriated terms according to similarity (with the personal properties) and dissimilarity (with creatures), Thomas demonstrates his theory of appropriations. Naming the divine Persons by means of certain essential attributes is another way of pursuing the distinction between the thing signified and the manner of signifying. The predication of each Person in terms of dissimilarity with creatures is simply another way of denying the (creaturely) manner of signifying of the personal names. For that reason, appropriation theory makes no sense apart from personal names, apart from the revelation of the Trinity. The appropriated terms give no insight into God, because they signify only by way of the Personal properties. Power, goodness, and wisdom are not really three in God, but one. Predicated essentially of God they are all the same thing being signified. To say that the three Persons are power, goodness and wisdom is to say either (1) these three attributes really are distinguished in God, or (2) the divine Persons are distin-

---

76. Cf. ST I, q. 43, a. 3 ad 2.

guished only according to reason or by reason as are these attributes. Using them for referring to the Three is therefore not a way of signifying distinctions. Rather, it is a way of clarifying our manner of understanding the divine Persons that helps us to distinguish the thing signified from our manner of signifying it.

Thomas' method in regard to appropriations is firmly rooted in the knowledge of the Persons, their proper names, manner of processing, and relations. The foundation of the discussion is that knowledge of the Persons had from revelation, the relational identity of the Persons had in the personal names. The dynamics of the appropriated terms themselves do not serve to illumine the mystery. The relation of power and goodness, for instance, is not used here to explain the Persons; rather, Thomas matches particular attributes to the properties of each Person according to a particular vantage point. Thus, the question of appropriation is not an absolute one. There is no one set of appropriations. There is no one way of revealing Personal differences by way of essential properties, because no group of attributes or triad of terms (or created image even) can accurately represent the Trinity. Thomas is accordingly not concerned with judging any one triad as better or worse than another.

The appropriation of essential attributes to individual divine Persons is, therefore, not an argument but a series of descriptive expressions that attempt to encapsulate aspects of the doctrine in correct speech about God. In this sense, appropriation theory fits into the practical aspect of theological investigation, which begins with a clarification of doctrine and leads to a meaningful communication of the truths of that doctrine in the same way that one demonstrates a knowledge of a grammatical rule by using it correctly. The end is right speech, and, in this case, right speech about God with the elimination of creaturely modes of understanding and signifying. Thus, no single attribute is to be asserted properly of one Person as if it belonged only to one Person. Such predication is meant to aid our understanding through similitudes and dissimilitudes. Another way to say that the Son is the image of the Father is to call the Son "beauty." Another way to say that the three Persons are one and that the Father neither proceeds nor is generated is to call the Father "unity." Another way to say that the Holy Spirit proceeds from the Father and the Son as mutual love and is the gift of sanctifying grace in us is to call the Holy Spirit "goodness." To investigate divine power absolutely does not reveal anything unique to the Father. In the same way, 'goodness' as a term or concept does not reveal anything more about the Holy Spirit than is known through the personal name of Holy Spirit.

The essential attributes contain no subtle differences that correspond to personal properties and distinctions. According to a particular manner of considering the Persons, one attribute may seem more suitable. But the more we think it properly suitable, the less we understand the mystery. Thomas goes so far as to say that the most proper name for God is *'Qui est'* because it is the least determinative, signifying only that in this One, being and essence are one—He is who is. The point of these efforts in manifesting the Persons is to avoid errors of projecting creaturely modes of being, to avoid thinking of three Gods, and to avoid the conclusion that one divine Person is less than another. Each divine Person is fully God, and one alone is equal to the other two or all three. Not three gods but one, and yet the Father is not the Son and the Son is not the Holy Spirit; these three are One God.

### 3.3 Thomas' Trinitarian Grammar
#### 3.3.1 Person and Essence

Aquinas explains that, in Trinitarian doctrine, Persons and essence cannot differ in fact but only according to our understanding. The Persons are distinguished from each other by relations, yet these relations are not adhering as accidents in the essence. Also, the simplicity of the divine nature necessitates that there is nothing but the divine nature in God. Thomas has already established that Persons are multiplied only by relations, and that relations must be subsistent in God because no accidents can be in the eternal divine simple essence.[77] The divine essence is then neither a merely abstract unity, as is humanity,

---

77. The teaching is directly in line with that of Augustine in his *De Trinitate* VII.2, 9 and of Boethius in his *De Trinitate* IV.

nor a unity existing prior (logically or temporally) to the Persons themselves. The Persons do not "come from" the divine essence.[78]

The most obvious difficulty in describing the identity of Person and essence is that one is countable and the other is not.[79] It is a logical contradiction for something to be distinct and not be distinct at one and the same time. Divine simplicity, however, demands nothing less than the identity of what is one in God with what is really three in God.[80] In ST I, q. 3, this simplicity was demonstrated by an absence of materiality (the principle of multiplicity in created beings). In q. 39, however, the issue is made problematic by the preceding long discussion of the multiplicity of Persons. Hence, it is a reasonable question to ask whether such multiplicity is really or accidentally present in the divine essence. For Thomas, if the divine relations are divine, they must be the divine essence itself and cannot in fact differ from it.

[D]ivine simplicity requires that in God essence and suppositum are the same and that in intellectual substances there is nothing other than Person . . . Just as relations in created things are present accidentally, so in God they are the divine essence. It follows then that Person and essence may not differ in reality, but nevertheless that Persons are really distinguished from one another.[81]

Divine relations of origin, unlike relations in creatures, are subsistent. They differ in fact from one another by virtue of being different supposita, but from the essence only according to our understanding.[82]

---

78. Cf. ST I, q. 39, a. 5.

79. 'One' as a principle of numeration is not predicated of God. To say "God is one" constitutes only the denial of multiple gods. Cf. ST I, q. 11, a. 3 ad 2.

80. Note that our language is strained and inaccurate even in describing the problem. There is nothing properly speaking "in God" but only God. The divine essence *is* God, and the three Persons *are* God. We use prepositions to signify such circumlocutions as "with respect to." It may be more accurate to say "the identity of the respect to which God is one with the respect to which God is three," but such verbosity is unacceptably burdensome.

81. [D]ivine simplicitas hoc requirit, quod in Deo sit idem essentia et suppositum; quod in substantiis intellectualibus nihil est aliud quam persona. . . . sicut relationes in rebus creatis accidentaliter insunt, ita in Deo sunt ipsa essentia divina. Ex quo sequitur quod in Deo non sit aliud essentia quam persona secundum rem; et tamen quod personae realiter ab invicem distinguantur." ST I, q. 39, a. 1 c.

82. ST I, q. 39, a. 1 ad 1.

Even one who has carefully read all the preceding questions would likely find this article a bit cavalier. Thomas presents the reader with several difficult points only cursorily substantiated. One is left wondering in what way the divine essence is really one and not just a form. Is it merely the *fiat* of the theologian's pen that makes it so? One would expect this particular article, because of its highly controversial and difficult question, to be quite long. It is not. It is almost matter of fact in its presentation. It is important, however, to keep in mind the way in which Thomas leads the reader—he is a very careful teacher. He has in previous questions carefully built up a Trinitarian grammar concerning the proper ways of talking about divine unity, simplicity, etc., and the distinction of Persons. By recalling the material of q. 3 and q. 28 here in q. 39, he invites the reader to incorporate the details of earlier discussions in this question in order that the answer here appear quite evident. Indeed, the reader might exclaim, "Of course!" Parts of the answer are as much stated already in several places and need only to be brought together here for the complete answer to be realized.

Thomas' third response in this article recalls an important point made in the middle of the discussion of divine unity.[83] Having made a great deal of progress thus far in the *Summa* in expounding the revelation of God—of God's self so to speak—we may have become quite comfortable with our precise and descriptive theological language. Thomas reminds us as we venture into the thicket of logical difficulties concerning the Trinity that we are attempting to describe something we cannot know directly or accurately describe in human terms. Our use of the term 'Person,' for instance, entails a twofold limitation on our knowledge of God: (1) a limiting or humbling of God in revelatory events of salvation history (including acts and speech of Christ); and (2) a limitation of our thoughts and words to understand and talk about that revelation (beyond merely repeating the words of Christ that serve as the basis for such doctrine). 'Person' is not a revealed designation, but it signifies what is many times asserted in the Scriptures.[84] It is our way of understanding what is revealed to us in

---

83. ST I, q. 13, a. 1.
84. "[M]axime per se ens et perfectissime intelligens." ST I, q. 29, a. 3 ad 1.

Christ about who God is: one God, Father, Son, and Holy Spirit. Even the revealed names of Father, Son, and Holy Spirit are understood by us according to correlates in creation, that is, through the things that are made (Rom 1:20).

Nevertheless, we "impose names on divine things according to the mode of created things," not according to the mode of divinity itself.[85] We may refer to the Persons as *supposita* of the divine nature in much the same way as we refer to an individual existing human with the term 'human'. There are two important differences, however. The form 'humanity' is only notionally one; the divine essence is a true unity. Secondly, God is not composed of form and matter, or of form and supposita, or of essence and existence. God is simple and all is one in the divine (except where there is an opposition of relation).

The unity in question is best understood as being not of a nature but of an essence. We can say three persons of human nature, but we do not say three individuals of human essence. The essence is the form of the individual, not of the species—or rather, essence coming from "being" designates what is truly one being.[86] The emphasis on essence serves to reiterate the existential unity of the three Persons: not a unity of mind, or will, or love, or even of nature, but of essence. This point is based on the Lateran statement that is a longer version of the Greek *homoousion* of Nicea.[87] Thomas does not let the reader forget that questions about the language of the doctrine—the choice of words, their syntax, relation, and identity—are all attempts to coordinate the data of revelation and to portray accurately such revelation in a meaningful way.

### 3.3.2 Defining Theological Language
#### 3.3.2.1 *What Is Signified and the Manner of Signifying*

Central to the attempt to use language accurately is determining the way in which such terms *mean* in theological discussion. Thomas distinguishes between the thing signified and the mode of signifying

---

85. ST I, q. 39, a. 1 ad 3.    86. ST I, q. 39, a. 2 ad 3.
87. ST I, q. 39, a. 2 sc.

of terms in order to clarify their import for talking about God. In ST I, q. 13 on naming God, he uses the mode of signifying to demonstrate how a given name could be asserted of God while its creaturely mode (compositeness and such) is denied. Thomas uses the distinction here in q. 39 to solve some of the logical tangles that are part and parcel of Trinitarian doctrine. This distinction is not, however, an effort to attain to a higher knowledge of God but is made in the context of knowledge about God. It is a distinction imported by Thomas into theology that does not "adjudicate for metaphysics."[88] Thomas is not thereby affirming a direct univocal knowledge by way of a pure signification. When Thomas denies the appropriateness of our mode of signifying with respect to divine names, he is intending to

> separate from God the inevitable connotations of composition, abstraction, and concretion that arise wherever our mind forms and signifies any predication as well as the related connotation that would imply anything accidental in God.[89]

The negative judgment about our ability to signify God and the consequent effort to "square the grammar" is then based upon what we already know about God—infinite, simple, subsistent being, etc. coupled with the inescapable creaturely orientation of our language.[90]

By denying that our manner of signifying can apply to God, Thomas is reminding us of the distance between our manner of understanding and God's manner of being (modelessness). When positing a perfection in God, there is an inescapable creaturely connotation in our language and thought. The reason is this: we signify things with words with a mediating conception in our minds.[91] Hence, we name something as we are able to understand it. We cannot know God except from creatures, and so we cannot name God except by way of the

---

88. K. Buersmeyer, "Verb and Existence," *New Scholasticism* 60 (1986): 152–55; cf. also M. Jordan, "Modes of Discourse in Aquinas' Metaphysics," *New Scholasticism* 54 (1980): 401–46.

89. Gregory Rocca, O.P. "The Distinction between *res significata* and *modus significandi* in Aquinas' Theological Epistemology," *The Thomist* 55 (1991): 189.

90. Ibid., 193.

91. Cf. ST I, q. 13, a. 1.

same things. For example, we name God as the source of things ("God is good" = God is the source or cause of goodness) or as possessing an attribute in a more excellent manner since all perfections exist preeminently in Him ("God is good" = God is goodness itself).

Whatever is said of God and creatures, is said according to some order of creatures to God as to their principle and cause in whom the perfections of all things preexist in a more excellent manner.[92]

Because we must deny of God any creaturely imperfection and limitations, we must deny the creaturely modes of being to God. Anything that we say of God "can also be denied of Him since they are not fitting to Him in the way that they are found in created things and as they are understood and signified by us."[93] The separation from God of creaturely imperfections and of the imperfect manner in which creatures possess perfections is the basis for Thomas' insistence that we separate our manner of signifying from what we are signifying when we name God.[94]

It would be a mistake, however, to conclude on the basis of such negations that nothing is really known and signified. The denial is not of the thing signified itself but only of the way in which that thing signified pertains.[95] Augustine, for instance, is often read as positing a creator-based referent system whereby "Father" is properly signified of God the Father and, by analogy, of earthly fathers. In this case the denial or subtraction of our manner of signifying from the thing signified would leave us with the pure, "original" meaning. Hence, our ig-

---

92. "Et sic, quidquid dicitur de Deo et creaturis, dicitur secundum quod est aliquis ordo creaturae ad Deum, ut ad principium et causam, in qua praeexistunt excellenter omnes rerum perfectiones." ST I, q. 13, a. 5 c.

93. Aquinas, *Super Librum Dionysii De divinis nominibus* (Marietti, 1950) Bk. 5, ch. 3, n. 673.

94. Rocca, "Distinction between *res significata* and *modus significandi*," 185.

95. Rocca notes that some modern authors read Thomas' argument in the following way: "the RS [*res significata*] is what the word really means, but we do not know what that is"; the RS is a "core meaning" that has picked up limited connotations by being applied to creatures for so long; supposedly, after stripping away the "encrustations" of the MS *(modi significandi)*, we are left with the "pure" meaning. But at this point no one can describe that pure meaning, and so in the end it is no meaning at all. Ibid., 175.

norance of God's true perfection entails a complete ignorance about the name "Father," which would consequently remain without meaning. If, on the other hand, we affirm that our knowledge of God is by means of creatures, then we can at once affirm the fact of such knowledge while noting the non-univocal character of our naming of God. When we predicate 'wisdom' of God, for example, we are denying that wisdom pertains in the same way, i.e., as an accident. The term 'wise' signifies properly in some way, but we cannot know how. That it applies, that the concept *qua* concept posits correctly some reality in God, is then a factual, not an explanatory, knowledge. We can use it but not conceive it.

> We never really know in a clear conceptual fashion what a divine name might mean for God, and whatever we do know about such a name is always a consequence of the judgments we have already made about God.[96]

The remainder of the thing signified left when the manner of signifying is stripped away is then based upon judgment, the judgment that what we are signifying is the same thing in God and creatures, the same thing signified only in an analogous manner.

The key to the affirmative divine attributes lies in the intelligibility of the claim that perfections found in a limited way in creatures are thinkable while negating those creaturely limitations.[97] Just as "white" can be signified as an abstract or concrete term, so "wisdom" is never grasped apart from its modes in the created order. To say "God is wise" without knowing exactly how God is wise does not detract from the intended truth of the statement. Because God is the source of all perfections, we affirm that such perfections pertain to God preeminently and substantially. On the other hand, because this intention within the term is negatively qualified, we cannot reason about it. Such insight into religious language is corrective indeed but not a license for "transcendent predication *tout court*."[98] The statement that the three divine Persons are of one essence is judged correct insofar as it signifies what

---

96. Ibid., 194.
97. R. McInerny, "Can God Be Named by Us?" in *Being and Predication*, 276.
98. D. Burrell, *Aquinas: God and Action* (Notre Dame: University of Notre Dame Press, 1986), 10.

is found in Scripture and encapsulates narrative statements into a systematic one. If one seeks the meaning of the expression, one then returns to its scriptural foundation (John 10:13, 38; 14:10, et al.).[99] This procedure is valid as long as one allows the manner of understanding to mediate between our manner of signifying and the divine mode of being. As our signifying falls short of understanding, so much more does our understanding fall short of the mode of being in God. That is, we must note that such predication is neither the same in every way with creatures nor completely different. This kind of affirmative predication can only be analogical.

### 3.3.2.2 *The Analogous Nature of Theological Predication*

Aquinas' primary model for explaining analogous terms is that of "health"—in a subject or in one causing it or in one signifying it. The analogous term is used according to a proportion or order to one thing—in this case, in the subject who possesses health. A treatment is healthy because it promotes or causes health. Skin tone may also be healthy as a sign of health. Proportion is then not to be understood as a measured proportion whereby one subject possesses health in a greater or lesser degree; rather, one referent *is* healthy whereas other referents cause or signify such health. There is no one meaning at root but an order to one proper significate (the healthy subject). When we use the term 'wise' to refer to God, we are not assuming a meaning common to creatures and God but noting that there is the same thing signified in both God and creatures. The signified wisdom in God is the cause of wisdom in creatures, not a higher example of wisdom in which case the term would be univocal.[100] Terms used of God and creatures cannot be univocal precisely because God is infinite and perfect. We know God from creatures, and our language is creaturely.

If we stopped there, it would be difficult to avoid the charge of equivocation. To say that God simply causes wisdom is not to say anything definite about God. A strict father, for example, may be the

---

99. Cf. ST I, q. 39, a. 2 ad 2.
100. Cf. ST I, q. 13, a. 5 ad 3.

cause of extreme politeness in his young son, yet the father may be personally very rude. In this case the only quality present in the father that caused something was strictness. When we say "God is wise," do we mean anything more than that God causes wisdom? Can we for that reason say "God is body" because God is the cause of corporeality?[101] Another aspect of Thomas' theory of naming is the doctrine of divine simplicity. Not only is God cause of wisdom but He is wisdom itself, for His causality and being are one with His intellect and power. It is not one thing for God to be and another for God to be wise. We name God properly when we deny any distinction between the divine attributes. God causes goodness by being (goodness); God causes humans to be wise by being Himself (wisdom). He is the cause of such perfections, and those perfections preexist preeminently in Him (substantially). Affirmative names are then said of God both causally and essentially.[102]

The nature of analogical language is, however, made somewhat problematic by an example Thomas gives in ST I, q. 13, a. 10. The question in that article concerns the semantic value of 'God' as used by the pagan. This name does not denote a perfection, nor is it a proper name. According to Thomas, the pagan and the Christian are not being equivocal in using the name 'God.' When a Christian says to the pagan that his (the pagan's) idol is not God, the pagan understands his own belief to be attacked. Both pagan and Christian use the name 'God' to signify the true God. The problem is that the pagan is wrong in his beliefs about the divine nature (e.g., thinking that it is local or material). Thus, the use of the name 'God' according to truth and according to opinion is neither wholly equivocal nor wholly univocal, but analogical.

The name 'God' is "understood according to one accepted signification that is included in the definition of the name [even] when used

---

101. Cf. ST I, q. 13, a. 2 c.
102. ST I, q. 13, a. 6 c. The importance of this point is seen in the consequent distinction between metaphorical and analogical naming. A purely negative way of naming would not be able to distinguish levels of predication, because all things can be predicated of God causally; more about this point in ch. 5.

for other things."[103] The pagan is right in intending by the name, 'God' the one true God, but is mistaken in the manner of signifying. The Christian correctly signifies the true God by the name, 'God', with the knowledge that the manner of signifying is inadequate. In the same way, one can call a big steak dinner or a huge appetite "healthy" with reference to the health of the subject in which health obtains but be mistaken in thinking that these things are true signs of or causes of health. The problem is not in knowing what health means but in knowing what is the proper manner of health in a subject, what are its true causes and signs and its true nature. Weighing over two hundred pounds and being half drunk, a man may be considered "healthy" on the streets of New Orleans, but the truth is otherwise. Yet that mistake does not mean that the term is used with a totally different meaning. The thing signified is found in various uses of the analogical term, but only one thing signified is prior and the basis for predication in other instances. The difficulty is in knowing which referent is signified properly and in what way, i.e, which analogate includes the proper meaning *(ratio propria)*.[104] In the case of 'wise', it is evident that the primary significate is the wisdom in God, for that wisdom is the cause of wisdom in creatures as well as the very subject of wisdom. Moreover, when wisdom is said of God, the thing signified "exists in a way we cannot comprehend, as one with His essence and other perfections."[105]

The term 'God' brings to the fore the question of accuracy in signifying, because this name is not common to creatures. On the one hand, it is not a proper name, because it is common to three. On the other hand, it has only one subject. To use it improperly is to mistake the sign for the subject itself. In dealing with this problem, Thomas is concerned with more than the correctness of grammatical constructs. The pagan, for instance, could say "God is just," but the proposition is inaccurate insofar as his use of 'God' is only analogically related to the true God.

---

103. "[I]n analogicis vero, oportet quod nomen secundum unam significationem acceptum, ponatur in definitione eiusdem nominis secundum alias significationes accepti." ST I, q. 13, a. 10 c.

104. McInerny, "The Analogy of Names," in *Being and Predication,* 284.

105. Ibid., 285.

### 3.3.3 A Most Elusive Theological Term: 'God'

In Trinitarian theology the use of the term 'God' is especially troublesome. We call the Father "God" and the Son "God," yet there is only one God. The traditional reading on this question is that 'God' signifies the divine essence or nature. The term 'essence' signifies the divine as form even though we deny the mode of form to it. That is, we affirm that the unity of divine nature is not merely abstract even though we can talk about truly simple things only in abstract terms.

Thomas divides essential names into two categories: substantive and adjectival. Names such as 'wisdom' or 'uncreated' or 'God' that signify substantially are used in the singular only—one uncreated, one wisdom, one God. Those names used adjectivally are used in the plural of the three Persons—three existent ones, three wise ones, three having deity, and so forth. The term 'God' is more difficult to define categorically, because 'God' and what it signifies, the divine essence, are not used in the same way. We do not say "divine essence from divine essence" or "three Persons of one God." The first step in dealing with the problem, according to Thomas, is to see that, although the divine essence is identical to God, 'God' is used of the divine Persons in a manner that divine essence is not. Take for example the common pronouncement that the Father is God, the Son is God, and the Holy Spirit is God, yet they are not three Gods. We do not say conversely that God is the Father and so forth, because not only the Father but also the Son and the Holy Spirit *are* God. We can say 'God generates' or 'is generated' to signify one of the divine Persons, but we do not say that the divine essence generates. It is not a principle of action; or rather, it is not a supposit, but exists in supposita. In other words, the formal character of 'essence' precludes certain types of expressions. The manner in which 'God' signifies, however, allows for a greater range of predication—and confusion.

Thomas takes his cue from the properties of speech. Instead of beginning with the differences between speaking about God and speaking about creatures, he allows the rules and modes of the latter to influence and guide the former because, as Thomas insists, we name things as we know them, and we know God from creatures. Our speech can only be in the creaturely mode, of course with the qualifications gained from reason and revelation that inform us about what God is not.[106] Theological understanding does not function as a privileged or higher-order language. As the Word clothed Himself in flesh, so God spoke through the prophets and to the prophets and in Christ in human language. We must use that same creaturely oriented language, stretching it as far as we can to signify that which is not creaturely. We cannot move beyond creaturely modes of expression, but we can deny the applicability of such modes owing to divine simplicity and so forth. It is a failed enterprise to attempt to formulate speech directly applicable to God. Such language would be meaningless for purposes of communication.[107] What we end up with in theological language, according to Thomas, is not a neat definition of God but a series of statements or, rather, a dialectical circumlocution that both affirms and denies things of God based upon judgments, not conceptualization. The distinction between God and the world demands that the rules of created existence do not apply to God, and yet these realms are not wholly discontinuous. This distinction does not preclude knowing something about God as cause or as Trinity. The difficulty is in knowing where our language obtains a positive hold on the truth about God and where it fails, i.e., knowing where it functions in the mode of predication.

The problem becomes more complex when we consider creedal statements such as "God begat God." The divine essence does not beget nor is it begotten, for the essence is not a suppositum except in the Father and in the Son and in the Holy Spirit. There are three Persons *of* one essence, not three Persons *and* one essence. 'God' signifies the divine essence only in "one having deity" as 'man' signifies "one having

---

106. Cf. ST I, q. 13, a. 1, and q. 39, a. 1. Also, for a similar attempt in the modern context to clarify the way in which God is both distinct from creatures yet knowable by them, see R. Sokolowski, *God of Faith and Reason* (Notre Dame, Ind.: University of Notre Dame Press, 1982).

107. Cf. St. Paul in 1 Corinthians. The use of tongues is useful only for the speaker unless someone can interpret, that is, put the "inspired" speech into intelligible form. The value of meaningful speech far outweighs any other form of utterance.

human nature." The verb (or notional adjunct) such as 'begets' or 'spirates' specifies which Person is signified, which is the one "having the divine essence." Humanity is a separate form in every human person, yet divine nature is substantial, metaphysical unity. 'Man' then signifies the individual having humanity or the collective of ones having humanity. 'God' may signify the one(s) having deity or the unity of divinity itself. Thus, 'man' has one manner of signifying while 'God' has two. 'God' signifies in the singular adjectivally and substantially.[108] Although "there are three having deity, there is only one deity, one God and not three."[109] For this reason, Thomas overturns the common manner of using the term 'God;' namely, that it supposits naturally for the divine essence. He argues that although 'God' signifies naturally the divine essence, it supposits naturally for the Person(s) inasmuch as it signifies the essence in the ones having it. Here again, Thomas' attentiveness to "the proprieties of speaking" determines that our use of 'God' will be more like our use of 'man.' 'God' then signifies a nature or essence, but supposits for the Persons. Its manner of signifying determines that a Person or Persons are intended. Only acts *ad extra* adjoined to 'God' would specify the divine essence itself being supposited (intended).[110] The divine essence can be the subject of supposition because it is truly one with the Persons.

It is noteworthy that in discussing modes of signification and supposition, Thomas does not refer to the Boethian distinction between *id quod* and *id quo*. This distinction was used by many of Thomas' predecessors to describe the simplicity of God and the different modes of linguistic expression. Thomas, however, refers to the essence not as a *quo* (that "by which") but as a *quod habetur* (what is had). In so do-

---

108. The commonly used Boethian distinction between the *quo est* and *quod est* is found in Thomas' *Scriptum* but not here, even though it would serve quite well in making his point clear. Thomas may, however, be wanting to say more than that the essence is the *quo est*, and therefore he looks for a better way of making his point. To say that God is one yet a different kind of unity than in creatures demands that the divine essence is not merely a *quo est*.

109. "[L]icet sint tres habentes deitatem, non tamen sequitur quod sint tres dii." ST I, q. 39, a. 3 ad 1.

110. ST I, q. 39, a. 4.

ing, he has more strongly suggested a unity and substantiality to the essence. It is not an abstract form as humanity is. The identity of Persons and essence allows the divine essence to be causal in this sense: when the Father, Son, and Holy Spirit create, the Father, Son, and Holy Spirit *as* divine essence create.[111] The divine Persons are distinct really but only with reference to one another, not with reference to the divine essence. They are distinct by means of opposition, i.e., relations. Attempts to prioritize essence or Person or attempts to answer questions of priority inevitably lead to problems. On the basis of divine eternity (naturally known) and equality (revealed), there can be no beginning or process in God. Is the Father the Father because He generates? Thomas says, "No"—the Father generates because He is the Father.[112] Person and essence remain equally fundamental. The difference in our language concerns the distinction between our modes of signifying. We signify what is simple with abstract terms, even though what is simple in this case is not an abstract form but concrete.

Thomas' concern throughout this discussion typically focuses not on God in Himself but on our manner of signifying God. Thomas shies away from an answer as to exactly how the divine essence can be truly one and the Persons identical to it but distinct among themselves. His efforts are aimed at making our speech conform to theological insights. He can do so not with an explanation *per se* but with the proper speech—precise terminology used in a careful manner. What is gained then is a set of rules governing theological language that prevents error or dishonor to God; that is, a multiplicity of guidelines for theological language that provides the many circumlocutions necessary to talk about what is beyond creaturely language and understanding. When speaking of what is beyond us, we are limited to our ways of understanding and naming informed by judgment by which we remove from our thinking whatever is inappropriate to God. The precision of language is a way of obeying the multiple dictates of revelation, not an explanation of God's being. Thus, in the end, theological investigation remains exegetical.

---

111. Creation is not proper to any one Person. Cf. ST I, q. 45, a. 6 c.
112. ST I, q. 33, a. 3.

### 3.3.4 Trinitarian Applications

The revelation of the distinction of divine Persons and their proper names brings another issue to the project of divine naming. It is one thing to qualify terms of perfection that are common to creatures, but should we proceed in the same way with revealed names? Do we in fact proceed in the same way with 'Father' as we do with 'wise'? The question concerns the primary referent of such terms. Are these personal names predicated more properly of God or of creatures. Which naming is prior logically?

Thomas argues that 'paternity' said of humans seems to derive from the preeminent paternity of God the Father. All earthly references to paternity are ordered to the divine and include in their definition an order by which they approach the prior instance more or less.[113] Two things should be noted: (1) paternity is not a perfection of the divine essence, but a personal property known by revelation; and (2) paternity is like an essential perfection term in that it pertains to God substantially and is understood by us in its creaturely mode. On the other hand, the class of analogous names is of two types: terms whose multiple uses are ordered to the creaturely and those whose uses are ordered to the divine. For example, names are used metaphorically of God with the primary referent in creatures. God can be called "lion" insofar as He has in the divine nature a similitude for doing all that He wills, as the lion does. Other names such as 'good' or 'wise' are ordered primarily to God because they are said of creatures with reference to the cause.[114]

We understand 'good' or 'wise' in creaturely terms and therefore distinguish the thing signified from the manner of signifying in order to predicate it accurately of God, with the qualification that we know its applicability but not the reason why. Does this distinction work the same way with the terms "Father" or "Trinity"? We say that God *is*

---

113. Cf. ST I, q. 13, a. 6.
114. In both cases, the various uses of the terms are ordered to one, i.e., to one which is proper. According to what is signified by the name 'wise', it is literally said of God *(proprie competunt Deo)* ST I, q. 13, a. 3.

good or wise not only because God causes goodness and wisdom, but also because God *is* goodness and wisdom substantially. Do we mean to say that God causes paternity and thus is paternity in the same way that God is wise because God is cause of and source of wisdom? Goodness is not an accident, nor is it present in God as it is present in us; it *is* God. In the same way, one would be able to say that paternity is present in God, but we do not know in what way it is present. It is substantial in God as is goodness, lacking all composition or any character of an accident. On the other hand, goodness and wisdom really are the same in God and differ only according to our understanding. Paternity and sonship, however, are not the same in God. These signified relations really are distinct, though the One in whom they are distinct remains one.

When Thomas attempts to clarify our use of these revealed names, he does not argue about what paternity must mean in God or what the first Person of the Trinity must be like. Instead, he describes how we in fact understand the creedal language, what we mean by certain terms and statements, all the while qualifying them in the same way he qualified terms of perfection. He explains that the term 'Father' signifies "that through which this Person is distinguished from all others" insofar as it signifies 'paternity'.[115] 'Paternity' in turn is said with respect to the Son and indicates that the Father is not from another, but unbegotten. The Persons differ both according to origin and according to relation, the relation following upon the act (of generation or of spiration). The Father alone is unbegotten, and the other two proceed from Him in two different ways, and it is by these two different kinds of origin that the Son and Holy Spirit are distinguished. However, these three are eternal and equal, and it is only our way of thinking that posits a beginning in procession and a relation coming to a subject rather than being subsistent.

Thomas qualifies this term 'paternity' by separating out the connoted creaturely modes of being. That is, he must distinguish the paternity we signify in God from our manner of signifying it. 'Paternity'

---

115. "[I]d per quod illa persona distinguitur ab omnibus aliis." ST I, q. 33, a. 2.

in God does not denote a "first one," nor one who becomes "paternal" after a begetting. 'Paternity' signifies a relation that alone differentiates the three Persons, a relation that subsists eternally and, for that matter, is not simply a property but a hypostasis. 'Father' signifies an individual divine hypostasis distinct from the Son and Holy Spirit by the very relation which is a distinctive and constitutive hypostasis.[116] For Thomas the origins and relations of the Persons are not distinct at all, not even according to our understanding.

For two things to be understood as distinct, it is necessary that the distinction be understood through something intrinsic to both, just as in created things such distinction is understood through form or matter. The origin of a thing, however, is not signified as something intrinsic but as a certain way from a thing and to a thing. Generation is then signified as a way to the one generated and as a proceeding from the one generating. Hence, it is not possible that the generated one and the one generating are distinguished by a single generative act, for it must be the same thing in both that distinguishes them. In the divine Persons, there is nothing for us to understand except essence and relations (or properties).[117]

The divine Persons are distinguished from one another only by relations. Origin signified as an active or passive act does not constitute a hypostasis. We must separate our manner of signifying relation and origin from the signified thing. We know relations are in God because the revealed proper names are relational, but such relations are not accidents coming to be in a subject in any way. Hence, the connoted origin in the personal names must be denied altogether in its temporal, causal, and logical mode.

What is most revealing in Thomas' discussion of these issues is the

---

116. ST I, q. 40, a. 2 c.

117. "[A]liqua duo distincta intelligantur, necesse est eorum distinctionem intelligi per aliquid intrinsecum utrique; sicut in rebus creatis vel per materiam, vel per formam. Origo autem alicuius rei non significatur ut aliquid intrinsecum, sed ut via quaedam a re vel ad rem: sicut generatio significatur ut via quaedam ad rem genitam, et ut progrediens a generante. Unde non impotest esse quod res genita et generans distinguantur sola generatione: sed oportet intelligere tam in generante quam in genito ea quibus ab invicem distinguuntur. In persona autem divina non est aliud intelligere nisi essentiam et relationem sive proprietatem." ST I, q. 40, a. 2 c.

way in which he "pulls back" from affirmative language. When treating various terms and questions regarding each of the Persons in turn (qq. 33–38), he was willing to let the affirmative language stand insofar as he could shed light on the theological terminology, especially the proper names. When discussing the more investigative questions of distinguishing the Persons from the essence or from the relations or from one another, Thomas is always careful to remain at the level of our manner of understanding, not assuming that we have through revelation a privileged access to the inner life of God. Hence, in q. 40 (cited above), Thomas points out what can and cannot be understood, what can and cannot be signified in God, all the while not supposing that we actually know in a positive way. He does not say "there is nothing except essence and relation in God" but that there is nothing else for us "to understand," nothing else for us to think about than essence and relation.

According to Thomas, then, one cannot proceed from 'Son' to the proper divine identity of this one signified by 'Son'. The way such realities obtain in God is unknown, just as the way in which God is wisdom is unknown. We can give an account of why we predicate wisdom of God, i.e., an account of how we know that God is wisdom, even though we cannot give an account of how wisdom pertains. To know the way in which God is wisdom is to know the very being of God, for it is the being of God that constitutes rather than is measured by wisdom. So also we cannot give an account of how sonship or paternity obtains in God, only an account of our affirmation—from the revealed personal names. Our explanation in both cases is limited to explaining how we came to that proposition, through reasoning or through revelation, and denying any creaturely modes of being to such signification. We still are unable to describe how the second Person is the Son and how that one really differs from the other two. Proper differences remain veiled, not the fact but the character. The fundamental differences between rationally attained names and revealed names are, in the end, negligible, because in neither case do we have a knowledge of the mode of being for such realities.

Revealed names differ only in their appropriateness. It is more proper to say Father, Son, and Holy Spirit than to say wise, simple, etc.[118] On the other hand, constructing an appropriate concept *(ratio)* or meaning is more difficult for the personal names than for the perfections. We know wisdom, for instance, only in its creaturely instances, but our participation in that perfection brings us closer to God. Hence, we may construct a concept for wisdom by way of eminence because the being of God defines wisdom and causes it in us. Hence, it is said of God more eminently. Paternity, on the other hand, is not causal. It is known in its creaturely modes and also connotes such modes. To say that it is a constitutive (eternal, subsistent) relation stretches language almost to the breaking point. The concept *(ratio)* by which we signify the Father is, then, less a definition than a pointing. When we say "Father, Son, and Holy Spirit," we are necessarily speaking in a religious manner, addressing the One God rather than speaking about Him.

In answering the question of the accuracy of Trinitarian formulations, Thomas keeps this analogous theory of naming at the fore. He strives at every turn to distinguish carefully what we know, what we understand and do not understand, how we signify and the truth of things. He analyzes the statement 'three Persons of one essence' not first according to God's mode of being but according to our mode of understanding. Because we understand individuals of a nature to be individuated through matter, we call them 'subjects' or 'supposita.' Hence, we name the divine Persons in this way "not because there may be some suppositum or subject in the sense of a thing."[119]

Thomas explicitly distances himself from the effort to gain insight into the divine distinctions themselves. We name God according to the manner in which such names are found in creatures, not in the divine itself.

---

118. ST I, q. 39, a. 3 ad 4. Note that according to q. 13, a. 10, *Qui est* is the most proper name for God because it is the least determinative. Hence, Father, Son, and Holy Spirit are most proper when seen as less rather than more determinate.

119. "Et propter hoc etiam divinae personae supposita vel hypostases nominantur; non quod ibi sit aliqua suppositio vel subjectio secundum rem." ST I, q. 39, a. 1 ad 3.

Our intellect does not name divine things according to their [proper] mode, because we cannot know them in their proper mode; instead, we know them in accord with the manner of creatures.[120]

We name God as one and three according to the way in which creatures are individuated, as form and suppositum. We say, "This is a man of perfect virtue," to signify the virtue as a form. So when we wish to signify the divine essence, which is not multiplied by way of the Persons, we predicate the essence of the Persons as a form.

[B]ecause 'nature' designates the principle of action and 'essence' is said of one being, something can be said of one nature that pertains to some act as everything that heats [possesses the nature of heating]; but "of one essence" cannot be said of something unless it is one being. Therefore, the divine unity is better expressed by the statement "three Persons are of one essence" than if it is said that they are of one nature.[121]

The truth of the creedal statement is measured by the sense of it in Scripture. The sense being found, the statement is judged permissible. Moreover, by attending to our creaturely manner of understanding and signifying, Thomas contends that 'essence' is preferred over 'nature' as the signified "form." Nature is generally understood to be the principle of action rather than of being *per se*. And in expressing the "form" of God, it is better to use the principle of being, i.e., essence.

In defending the accuracy of Trinitarian propositions, Thomas is at every point concerned foremost with the fundamental principle that our understanding is limited to the manner of created things and that our naming follows accordingly. The accuracy of such propositions about God is determined by the negation of creaturely modes. Thomas

---

120. "Intellectus noster res divinas nominat, non secundum modum earum, quia sic eas cognoscere non potest; sed secundum modum in rebus creatis inventum." ST I, q. 39, a. 2.

121. "Ad tertium dicendum quod, quia natura designat principium actus, essentia vero ab essendo dicitur, possunt dici aliqua unius naturae, quae conveniunt in aliquo actu, sicut omnia calefacientia: sed unius essentiae dici non possunt, nisi quorum est unum esse. Et ideo magis exprimitur unitas divina per hoc quod dicitur quod tres Personae sunt unius essentiae, quam si diceretur quod sunt unius naturae." ST I, q. 39, a. 2 ad 3.

is not so much probing the mystery as protecting it by clarifying our language as an instance of speech governed by rules of analogical naming. Speech about God is meaningful insofar as it adheres to rules of grammar and reflects truths known about God, with the added qualification that such language does not accurately represent the divine, though it can signify properly. The perfective terms are unique among the rationally known terms in being literally applicable to God. Because we know God by means of these perfections proceeding from God to creatures, such perfections are indeed in God though in a more eminent mode. What is signified by the term 'wisdom' is literally true of God *(proprie competunt Deo)*.[122] It is only our manner of signifying this perfection that renders the term more proper to creatures.

Theological language functions within the bounds of everyday grammar even as it serves to signify what is quite beyond human understanding and human language. If theological language were to break the rules of grammar, it would to that extent cease to be intelligible. What it signifies, its suppositional trajectory, is accurate because it is guided by revelation, even though the manner of its signification is according to created things. Distinguishing what is signified from the manner of signifying does not leave us with a core concept or root definition. Thomas' theory of analogical naming is dependent simply upon "recognizing the truth about God."[123] This is not the same thing, however, as a disavowal of suppositional accuracy. Some modern theologians would deny the manner and fact of our naming God as one and three. Thomas, on the contrary, is insistently working on the foundation of revealed truths and terms. Thomas' confidence is not due to the power of human understanding to grasp the divine nature but rests upon the assurance of God's communication in a human manner.[124] That God became man and that God has spoken through men and women throughout history provide an even more solid foundation for speech about God, especially what cannot be known by reason.

---

122. ST I, q. 13, a. 3 c.
123. G. Rocca, "Distinction between *res significata* and *modus significandi*," 196.
124. Cf. ST, q. 1, a. 1, and q. 32, a. 1.

## 3.4 Conclusion

In order to speak properly about Christ, one cannot avoid the necessity of clarifying the complex if not contradictory language about divine Persons and divine essence. It is precisely at the juncture of these terms that error most often erupts, error that dishonors God and detracts from the glory of God. Arius supposed that the sending of the Son entailed created aspects. Sabellius thought that it is only according to our understanding that God is three. Gilbert of Poitiers was accused of saying that the personal properties were mere accidents to the divine essence. Peter the Lombard was accused of teaching a reified essence, making God into a quaternity. All of these problems resulted from attempts to talk about the oneness and threeness of God at the same time. The difficulties of talking about the divine essence and divine Persons coherently proved virtually insurmountable without denying or calling into question some part of the doctrine itself. Clumsy use of terms implied a multiplicity of Gods, a denial of real distinction between divine Persons, or even a reification of the essence prior to or apart from the Persons.

Aquinas took it upon himself to pursue a path around these errors by defining the unity of divine nature first and then determining the character of revealed distinctions in God. Only then does he take up the discussion of the systematic language needed to talk about God as One and Three at the same time. The difficulty is formulating a language that brings together expressions of the divine unity and expressions of the inner divine distinctions. That is, to bring together in a meaningful way language about Person and language about essence. Thomas' success in this regard owes as much to the clarity of his earlier discussions as to his constant attention to the nature of theological language. He places at the center of his theory of naming the necessary qualification that we name God in the way that we know God, through creatures. Revealed names and revealed truths for which we formulate names (e.g., Person) provide a solid foundation for our imperfect speech about God. It is the condescension of God in the revelation of salvation history that guides our speech. Such revelation gives license to our use of such terms but does not provide further insight into the being of God. With or without revelation, God's manner of being is beyond us, because we cannot understand apart from creatures and creaturely modes. We cannot but understand "Father" according to its reference within creation. We say that this one is power or unity or eternity not as a way of identifying this divine Person as opposed to the other two but as a way of affirming that this one is not weak but is powerful because He is God. What is signified, the proposition's semantic value for theological discourse, is not an inner divine distinction but the unity and equality of the Father with the Son and Holy Spirit, three Persons and one essence.

# 4. Theological Language
## A Question of Context and Character

Thomas Aquinas' discussion of naming God is based upon two principles: (1) we name God as we know God; and (2) we do not know what God is but only what God is not. These two principles taken together seem to suggest that our language about God does not "hook up" with the divine reality. Indeed, Thomas states that there is a sense in which "God does not have a name . . . because his essence is beyond that which we understand about God and signify with words."[1] Consequently, the clarification of theological language does not appear to move beyond human experience, for our speech and concepts about God cannot but remain immeasurably distant from the subject of such speech. One may conclude that theological language is merely a function of a community, its expression of the community's own experience. There is no one theological language but a plurality of theological languages. No one language is universal or even translatable because it is not dependent upon truth beyond the community.[2] On the other hand, when we say that God is good or wise, we do in fact, according to Thomas, signify the divine substance, albeit analogously.[3]

---

1. ST I, q. 13, a. 1 ad 1.
2. The similarity between certain apophatic readings of Thomas' theology and "functional linguistics" is uncanny. Cf. B. Whorf, *Language, Thought, and Reality: Selected Writings* (Cambridge: MIT Press, 1956), 246–70. In Whorf's view, the radical disjunction between language and reality renders the question of "truth" merely functional.
3. Cf. ST I, q. 13, a. 2 c.

Moreover, we can define and distinguish certain theological terms such as 'person,' 'essence,' 'God,' and 'divinity' by the different ways in which they signify God. The question is whether these terms in their theological use really have anything to do with the truth about God. If they do, then we would have to admit that we can signify better than we can understand.

## 4.1 The Question of Context

Many scholars have argued that Aquinas cannot be understood apart from his relation to the medieval tradition of speculative grammar. They argue that reading Thomas without knowing speculative grammar is precisely to miss the point of his work or at least the genius of it. Indeed, says F. A. Cunningham, "to study St. Thomas without studying speculative grammar . . . is like studying Shakespeare in translation."[4] The genealogy of this grammatical tradition is thought to stem from Abelard and culminate in the refinements of the speculative grammarians contemporary with Aquinas. Thus, in order to understand Thomas' philosophy of language, particularly his theological language, one must read him in the context of the grammar which culminated in the late-thirteenth-century works commonly entitled *Grammatica speculativa*.

The speculative grammarians believed that the causes of grammar lie in things, and they claimed that there is "one universal grammar dependent on the structure of reality." They defined the parts of speech in semantic terms, "using a terminology which they derived from the metaphysical and logical theories of their contemporaries."[5]

---

4. F. A. Cunningham, "Speculative Grammar in St. Thomas Aquinas," *Laval théologique et philosophique* 17 (1961): 86. Cunningham cites a common misattribution of a speculative grammar to Thomas as justification for his suggestion. He is misleading, however, in citing the more well-known Breslau manuscript as the source of the suggested Thomistic authorship (cf. nn. 22–24 below). For evidence of the continued interest in Thomas' relation to speculative grammar, see H. J. M. Schoot, *Christ the 'Name' of God: Thomas Aquinas on Naming Christ* (Nijmegen: Peeters Leuven, 1993); and S.-C. Park, *Die Rezeption der Mittelalterlichen Sprachphilosophie in der Theologie des Thomas von Aquin* (Leiden: Brill, 1999).

5. G. L. Bursill-Hall, *Speculative Grammars of the Middle Ages* (The Hague: Mou-

In speculative grammar, one investigates syntax, meaning, and reference with recourse to the being of things. The grammarian must, therefore, study the things of grammar and philosophy. In so doing, Boethius of Dacia writes, the grammarian must be a "philosopher of the real so that he is able to consider the properties of things from which he takes the modes of signifying."[6] Though not identical, the modes of signifying are directly related to the modes of being of things themselves as effects to their cause. According to E. J. Ashworth, the modes of signifying come from the modes of being and correspond to them such that "a word has not only its significates but also its *modi significandi*, before it enters a sentence, . . . [and] these *modi* cannot be altered by the role the word plays in a sentence."[7] Use and context are remotely secondary because analogy and equivocation are not functions of supposition but of imposition, i.e., properties of the word itself.[8]

---

ton, 1971), 35. Cf. J. Pinborg, "Speculative Grammar," in *The Cambridge History of Later Medieval Philosophy*, ed. N. Kretzmann, A. Kenny, and J. Pinborg (Cambridge: Cambridge University Press, 1982), 254–70.

6. "[P]hilosophus realis, ut possit considerare proprietates rerum a quibus modos significandi accipit." Boethius, *De modi significandi sive Quaestiones super Pricianum majorem*, ed. J. Pinborg, H. Roos, and S. Jensen (Copenhagen, 1969), q. 12, p. 50.

7. E. J. Ashworth, "Signification and Modes of Signifying in Thirteenth-Century Logic: A Preface to Aquinas on Analogy," *Medieval Philosophy and Theology* 1 (1991): 62; cf. also Schoot, "Aquinas and supposition: the possibilities and limitations of logic *in divinis*," *Vivarium* 31 (1993): 193–225. Schoot presents a position very similar to that of Ashworth and relies heavily upon William of Sherwood and Lambert of Auxerre to interpret Aquinas' theological language. The resulting interpretation, however, suggests that linguistic rules are not the result of theological investigation but its very starting point and guide (p. 43). But is there anything to be learned from the fact that the issues of supposition and signification, the rules by which one might speak about the oneness and threeness of God in coherent speech, are found not at the beginning of the *Summa theologiae* but in q. 39, near the end of the treatise *De Trinitate* and after a complete survey of the revealed doctrine? The linguistic discussion in question 16 of the treatise on Christ in the *tertia pars* is also central to Schoot's interpretation in his *Christ the 'Name' of God: Thomas Aquinas on Naming Christ*. One cannot help but wonder why Aquinas waited so long to introduce these important notions. Could it be that, for Aquinas, correct speech follows upon correct understanding and not *visa versa*?

8. By "imposition" Ashworth means to indicate the complete endowment of a word; she is thereby following Abelard, not Aquinas. Ashworth, "Signification," 45.

Assuming that Thomas was familiar with and sympathetic to this speculative view of grammar, one question comes to mind: What is the force of the apophatic critique or correction of theological language in this context? When grammar and things are so closely linked, the denial of any explicit knowledge of the being of God would appear to empty language of virtually all meaning. Indeed, it is often asserted that Thomas is profoundly influenced by the apophaticism of Maimonides and Ps.Dionysius. Assuming this influence and its "critique of linguistic immediacy," M. Jordan reads Thomas' theology as an interplay of a number of competing "languages" concerning the same divine reality.[9] Because God cannot be known by us, it seems that we must loosen our grip on any one way of talking about God. Holding too firmly to one system of language would be idolatrous insofar as such language falls short of "hooking on" to the being of God yet is wielded as though it does. The very multiplicity of "languages" in Scripture may be taken to show that there is no one correct theological language, and so even revealed languages "shatter against the divine."[10]

For Thomas, however, the fact that we name God as we know God results in neither a series of anthropomorphisms nor sets of terms or languages that are hopelessly metaphorical. He argues that terms of perfection "signify the divine substance and are predicated of God substantially."[11] We can signify the divine essence, although our signifying is not perfect. In other words, in those names we attribute to God, we must consider both the perfections signified and the manner of signifying. Such names are deficient in their manner of representation. For Thomas, certain terms do indeed signify God and do so properly, even though the connoted "mode" is according to our understanding and not according to God's manner of being.[12] Thomas explains:

---

9. M. Jordan, "The Competition of Authoritative Languages and Aquinas' Theological Rhetoric," *Medieval Philosophy and Theology* 4 (1994): 88.
10. Ibid., 89–90.
11. "Et ideo aliter dicendum est, quod huiusmodi quidem nomina significant substantiam divinam, et praedicantur de Deo substantialiter." ST I, q. 13, a. 2 c.
12. ST I, q. 13, a. 9 ad 2.

That by which a name is imposed for signifying is not always identical to the thing actually signified by the name. Just as we know the substance of a thing from its properties or operations, so we denote the substance of the thing itself.[13]

Linking our knowing and our naming of God does not mean that we cannot name God accurately. We know such things as stones by their effects but signify the thing itself in our naming. We signify God in the same way. That is, we signify God by means of effects, and such effects function as a definition.[14] Our naming is indeed limited because it follows the mode of being in our minds rather than God's mode of being God, yet the signification appears to be valid.[15] Thus we judge that certain perfections are in God, though in a more eminent manner than we can understand.

Reading Thomas' theology in the tradition of speculative grammar demands that one root all semantic import in the word's natural signification such that it can only "shatter against the divine." This view denies that language can function outside the realm of its natural modes. Hence, one must ask whether proposing such a context for Thomas' theology illumines his teaching or actually obscures it. In order to answer this question, we must investigate more thoroughly the nature of speculative grammar and Thomas' relation to it.

### 4.1.1 Speculative Grammar

The speculative grammarians, or "Modistae" as they came to be known, comprised a group of grammarians teaching in the University of Paris Arts Faculty between 1260 and 1350.[16] These speculative gram-

---

13. "Quod non est semper idem id a quo imponitur nomen ad significandum, et id ad quod significandum nomen imponitur. Sicut enim substantiam rei ex proprietatibus vel operationibus eius cognoscimus, ita substantiam rei denominamus . . ."; ST I, q. 13, a. 8 c.

14. Cf. ST I, q. 2, a. 2 ad 2; q. 13, a. 1 c.

15. ST I, q. 13, a. 9 ad 2.

16. The term "Modistae" was first used by J. Müller in *Anzeiger für deutsches Altertum* 25 (1878): 232–38, 352–55. For an overview of the texts of the Modistae, see M. Grabmann, *Mittelalterliches Geistesleben* I, 115–46. Grabmann assumed that speculative grammar was a much larger phenomomenon than is admitted today. Recent bibliogra-

marians had set aside humanistic or literary considerations and pursued their work entirely in terms of philosophy.[17] Grammarians such as Martin of Dacia, Michel of Marbais, and Siger of Courtrai focused on the relation between the modes of signifying and modes of being. Where there are two modes of signifying in grammar, these grammarians would argue for two corresponding modes of being. They read Aristotle's *Categories,* for example, as an introduction not to logic but to metaphysics. For them, the multiplicity of abstract modes of thinking demanded a corresponding multiplicity of modes of being, and it was the modes of being that really mattered. One could not be *merely* a grammarian. Animality, humanity, and personality were for them not merely ways of thinking about Socrates but ways in which Socrates *is.* Moreover, grammar was understood to be a distinct philosophical science whose principles can be investigated. One explained grammatical structures not according to classical usage but according to logic, and the logic of grammar was directly dependent upon the logic of things. In the hands of the Modistae, grammar ceased to be an art whose practice one must learn through imitation and instead became a science, a study whose rules can be known by their causes, by reference to things in themselves, *extra animam.*

One can easily identify the Modistae by their works, for these grammarians alone wrote treatises whose very subject was the modes of signifying. There are only slight differences among these texts, primarily that of greater clarification in the later writers such as Thomas of Erfurt and Radolphus of Brito. In the writing of the two most prominent members of the group, Martin and Boethius of Dacia, we can discern several key tenets: (1) the parts of speech have their causes in things; (2) the modes of signifying are derived from the modes of being as effects from their causes; (3) there is a direct correspondence

---

phy can be found in G. Wolters, "Die Lehre der Modisten," In *Sprachphilosophie. Ein internationales Handbuch zeitgenössischer Forschung,* edited by M. Dascal, K. Gerhardus, K. Lorenz, and G. Meggle (New York: de Gruyter, 1992), 596–600.

17. M. Grabmann, *Thomas von Erfurt und die Sprachlogik des mittelalterlichen Aristotelismus,* in *Sitzungsbericht der Bayerischen Akademie der Wissenschaften* (Munich, 1943), p. 77.

between the modes of being, the modes of understanding, and the modes of signifying; (4) assuming that art imitates nature, the parallels between the modes of being and modes of signifying constitute the grounds of a universal grammar.[18]

The Modistae believed that the science of grammar is universal in scope such that all languages share common structures and have only accidental differences among them.[19] It was not necessary to investigate other languages, because the argument was not empirical and, further, its claim of a scientific character excluded the possibility of a non-isomorphic view. It is also evident that in this view of grammar, questions of syntax and meaning, grammaticality and truth are inseparable. What is striking about the Modistae is their naive view of the universality of (Latin) grammatical froms and their insistence that such forms are natural. The Modistae's assumption that grammar is an independent science is one held in common with certain twelfth-century grammarians and therefore cannot be used as an identifying characteristic.[20] References to the modes of signifying are also not pe-

---

18. Cf. Boethius of Dacia's comment: "omnia idiomata sunt una grammatica. Et causa huius est, quia cum tota grammatica accepta sit a rebus - non enim potest esse figmentum intellectus; illud enim est figmentum intellectus, cui nihil respondet in re extra animam - et quia naturae rerum sunt similes apud omnes, ideo et modi essendi et modi intelligendi sunt similes apud omnes illos, apud quos sunt illa diversa idiomata, et per consequens similes modi significandi, et ergo per consequens similes modi construendi vel loquendi. Et sic tota grammatica, quae est in uno idiomate, est similis illi, quae est in alio idiomate." Boethius of Dacia, *Modi signficiandi sive Quaestiones super Priscianum majorem*, ed. J. Pinborg and H. Roos (Copenhagen, 1969), p. 12. Cf. also Thomas of Erfurt, *De modis significandi sive grammatica speculativa*, c. 4 in the works of Scotus, ed. Wadding, vol. 1.

19. R. Anderson takes exception to the modern reading of grammar as a science. The view of Bursill-Hall and Pinborg presupposes an extreme autonomy and separation of the sciences corresponding to the modern division of disciplines. Cf. Anderson, "Medieval Speculative Grammar: A Study of the Modistae," unpublished dissertation (University of Notre Dame, 1989), 11–25. The Modistae provoked censure precisely because they were admittedly not being *grammaticus purus* within the subordinate and practical art of grammar. Cf. J. Jolivet, "Comparaison des théories du langage chez Abélard et chez les Nominalistes du XIVe siècle," in *Peter Abelard*, ed. E. M. Buytaert (Leuven, 1974), 163–78.

20. This view goes back to Peter Helias' *Super Priscianum* of the mid-twelfth century. We use "independent" to signify the pursuit of grammar as a speculative endeavor

culiar to the Modistae as such, for they are found in Boethius, Peter Helias, and many scholastics, yet without the direct corresponding connection with things outside the mind. It is rather the extremes to which Modistae argue for natural grammatical structures that distinguish them from their predecessors.[21]

There is, of course, some debate on whether the Modistae actually identified the modes of signifying with the modes of being.[22] According to the research of Bursill-Hall and Robins, this very close linking of reality and language (including virtually all of its grammatical complexities) is the most salient feature of the Modistae. The Modistae's efforts to pursue semantic rather than linguistic explanations of grammar could not but lead to the question of the nature of things at every point of syntax. Bursill-Hall points out that the Modistae did not *equate* the different levels, and in one sense he is right. The later Modistae, Thomas of Erfurt and Siger of Courtrai, both mark a material separation between the modes of being, the active modes of signifying, and active modes of understanding. But whether their "material" or "formal" separations mitigate Boethius of Dacia's contention for a numerical correspondence is debatable, and we shall soon return to this question.

Boethius of Dacia insisted that the grammarian most properly considers both the modes of signifying and the modes of being. These

---

wherein the very explanation of its principles, rather than the perfecting of their use, is the aim of the grammarian. "Independent" does not mean that such speculative work is a terminal endeavor with no practical application or wider use. Mathematics can be used by the other disciplines, but this science does not of itself provide for such uses.

21. In fact, the concept of *modi significandi* and its relation to both the intellect and things can be found in Aristotle's *Perihermenias*. K. Buersmeyer observes that speculative grammar self-destructed under the weight of its own elaborate meta-language. Buersmeyer, "Aquinas on the '*Modi significandi*,'" *The Modern Schoolman* 54 (1987): 79.

22. Pinborg says, "certainly not." Pinborg's suggestion that none of the Modistae was so naïve as to hold to this identification theory because of the multiplication of realities appears to ignore the many discussions of this very question in Modistic texts. Cf. Pinborg, "Speculative Grammar," 262–63. Rosier, *La grammaire spéculative*, 58–62. On the other side of the question are Bursill-Hall (*Speculative Grammars*, 35), R. Robins (*Ancient and Medieval*, 79–87), and K. Buersmeyer ("The Verb and Existence," *New Scholasticism* 60 [1986]: 145–62).

modes are equally involved, being numerically equivalent and rooted in each other.²³ The pure grammarian cannot explain such properties causally, according to Aristotelian science, and so he pursues only the art and not the science of grammar.²⁴ Boethius argues that the one who considers the properties of speech ought also be a philosopher of the real.

[First], so that one may consider the properties of things from which the modes of signifying are taken and by which one imposes a word for signifying; [second] so that he may be able to consider the modes of signifying.²⁵

In order to consider the parts of speech, the grammarian must inquire into all the things that are signified. Thus, according to the Modistae, one must have some recourse to the properties of things that are themselves the cause of the modes of signifying. The modes of signifying themselves come from the properties of the thing.²⁶

Just as the modes of signifying differ, so it is necessary that the properties of things differ which are themselves designated by and are the basis of such signification. Every mode of signifying is taken from a [corresponding] property of the thing which the meaning of the word designates. [Thus] ... if some thing is sufficiently designated by a word, one mode of signifying always designates one property of the thing and [consequently] all the modes of signifying [some thing] would designate all the properties of the thing.²⁷

---

23. Cf. Boethius of Dacia's *Modi significandi*, in which many of the questions, especially from q. 11 to q. 39, address directly the connection between the three levels. For example, question 26 "utrum modi intelligendi, modi significandi et modi essendi sint penitus idem." Response: "quod res et intellectus et significatum non sunt idem penitus; differunt enim saltem in ratione, quamvis realiter sint idem." Later, he states that the predication of genus corresponds to a *modus essendi* or property (q. 49).

24. The conflict between the scientific and the literary study of grammar can be seen in Henri d'Andeli's allegorical poem "La Bataille des Sept Arts," which can be found in L. J. Paetow, *The Battle of the Seven Arts* (Berkeley, 1914), ch. 1.

25. "Debet enim esse philosophus realis, ut possit considerare proprietates rerum, a quibus modos significandi accipit, sub quibus vocem ad significandum imponit, et debet esse grammaticus, ut modos significandi possit considerare." Boethius of Dacia, *Modi significandi*, q. 12, p. 50; cf. q. 18, p. 68.

26. Grammar is a science because it has demonstrable and knowable causes, knowable by the intellect as immutable. Boethius of Dacia, Ibid., q. 17. Cf. Thomas of Erfurt, *Grammatica speculativa*, q. 3.

27. "[S]icut modi significandi dictionis differunt, sic oportet proprietates rerum,

Just as modes of signifying differ so the properties of the thing must differ one to one, being not identical but determinate and proportionate one to the other.

The modes of being are the properties of a thing as it is outside the intellect. The modes of understanding are the same properties according their being in the intellect.... The modes of signifying are the same properties as in the thing signified in diction.[28]

Every different mode of signifying has a corresponding mode of being. The study of the modes of signifying in this case draws upon the modes of being because the assumption of a universal grammar demands this very relation.[29] Grammatical distinctions are rooted in real things such that the distinctions correspond. The mind as a *tabula rasa* does not contribute to the distinctions. In fact, the mind's relative passivity with respect to the modes insures the truthfulness of speech.

Since the whole of grammar is taken from things—indeed it cannot be a figment of the intellect, to which nothing in the thing beyond the soul corresponds—and because the natures of things are similar among all, (therefore) the modes of being and the modes of understanding are also similar among all. [Thus,] even among those with diverse linguistic idioms, the modes of

---

quas circa significata designant et a quibus accepti sunt, differre. Quilibet enim modus significandi ab eadem proprietate rei est acceptus, quam circa significatum dictionis designat. Vide etiam diligenter, quod si aliquae res sufficienter per dictionem significatur, oportet quod semper unus modus significandi unam eius proprietatem designat et omnes modi significandi omnes eius proprietates." Boethius of Dacia, ibid., q. 17, p. 65.

28. "Modi autem essendi sunt proprietates rei secundum quod res est extra intellectum. Modi autem intelligendi sunt eaedem proprietates rei secundum quod res est in intellectu et ut eaedem proprietates cum re sunt intellectae. Modi autem significandi eaedem proprietates sunt in numero secundum quod res est significata per vocem." Martin of Dacia, *Modi significandi*, q. 4, pp. 19–20 and prol., p. 3. Cf. H. Roos, S.J., *Die 'Modi significandi' des Martinus de Dacia. Forschungen zur Geschichte der Sprachlogik im Mittelalter*, Beiträge zur Geschichte der Philosophie und Theologie des Mittelalters, Bd. 37, Heft 2 (Münster, 1952).

29. The attempt to formulate a universal grammar can be see as early as Peter Helias' *Summa super Priscianum* (c. 1150). L. Reilly, however, contends that Helias borrowed the idea of universal grammar from William of Conches, who wrote his *Glose* in two versions shortly before Helias. The identification of subject and substance paved the way for later discussions of the correspondance of various levels of modes. Cf. Reilly, "Introduction," 30–41.

signifying must be similar. Therefore, the modes of expression and speaking will also be similar. The whole of grammar that is in one idiom then must be similar to that in another idiom.[30]

If, in fact, the modes of signifying of our speech do not correspond to the being of things, then there is no basis for asserting the truth of our expressions. Our knowledge of things is accurate only to the extent that our intellect is a passive mechanism.

Differences in the grammar of languages are necessarily confined to "accidental differences." The Modistae note structural differences among languages but do not seem to have noticed any differences other than an article in Greek or the variety of inflections in nouns.

> Grammar is then the same with all essentially but diverse in its incidental forms.... That is, grammar is the same with the Latins and the Greeks. Therefore, it seems that grammar is essentially the same with all.[31]

There was simply no alternative but to pursue universal grammar, once the mechanics of signifying were attributed no longer to the active powers of the mind, but to things alone as causes. The perceiving mind communicates only what is perceived as it is perceived, i.e., as it is in reality.

---

30. "[C]um tota grammatica accepta sit a rebus - non enim potest esse figmentum intellectus; illud enim est figmentum intellectus, cui nihil respondet in re extra animam - et quia naturae rerum sunt similes apud omnes, ideo et modi essendi et modi intelligendi sunt similes apud omnes illos, apud quos sunt illa diversa idiomata, et per consequens similes modi significandi, it ergo per consequens similes modi contruendi vel loquendi. Et sic tota grammatica, quae est in uno idiomate, est similis illi, quae est in alio idiomatae." Boethius of Dacia, *Modi significandi*, q. 2, p. 11.

31. "[Q]uod grammatica est eadem apud omnes essentialiter, est tamen diversa apud omnes accidentaliter.... Idem enim secundum speciem modus sciendi grammaticam est apud Latinos et Grecos. Ergo videtur, quod grammatica secundum speciem et essentialiter sit eadem apud omnes." Johannes of Dacia, *Summa Grammatica*, in *Johannis Daci Opera*, ed. A. Otto and H. Roos (Geneva: G.E.C. Gad, 1955), v. I, p. 54. His reasoning on this matter is typical of the Modistae: "Item grammatica est accepta a rebus, nam ipsa non est figmentum intellectus, quia figmento nihil respondet a parte rei extra animam. Sed nature rerum sunt eadem secundum speciem et essentialiter apud omnes, ergo et earum proprietates, que sunt modi essendi, a quibus accipiuntur modi intelligendi et per consequens modi significandi et postmodum modi construendi." Ibid., p. 55.

This activity of the mind is most evident in the Modistic distinction of passive and active modes of understanding and signifying. One of the last speculative grammarians, Radolphus of Brito, developed the distinctions between the active and passive modes to explain the problem of words signifying non-existent things.[32] The passive modes of signifying refer to the *thing* as understood by the mind. The passive modes of understanding refer to the *property* as it is grasped by the mind. These two passive modes are only formally distinguished from the modes of being of the subject in question. The active modes, on the other hand, allow for the activity of the mind in taking the modes of being of one thing and applying it to another. The active modes of signifying are properties of the word, and the active modes of understanding are properties of the thing as understood by the intellect. The mind can signify a substantial mode of being in the case of a non-existent such as blindness, because the mode of being is in the mind. The mode of understanding is in this case the mode of being.[33] Boethius of Dacia argues that such non-existents are patterns of thought derived from other really existent things. Yet the fact that blindness has no real mode of being leads Boethius to conclude that it has no real mode of signifying. Because the intellect must follow the properties of a thing, modes of understanding not rooted in some mode of being are not true modes.[34] For that reason, this solution to the problem of non-existents serves to reinforce the correspondence between modes of signifying and the modes of being.

According to later Modistae, the knowing and signifying subject is

---

32. It is noteworthy that Pinborg's study of the Modistae relies quite heavily upon this rather late figure, who alone among the Modistae does not affirm a one-to-one correspondance between word and thing.

33. Boethius admits, however, that certain things such as chimeras do not have a *modus essendi* outside the soul. In that case, the *modus essendi* signified is itself the *modus intelligendi*, i.e., in the soul. Cf. Boethius, *Modi significandi*, q. 20, p. 73.

34. "[N]on enim potest sibi fingere tales modos significandi. Unde cum res per suas proprietates sibi determinat modos intelligendi, ita quod non possit intelligi sub modis intelligendi, qui repugnant suae proprietati, intellectus enim intelligendo, sequitur rem in essendo, . . . ergo proprietates rerum sibi determinant modos significandi." Boethius, *Modi significandi*, q. 17. See also q. 20, p. 72.

not entirely passive. The active modes of understanding are based upon the properties of the intellect,[35] and the active modes of signifying are based upon the properties of the word itself.[36] On the other hand, these active and passive distinctions are not alternatives but distinctions within the intellective and significative processes. Formally, we can distinguish the properties of the thing from the properties as they are understood and as they are signified. But this awareness of the different modalities[37] should not obscure the identification of the modes signified and the real properties of things. The identity of language and reality remains. This correspondence reflects the Modistic assumption that the causes of grammar lie outside grammar itself, in reality, and are therefore derived from the structure of reality rather than being due to the plurality of our ways of thinking about things, in addition to the structure of reality. The alternative is not to divorce ways of speaking from ways of being, but to admit a more complex relationship in which our "levels of abstraction" need not correspond to levels of being in the thing.

Given this portrait of Modistic teaching, it may seem difficult to imagine why this tradition is so often invoked as a profound influence upon Aquinas. The many recent studies and editions of speculative grammars have not dampened the enthusiasm with which Thomas and other masters of theology are implicated with the Modistae.[38] Even the acknowledgment that Thomas did not know their technical elaborations, and consequently the texts themselves, has not prevented scholars from proceeding as if Thomas had been in contact

---

35. Cf. Thomas of Erfurt, *Grammatica Speculativa*, q. 13.

36. This particular notion goes back to twelfth-century writings of Helias, Abelard, and others, in which the signification of a word is a broad range of actual and possible uses determined by the word itself. William of Conches was the first to argue that words have basic and figurative uses such that the intention of the user also determines the semantic value of a term by inserting it into ever new contexts.

37. That is, intentional existence in the mind vs. existence in the thing, the former being permanent, e.g. Boethius, *Modo significandi*, q. 26.

38. Jordan contends that Abelard's relation to the Modistae is seen in the fact that he views the modes of significations as modes of the words themselves and not as they are used. It is the consideration of the sense of words rather than their reference that gives rise or at least roots these modes. Cf. Jordan, "Modes," 408–9.

# The Question of Context

with this movement and eagerly drew upon their teaching. One scholar simply assumes that "the larger development of semantic speculation which is evident in the *Modistae* did not escape [Thomas'] notice."[39] It is not clear, however, whether "being noticed" is anything like "being an influence."

### 4.1.2 Historiographical Considerations

Several factors have contributed to the general association of Thomas with the speculative grammarians of his day. A misattribution in the manuscript tradition, for example, planted the idea in Thomas' readers. A particular *Grammatica speculativa* of uncertain origin was attributed to several scholastic theologians, including Aquinas.[40] Another *Tractatus de modi significandi* was attributed to Thomas' arts master, Master Martin. The solutions to these errors in the secondary literature some sixty-five years ago have not curtailed the perpetuity of the idea that Thomas was greatly influenced by speculative grammar; the seed had already taken firm root.[41] Scholars have used the citation of the misattributions themselves as justification for continued association. Hence, the very possibility of these errors of attribution is offered as a kind of proof that the relation is real even if not demonstrated in that way.[42] On the other hand, in many of his

---

39. Ibid., 410. Park pursues a similar line of reasoning in his *Mittelalterlichen Sprachphilosophie*, 72–81.

40. One Breslau manuscript from the fifteenth century (Cod. IV, Q 81b) attributes a commentary on an anonymous *Tractatus de modis significandi* (known under the name *Grammatica speculativa*) to Thomas Aquinas. The *Tractatus* itself was for centuries attributed to Scotus—see note 4 above.

41. M. Grabmann was the first to note that the *Tractatus* was in fact a work by Thomas of Erfurt. Cf. Grabmann, "De Thoma Erfordiensi Auctore Grammaticae Quae Ioanni Duns Scoto Adscribitur Speculativae," *Archivum Franciscanum Historicum* 15 (1922): 273–77. Cf. also *Thomas von Erfurt und die Sprachlogik des mittelalterlichen Aristotelismus*, Sitzungsberichte der Bayerischen Akademie der Wissenschaften, Philosophisch-historische Abteilung, Bd. 2 (Munich, 1943). More recently, S.-C. Park cites a dubious *De modalibus* and the contemporaneity of Thomas and certain modistae as sufficient evidence of positive influence. Park, *Die Rezeption der Mittelalterlichen Sprachphilosophie*, 58–81.

42. Contrary to later citations, Grabmann never said that the *Tractatus* itself was falsely ascribed to Thomas Aquinas, only the commentary notes. There really was no

texts, Thomas uses the terminology so integral to Modistic thought.[43] Thus, while problematic, associating Thomas with speculative grammar is not without foundation.

The interest in speculative grammar has grown dramatically since the 1960s.[44] The recent appearance of a number of critical editions of grammatical works from the twelfth and thirteenth centuries has greatly increased our knowledge of this field. We know much more now about the Modistae and also about the development of grammar in the crucial stages of change in the twelfth and thirteenth centuries. The increasing precision with which some describe the speculative grammarians, however, has generally not led to any clarification of the earlier assumptions regarding the influence of this group. Speculative grammar as such is often invoked in arguments concerning the reading of Thomas and not explained. It is quite fair to ask then, what is "speculative grammar" when invoked as the background for reading scholastic theology?

The general characterization of speculative grammar offered by Grabmann some seventy years ago focused on the terminological sim-

---

"tradition of misattribution" prior to Grabmann's article. The myth of a Thomistic *Grammatica speculativa* was established and perpetuated by the misreading of Grabmann's article. Cf. for example, Bursill-Hall, *Speculative Grammars*, 34, n. 79; Cunningham, "Speculative Grammar," 76. The presence of the name "Thomas" would, of course, lead some to assume the great saint, but in actual fact only one manuscript indirectly suggests that Thomas Aquinas wrote a *Grammatica speculativa* (Melk, Cod. 181, f. 158). This manuscript, however, was not included in Grabmann's work but only in a 1952 study of Martin of Dacia. Cf. H. Roos, S.J., *Die 'Modi significandi' des Martinus de Dacia*, Beiträge zur Geschichte der Philosophie und Theologie des Mittelalters. Bd. 37, heft 2 (Münster, 1952), p. 40, n. 5. On a speculative grammar misattributed to Albert, see O. Meersseman, O.P., *Introductio in Opera Omnia Alberti Magni* (Bruges, 1931), 143; on Scotus, see P. O. Schafer, O.F.M., *Bibilographia de vita, operibus, et doctrina Joannis Duns Scoti*, vol. 1 (Rome, 1955), pp. 1–50, nn. 2038, 4977.

43. Cf. ST I, qq. 13 and 39.

44. Bursill-Hall outlined the state of current scholarship in this field in his "Toward a History of Linguistics in the Middle Ages, 1100–1450," in *Studies in the History of Linguistics*, ed. D. Hayes (Bloomington: Indiana University Press, 1974), 77–92. A bibliography of recent work can be found in William of Shyreswood, *Introductiones in Logicam*, trans. and comm. H. Brands and C. Kann (Hamburg: Felix Meiner, 1995), 317–20; also in S.-C. Park, *Die Rezeption der Mittelalterlichen Sprachphilosophie*.

ilarities between Arts faculties and Theology faculties in the late thirteenth century.[45] Following the foundational work of Thurot, Grabmann argued that the essential change in grammatical method from literary to logical considerations can be traced back to Abelard and William of Conches.[46] Abelard was one of the first to focus on the signifying power of words as determinative of the logical meaning of grammatical structures. Grabmann assumed that speculative grammar encompassed a broad range of persons, including R. Bacon and R. Kilwardby, and consequently had a measurable effect on the Theology faculty.[47] This broad classification of speculative grammar has subsequently been corrected on some points, yet Grabmann's argument for the centrality of logic in speculative grammar has been largely accepted. Thus, one can measure in some sense the move to-

---

45. This less-strict manner of referring to speculative grammar probably played a role in Grabmann's willingness to suppose that the Magister Martinus, Aquinas' arts master, mentioned by William of Tocco, was in fact Martin of Dacia. Grabmann in this early stage of studying the modistae overestimated the scope of this movement. Cf. M. Grabmann, *Mittelalterliches Geistesleben* I (Munich, 1926), 141–46, 250–51. His student, H. Roos, argued against this identification in his *Martini de Dacia Opera* (Copenhagen: G. E. C. Gad, 1961), xxxviii.

46. Ch. Thurot was the first to view Ablard as the pivotal figure in the development of grammar. *Notices et extraits de divers manuscrits latins pour servir à l'histoire des doctrines grammaticales au moyen âge* (Paris, 1868). And see M. Grabmann, *Mittelalterliches Geistesleben* I, 104–46, esp. 113–15.

47. Bacon and Kilwardby both advocated a universal view of grammar, at least in part. Kilwardby was also a grammarian of the first rank, working out many of the distinctions that would become part of Modistaic teaching. It is probably their assumption of the universality of grammar that gave them the appearance of Modistae. See R. H. Robins, *Ancient and Mediaeval Grammatical Theory in Europe* (Port Washington, N.Y.: Kennikat Press, 1971), p. 77f. They did not share, however, with the Modistae the pursuit of semantic explanations for syntax. For an example of the persisting tendency to define speculative grammar very broadly, see L. G. Kelly, "God and Speculative Grammar," in *L'Héritage des grammariens latins de l'antiquité aux lumière*, ed. I. Rosier (Louvain: Peters, 1988), 205–13. Kelly seems unaware of the value of aesthetics in medieval argumentation. He frequently identifies as demonstrative grammatical arguments that are in fact arguments from convenience. The medieval thinker, on the other hand, took great pleasure in finding congruence between the truth of some thing and its accidental properties. Grammar is no proof of such truth, but where the grammaratical form of a given term coheres with the argument, it is integrated. The result is a more complete, unified, and beautiful portrait of the subject under discussion.

ward Modistic teaching by the degree to which grammar became logic.[48]

The second generation of scholarship, represented by Fredborg, Pinborg, and Bursill-Hall, contends that the development of grammatical study from Peter Helias to the Modistae is a linear development encompassing scholastic work in general and is, in the real sense of the word, a "culmination" of scholastic reflection on language.[49] The narrative of these scholars' thesis dates the genesis of speculative grammar to the introduction of logic, as did Grabmann.[50] Grammarians turned to logic to explain grammatical features, on the assumption that the causes of the parts of speech were extra-linguistic and extra-mental. Speculative grammar then developed as it included more and more grammatical features within the domain of logic. Whereas Helias discussed the natural correspondence of nouns and verbs to things in the world, the later Modistae discussed adjectives, prepositions, and the gender of nouns in this way.

According to Pinborg and Bursill-Hall, grammar developed from Abelard to Aquinas in two stages:[51] (1) William of Conches' and Peter Helias' attempts to join grammar and dialectic in their work on systematic grammar; (2) Robert Kilwardby's and Roger Bacon's consoli-

---

48. L. J. Paetow reviews this period of change in the study of grammar and judges it to be one of decline with respect to language and the arts in general. What was proposed as grammar from about the midpoint of the thirteenth century was, according to Paetow, only logic. Paetow, *The Arts Course at Medieval Universities with Special Reference to Grammar and Rhetoric* (Champaign, Ill., 1910), 43ff.

49. Cf. K. M. Fredborg, "The Dependence of Petrus Helias' *Summa super Priscianum* on William of Conches' *Glose super Priscianum*," *Cahiers de L'Institut du Moyen-Age Grec et Latin* (CIMAGL) 11 (1973): 1–57; Bursill-Hall, *Speculative Grammars*; J. Pinborg, *Logik und Semantik im Mittelalter* (Stuttgart: Friedrich Frommann Verlag, 1972); and *Die Entwicklung der Sprachtheorie im Mittelalter*, Beiträge zur Geschichte der Philosophie und Theologie des Mittelalters, Bd. 42, Heft 2 (Copenhagen: Verlag Arne Frost-Hansen, 1967). Cf. also L. G. Kelly's review of Bursill-Hall's *Speculative Grammars* in *Canadian Journal of Linquistics* 18 (1973): 177–81. Kelly contends that Bursill-Hall's arguments are over-reaching due to his lack of acquaintance with scholastic teaching.

50. See also R. W. Hunt, "Studies on Priscian in the Eleventh and Twelfth Centuries," *Mediaeval and Renaissance Studies* 2 (1950): 39ff.

51. Pinborg, *Die Entwicklung*, 20–29, 55–56; Bursill-Hall, *Speculative Grammars*, 31–36.

dation and refinement of the earlier work. The idea of grammar having its causes in the properties of things, and the consequent goal of formulating a universal grammar, were both prevalent in grammatical treatises prior to the Modistae. The Modistae then are viewed as only the latest and best among speculative grammarians, proposing the most well-developed and technical system of grammar. By taking the coupling of logic and grammar as the essential feature of speculative grammar, one can draw a line of intellectual influence from Helias and Abelard to Boethius of Dacia, the earliest of the Modistae. The larger group (speculative gramarians) is identified by the logical concern with grammar and with the way words mean first and foremost as opposed to the art of word use. It is not so much the conclusions but the common questions and terms that define the target group and its antecedents.

This approach unfortunately has the consequence of grouping together Helias and Abelard—whereas in fact the latter disputed the relation between grammaticality and truth. That relation is not debatable for the later Modistae. For the Modistae, grammaticality concerns truth, because the modes of signifying are explained causally with reference to the properties of things. Helias, like the Modistae, contended that grammaticality or the grammatical sense of the text includes a consideration of reality. A noun, for example, signifies all members of that class, both real and potential. A sentence is meaningful only if it refers to something in the world. Terms of second intention (e.g., species) then refer to something in the individuals even if that something does not exist separately. Thus, one predicates natures of things because such natures inhere in things. Abelard, however, kept separate the questions of grammatical and logical sense.[52] He contended that

---

52. De Rijk defends Abelard against the charge that he used logic indiscriminately to determine the truth about the world. According to De Rijk, Abelard's foremost concern was with the truth of expressions, the accuracy of propositions, and distinguishing between valid and invalid arguments. Logic then must refer to the state of things in the world, at least as the world is known on the physical level. Abelard, for example, determines the proposition "p is true" to be equivalent to the proposition "the state of affairs referred to by p exists." L. M. de Rijk, *Logica Modernorum: A Contribution to the History of Early Terminist Logic,* vol. 2/1 (Assen: Van Gorcum, 1962–67), 52.

intellection is merely the multiplication of considerations that do not actually penetrate anything. Nouns signify existent things, but verbs have only to do with the intellect conceiving, grasping, considering, etc. Verbs then have no conceptual import. Second intentions are likewise functions of the mind on the basis of similarity. Nothing in actuality is signified other than the group of individuals.[53] Hence, Abelard argued that saying 'Socrates is an animal' is like saying 'Socrates is a stone.' Predicating genus is similar to unreal predications, i.e., acts of the mind only.[54] Proposing that grammar is generally conventional, Abelard argued that the modes of human understanding as well as the properties of things are the causes of the modes of signifying. How the Modistae define modes of signifying is unique precisely because they explain such modes almost entirely in terms of things in themselves, outside the mind. No predication is merely the act of the mind without real causes in things.

Alongside the work of Grabmann, Pinborg, and Bursill-Hall, there has been another trend in scholarship, which views the Modistae as very distinct not only from their predecessors but also from their contemporaries. We find this trend in the work of M.-D. Chenu, who contends that the Modistae are distinguished especially by their claim to have insight into the being of things.[55] Chenu locates the beginning of speculative grammar in the twelfth-century debate on the semantic unity of temporally conditioned propositions. In that debate, Bernard

---

53. Such a view contrasts with that of Helias, in which sense and reference are not strongly contrasted but, like the view of the later Wittgenstein, all uses of the word are included; i.e., its meaning is the complex of uses. Thus even connotation and denotation are included in this simple apprehension. Thus, Helias disagrees with William of Conches in seeing a basic significate and then related figurative uses. Cf. L. Reilly, "Introduction" to Peter Helias, *Summa super Priscianum*, vol. I, ed. L. Reilly, C.S.B., in Studies and Texts 113 (Toronto: Pontifical Institute of Mediaeval Studies, 1993), 1–41.

54. Abelard also juxtaposed these sentences in order to show genus predications are more like unreal predications than like accidental predications. And though the inherence theory finds its way into Abelard's work, it is the identity theory that is prevalent, especially when the issue is confronted directly. Cf. De Rijk, ed., *Dialectica. First complete edition of the Parisian manuscript* (Assen: Van Gorcum, 1970).

55. Reilly, "Introduction," *Summa super Priscianum*, 1–41; M.-D. Chenu, *La théologie au douzieme siècle* (Paris: J. Vrin, 1957).

of Chartres argued that the element of time is irrelevant in questions of truth. The propositions "Socrates will run," "Socrates runs," and "Socrates ran" all have a semantic unity signifying the same thing, differing only according to our connotation of time, which is accidental to the truth of the sentence. According to Chenu, certain thirteenth-century theologians criticized this supposed semantic unity by pointing to the inescapably temporal character of our knowing and signifying. They claimed that the diversity of our ways of understanding the same reality determines the diversity of our modes of signifying. Moreover, the element of time is included in the judgment of truth and is therefore essential. "Christ has come" is not true at a certain time prior to the actual event.

> The laws of truth in our mind are not established solely by the mind itself and its psychological modes. The more radical and weighty consequences of this are in [the mental acts of] composition and division, the abstractive procedure and the temporality of judgment. [That is], by composing and dividing, one (co)understands time.[56]

What is at stake is the fundamental correspondence between the modes of signifying and the modes of being. The interplay of the element of time indicates that our understanding, our point of view as knowing subject, impacts the semantic value of a statement.

In his 1957 work, *La théologie au douzieme siècle*, Chenu offers a somewhat corrected form of his earlier thesis on this subject, especially on the theologians' use of grammar.[57] He dropped the notion that the scholastics were pursuing speculative grammar and referred instead to their observation of grammatical rules. The scholastics' insight was precisely to follow the rules of grammar and the rules of theology according to their respective subjects and not to allow one to rule the other. The theologian should not alter proper syntax, nor should the grammarian suggest insights into theology on the basis of grammar. Grammar was not ousted from the speculative sciences or

---

56. M.-D. Chenu, "Grammaire et Théologie aux XIIe et XIIIe Siècles," *Archives D'Histoire Doctrinale et Littéraire du Moyen Age* 10 (1935): 21.

57. Compare Chenu, "Grammaire," 8, with *La théologie*, 91.

from theological work but was limited such that it was not allowed to "command" theology. Chenu argues,

> the rules of Donatus do not govern theology, for the mystery thwarts them. Sacred doctrine employs them as servants, as means for pentrating the word of God. Yet the more that theology is faithful to its transcendent object, the more that grammar must abide by its own laws. . . . In the twelfth century, it was those who practiced the better grammatical critique who were likely to be the better theologians.[58]

No longer did Chenu see the twelfth century as the first stage in speculative grammar.[59] In fact, the influence of Bernard of Chartres was sharply curtailed not so much by Thomas and other theologians in the thirteenth century but by Gilbert of Poitiers, Alan of Lille, and Jean of Salisbury in the twelfth century. It was, in fact, Gilbert who transposed the epistemology of Bernard of Chartres by analyzing the modes of signifying according to an Aristotelian psychology of forms.[60] By showing the way that grammar functions as opposed to what theology claims, this grammatical critique remained quite useful for theologians. Thus we say one thing according to our modes of signifying but we mean it in a special way according to our modes of understanding. Grammar provides insight into our way of thinking, not God's way of being. The triumph of theology consists in treating and using grammar according to its laws.[61]

Unfortunately, in many recent studies, there has been a tendency to classify the development in grammar prior to the Modistae as "speculative grammar" in a loose sense or as "pre-Modistic" as in Chenu's earlier work.[62] The growing knowledge about the Modistae

---

58. Chenu, *La théologie*, 107.     59. Chenu, "Grammaire," 28.
60. Chenu, *La théologie*, 96.     61. Ibid., 91.
62. Cf. *Grammatica Speculativa of Thomas of Erfurt*, ed. and trans. G. L. Bursill-Hall (London: Longman, 1972), 18f. Pinborg also reserves the term 'modistae' to signify the particular group from 1260 to 1320. Hence, he discusses Thomas only within the larger category of 'speculative grammar.' J. Pinborg, *Entwicklung der Sprachtheorie im Mittelalter*, in Beiträge zur Geschichte der Philosophie und Theologie des Mittelalters, Bd. 42, heft 2 (Münster, 1967), 30–45. See also Pinborg, *Logik und Semantik im Mittelalter: Ein Überblick* (Stuttgart: Frommann-Holzboog, 1972), 88–101.

and the development of grammar during the twelfth and thirteenth centuries has led to an artificial separation of the terms "speculative grammar" and "Modistae." What Chenu realized was that the arguments, as well as a fuller terminology, were virtually confined to the University of Paris and especially to the Arts Faculty. There were some proponents of a Modistic-like view of grammar, such as Bernard of Chartres. Yet many in the twelfth century opposed such a view. The Modistae are the revival of one side of this conflict; not a culmination but an aberration of grammatical thought in the late thirteenth century. It is doubtful then, according to Chenu, whether masters of theology such as Thomas who received their arts education from other institutions would have been directly influenced.[63] Also, the only evidence of influence between these two faculties is quite contrary to the one commonly assumed. It is more likely that the junior Arts faculty took their cues from the senior Theology faculty and not *visa versa*.[64] One need only consider modern graduate and undergraduate faculties at any major university to see the simple logic involved here. Of course, pointing out problems in the secondary literature is not itself a demonstrative argument.

### 4.1.3 Development of Grammar

As Chenu has pointed out, an important factor in considering the relation of Thomas to speculative grammar is the actual development

---

63. Thomas studied the arts in Naples under Master Martin and Master Peter of Hibernia. Cf. J. A. Weisheipl, O.P., *Friar Thomas D'Aquino* (Washington, D.C.: The Catholic University of America Press, 1983), 17. Albert pursued his arts studies in Germany prior to entering the Dominican house of Saint Jacques. M. Entrich, O.P., *Albertus Magnus* (Cologne: Verlag Styria, 1982), 16ff; Bonaventure went through the Arts faculty in Paris (1236–41) but was too early to have been influenced by the earliest of the Modistae, Boethius of Dacia (Master of Arts c.1265 at the earliest).

64. The later Modistae, such as Siger of Courtrai, often quote Thomas. Siger cites him heavily in his commentary on the *Perihermenias*. Gauthier suggests that Martin of Dacia also borrowed from Thomas as he pursued his own commentary on Aristotle's *Perihermenias*, especially in book *Lambda*. Thomas Aquinas, *Opera*, Leonine edition, p. 72. For Siger of Courtrai's extensive borrowing from Thomas, see P. Verhaak, *Zeger van Kortrijk Commentator van Perihermeneias* (Brussels, 1964), pp. cxxxiii–cxl.

of grammar up to the time of the Modistae. If one does not assume that Modistic grammar was the "culmination" of grammatical development, other ways of interpreting similarities can be seen. From the time of William of Conches, many authors applied logic to the study of grammar.[65] Throughout the twelfth and thirteenth centuries, one can find discussions of the modes of signifying. What sets the Modistae apart is their philosophical view—namely, that grammar in its complete form can be universally understood and demonstrated by its cause in things in themselves. With some of their predecessors, they shared the idea that grammar was a science and that some syntax (noun and verb) has its causes in things. Moreover, both Peter Helias and the Modistae held an *inclusive* view of the relation between grammaticality and sense. A sentence could not be called correct syntactically without also being true logically. Others such as Abelard proposed an *exclusive* view whereby a proposition could have a coherent sense but not be true, i.e., not refer to anything in the world.[66] Syntax is in that case somewhat distinguished from logic.

These two groups, however, seem to share a common view of word use. Helias, Abelard, and the Modistae held that words naturally have a range of meanings. The meanings of words are said to be "complexive" of the word. All meanings or significates, both potential and real, are included connotatively. Some uses of a word are broader than others. Helias, for example, argues at length against the tendency in logic to restrict the meanings of words. He does not make his case by distinguishing proper and metaphorical uses but maintains a broad range of meanings according to a broad range of actual uses.[67] Others,

---

65. R. W. Hunt was the first to point out that the early twelfth century saw the influence of grammar on logic and the later half saw a reversal of that influence. Cf. R. W. Hunt, "Studies on Priscian in the Twelfth Century," *Mediaeval and Renaissance Studies* 2 (1950): 1–56.

66. Abelard also held a correspondingly strict view of the work of the grammarian vs. that of the logician.

67. Cf. Reilly, "Introduction," in *Summa super Priscianum*, 19–28. Abelard, on the other hand, argues that this range of meanings is restricted to the words themselves, their "natural supposition." From 1300 onward, the proposition rather than the term became fundamental. Cf. L. M. De Rijk, "The Development of *Suppositio naturalis* in Medieval Logic," *Vivarium* (1971): 71–107.

such as Helias' predecessor William of Conches as well as a number of scholastic theologians, would argue that a word has certain basic meanings and other metaphorical meanings. The intention of the user can determine new uses for a term in a different context. This procedure then allows a greater range by reason of intention such that language is seen as a pliable tool for communication.[68]

We then have two key sets of factors in distinguishing views on grammar: (1) exclusive vs. inclusive view of the relation between syntactic sense and reference to extra mental reality; and (2) complexive vs. basic/metaphorical signification. Including only those figures who are normally included in the retelling of the development of grammar, we can distinguish three identifiable groups.[69] For ease of reference, we offer the divisions found in Diagram 1. Note that the key axis extends from "universal grammar" (upper left) to "social linguistics" (lower right) thereby providing a key orientation for all four groups such that the positions of Abelard (group 3) and Aquinas (group 2) are closely related in the whole schema though distinct among themselves.[70]

Based upon the assumed connection between grammatical sense and truth (inclusive vs. exclusive) and the principle of coordination for a word's many uses (complexive vs. basic), we can discern three branches in medieval grammar. Members of the first group, consisting of the Stoics, Helias, and the later Modistae, do not separate sense

---

68. This view does not exactly correspond to Jordan's "inert tokens," because the basic meaning of the word, or rather the *ratio significata*, is retained. Cf. Jordan, "Modes," 408.

69. The fourth category is occupied only by certain modern linguists and is not relevant for our purposes except as a corrective showing what cannot be the case for medieval thinkers. NB: The list in each group is not meant to be complete. The membership consists simply of important representative figures, those normally included in these discussions.

70. B. Whorf's social linguistics can be seen as the polar opposite to universal grammar. Popularizing E. Sapir's thesis that each language shapes the conceptual world of its speakers, Whorf argued that one learns not only a language but also a way of thinking from one's community. The structure of thought itself is in that case conventional. Cf. J. A. Lucy and J. V. Wertsch, "Vygotsky and Whorf: A Comparative Analysis," in *Social and Functional Approaches to Language and Thought*, ed. Maya Hickman (Orlando: Academic Press, Inc., 1987), pp. 67–85.

DIAGRAM 1

| Universal Grammar | Inclusive view of grammar and truth | Exclusive view of grammar and truth |
|---|---|---|
| *Complexive Signification* | Modistae (Arts Faculty) Helias  Stoics      1 | Abelard  Ockham      3 |
| *Basic and figurative significations* | William of Conches  Thomas Aquinas (and other thirteenth-century Masters of Theology)      2 | Whorfian Social Linguistics      4 |

from reference; neither do they separate grammar from questions of logic. Moreover, a word can have many different uses, none of which essentially change the word or threaten equivocation, because the word's meaning is the complex of these uses. The basic semantic unit then is the sentence, in which the individual words find definite meaning.

The second group, consisting of William of Conches[71] and Thomas Aquinas, differs from the first in attempting to define a word's basic meaning as opposed to the more figurative uses. Likewise, a word's signification is at least partly determined by its use in a proposition. For instance, the metaphorical use of the term 'anger' in reference to God is allowed because the strange, non-literal context can alter the term's signification. Hence, signification is directed as much by the word as by the speakers' imposition of the word in a particular context. The first group, on the other hand, would contend that the term is no less proper in any one context but reveals the breadth of the term's uses.

---

71. Cf. K. M. Fredborg, "Some Notes on the Grammar of William of Conches," *Cahiers l'Institut du Moyen-Age Grec et Latin* 37 (1981), pp. 21–28. For a survey of William's thought and relevant bibliography, see H. R. Lemay, "The doctrine of the Trinity in Guillaume de Conches' Glosses on Macrobius: texts and studies" (unpublished dissertation from Columbia University, 1972).

The third group consists of Abelard, Ockham, and possibly Radolphus of Brito.[72] This group is defined particularly by the subordination of word use (sentences or propositions) to signification. A word must signify a really existing thing in order to be used in a true proposition. Second-order terms such as species terms then signify the individuals collectively. With this separation of meaning and reference, the rules of grammar and logic are no longer intertwined as they are in the Helias-Modistic tradition. Far from drawing upon grammar, logic was upheld as the more autonomous method of inquiry.

This schema illustrates the fundamental differences between Thomas and the Modistae on the one hand and between Thomas and Abelard on the other. The common reading of the development of speculative grammar, beginning with the co-mingling of grammar and logic in the mid-twelfth century and culminating in the universal claims of the Modistae, smoothes over such differences. Abelard himself stated that he was concerned only with words and not with the nature of things. Abelard's statement comes at two very important places in his *Dialectica:* in the context of terms signifying non-beings (chimeras), and in the discussion of universals.[73] Abelard takes exception to those who multiply abstract beings and speak of the being of universals, i.e., as inhering in a subject yet being *per se* one. Along the same lines as his teacher, Roscelin, Abelard contends that essential natures have no being of their own. Words signify by reason of human intellection. For example, our intention to signify a group displaying some similarities is the basis for genus and species predication. There is no essential correspondence between language and reality. On this

---

72. For Abelard's discussion of the priority of signification over construction, see his *Dialectica*, 125ff. Radolphus, as the last of the Modistae, does appear to have distanced himself from the earlier formulations of Boethius of Dacia. Pinborg's heavy reliance upon Radolphus would explain in part his disagreement with Bursill-Hall and Robins on the fundamental tenets of speculative grammar. Cf. J. Pinborg, "Some Syntactical Concepts in Medieval Grammar," *Classica et Mediaevalia Dissertationes* IX (1973): 501ff.

73. *Logica Modernorum*, vol. III, ed. DeRijk (Assen, Van Gorcum, 1962–67), 388 and 286. These contexts match exactly that of Boethius of Dacia and Thomas of Erfurt's consideration of the linking of words to things.

point it is clear that Abelard is no speculative grammarian and disagrees fundamentally with those who are in fact the philosophical predecessors of the Modistae (e.g. Bernard of Chartres, William of Champeaux). The notion of a universal grammar does not emerge from Abelard's work for the very reason that he endeavored to distance the logical meaning of grammar from the structures of reality.

In the broader narrative of the development of grammar, it is useful to link Abelard and Aquinas in their shared attempt to provide a sophisticated way of distinguishing and managing the relation between our speech and the being of things by means of our active and passive intellectual acts. Where they part ways is in the degree to which our understanding attains to the being of things. The pursuit of metaphysics has no real place in Abelard's system of thought except as an exercise in logic. Genus and species refer only to classes of individuals who are determined to share certain traits. Such predication is based on likeness rather than unity: as a white horse and a white man are both white, so Socrates and Plato are both human.

Thomas, like the Modistae, views the mind as a *tabula rasa*, in which there are powers both active and passive.[74] For Thomas, however, these powers, in addition to the being of things, are the basis for a multiplicity of modes of understanding. The mind's activity in composing, separating, and reasoning on the basis of sense objects produces images in the mind that do not correspond to the being of the thing itself.

The similitude of the thing is in the intellect according to the mode of the intellect and not according to the mode of the thing. Thus, the [conceptual] composition and division of the intellect correspond to something on the part of the thing [known] but such is not in the thing in the same manner as in the intellect.[75]

---

74. ST I, q. 84, a. 3. Thus, the being of the thing in the intellect is not equal to the being of the thing itself. Cf. ST I, q. 85, a. 5 c.

75. "[Q]uod similitudo rei recipitur in intellectu secundum modum intellectus, et non secundum modum rei. Unde compositioni et divisioni intellectus respondet quidem aliquid ex parte rei; tamen non eodem modo se habet in re sicut in intellectu." ST I, q. 85, a. 5 ad 3.

The sophistication with which Thomas describes the functioning of the intellect in regard to the being of things is seen in his division of the sciences. Only in physics does the mind consider things as they are in matter and in motion. In all other sciences, the mind considers things abstracted from their very mode of being in matter.[76] The speculative sciences are distinguished according to the different ways the mind abstracts or separates the subject from matter and motion. This division according to intellectual procedure is a decisive point of difference between Thomas and the Modistae and between Thomas and Abelard.[77] The division guides one's reasoning in each science, thereby determining the scope of logic. Logic is neither a distinct science nor the blunt instrument of all sciences. Rather, logic functions according to the nature of each science.[78]

Thomas argues that we can consider things only in terms of matter because our knowledge begins in sensibles. We cannot know insensibles directly, but only by means of and in terms of sensibles—Creator only in terms of creatures.[79] Hence, our mind is not a completely passive power standing in utter potency to whatever is, but whatever is in matter or known by means of matter (as effects).[80] For that reason, Thomas centers his discussion of naming God on the premise that our modes of signifying are not equivalent to God's mode of being.

The differences among these groups reveal the divergence of opinion on fundamental matters concerning our knowledge of the world and our ability to signify it. One's views on the priority of signification

---

76. Thomas, *Super librum Boethium De Trinitate*, q. 5, aa. 1 and 3.

77. For Thomas, we have a natural capacity for metaphysical inquiry, although we know such insensibles by means of the sensible.

78. The speculative sciences are defined according to their method: *rationaliter* in the natural sciences, *disciplinaliter* in mathematics, and *intellectualiter* in metaphysics. Cf. Thomas, *Super Boethium*, q. 6, a. 1.

79. ST I, q. 13, a. 1 c.

80. ST I, q. 88, a. 1 c. The mind is dependent on recourse to phantasms and hence, without such cognition, we are not able to know anything. However, the proportion of immaterial things to material things allows us to know the latter by way of negation, namely, in terms of what they do not have. Cf. also Aquinas, *Sentencia Libri De anima* III.4, lect. vii.

and supposition (or meaning vs. use), the principle of coordination for the range of a word's use, and the relation between [grammatical] sense and [logical] reference all profoundly influence one's understanding of grammar. Those who hold to a basic/figurative coordination of word use are in fundamental disagreement with the Modistae. The Modistae connect word and thing according to their modes, such that the idea of a figurative use would be a violation of that relation. The figurative use of a term in modistic grammar would not be a function of human experience and would consequently be set loose from the mooring in reality that guarantees its truth.

Likewise, those who, like Abelard, separate grammatical and logical pursuits are distinguished from the Modistic investigation of grammar as a means of understanding reality. This point is most readily seen in Abelard's discussion of the distinction of divine Persons. By giving full reign to logic, his investigation proceeds only on the basis of demonstrable truths; logic, as the grammar of the mind, cannot in any way learn from revelation because that would constitute the subjection of logic to another grammar, to another terminology. Neither the literary constructions of grammar nor the revealed names for the divine Persons can add anything to logic. Revelation is only another way of speaking, not the identification of truths not yet and otherwise unknowable.[81] Abelard's logical nominalism forces him into a corner with regard to revelation. Just as the acts of the mind cannot be trusted to attain to truths beyond the senses, so verbal revelation cannot be assumed to reveal unknown realities. Divine names are ways of talking about what is already known about God, i.e., mere mental constructions for communication. What cannot be demonstrated, cannot be revealed by another speaker, human or divine.

This division of groups also highlights the differences between Modistic and Thomistic word use. For both, the propositional context

---

81. On a related note, Abelard can be seen as the forerunner of the Gilsonian reading of verbs. Cf. E. Gilson, *Being and Some Philosophers* (Toronto: PIMS, 1952). For both, the verb is a judgment of the mind and not a concept, hence, the verb "is" by itself means nothing. According to Thomas, the verb has a conceptual force, for the first thing grasped by the mind is being. Cf. R. McInerny, *Being and Predication,* 173–228.

for the word is important for determining signification, but less so for Thomas. According to Thomas, human language can be extended to communicate revealed truths. The connoted modes of creaturely being or the modes of signifying in human discourse must, of course, be denied as repugnant to the divine reality, but language can be directed and clarified by its revealed use.

### 4.1.4 The Theological Conflict

The central difficulty with assuming a Modistic background for Thomas' philosophy of language is that there is no room for the acknowledgment of radical imperfection, no room for an "apophatic critique." The admission of imperfect knowing and signifying robs Modistic grammar of any and all semantic value. Modistic modes of signifying are derived from and caused by the modes of being, the properties of things. The mind as a *tabula rasa* and passive instrument is not moved except by things. Hence, the human speaker, according to the Modistae, cannot signify in a manner that is repugnant to things.

> Since through its own properties the thing determines for itself the manner in which it is understood, the thing cannot be understood in a manner that does not correspond to such properties. Indeed, the intellect in its understanding follows the thing in its being; and through these modes of understanding, the modes of signifying are determined. The modes of signifying are then likenesses of the modes of understanding. The modes of signifying then follow the modes of understanding, for the former cannot be without the latter. Therefore, the properties of things themselves determine the modes of signifying [them].[82]

Without access to the modes of being, there is no guarantee of the truth of language. To say that the modes of being of the subject in

---

82. "Unde cum res per suas proprietates sibi determinat modos intelligendi, ita quod non possit intelligi sub modis intelligendi, qui repugnant suae proprietati, intellectus enim intelligendo sequitur rem in essendo, et per suos modos intelligendi determinat sibi tales modos significandi, qui sunt similes illis intelligendi; modi enim significandi sequuntur modos intelligendi et sine illis non sunt possibiles, ut de se patet - ergo proprietates rerum sibi determinat modos significandi." Boethius of Dacia, *Modi significandi*, q. 17, pp. 64–65; see also, q. 114.

question cannot be known is to eliminate any real possibility for speech, for any predication whatsoever.

This point can be seen in a related context. The idea of a universal grammar means that ordinary syntax—nouns, verbs, adjectives, and so forth—is directly related to things and their properties as effects to their cause. The way one talks about a given thing is not the work of the mind perceiving, considering, abstracting, separating and grouping things. For the Modistae, either the mind is perceiving something as it is, or the mind is being deceived. The Modistae refer to the active modes of understanding, but by this term they mean the property of the thing *as* understood, and thus they make only a formal distinction between the property in the thing and in the understanding mind.[83] In a very real way then, things in the world determine the way we talk about them and the way we signify them. Concrete and abstract modes of signifying correspond to different modes of being and are not results of operations of the mind. Without access to the modes of being, the mind remains immobile. Pointing out the imperfections in our naming of God calls into question the truthfulness of language, if one assumes that the modes of signifying are dependent upon the modes of being. To signify falsely is precisely to signify something not according to its own modes of being, the properties of the thing.[84] Eliminating this direct causal connection between our modes of signifying and God's mode of being renders any theological discourse seriously suspect, if not vacuous.

---

83. See, for example, the causal link from thing to intellect to speech: "quod quaedam sunt, quae habent esse extra animam, quae, si intelligantur ita quod intellectus intelligendo illa non errat, habent modos intelligendi secundum suos modos essendi, ut quilibet modus intelligendi apud intellectum sit proportionalis modo essendi in re ipsa, et ut distincti sint modi intelligendi secundum distinctionem modorum essendi; oportet etiam, quod modi significandi in dictione sunt proportionales modis intelligendi et modis essendi talium rerum; non enim possunt tales res intelligi et significari contra repugnantiam suarum naturarum." Boethius of Dacia, *Modi significandi*, q. 20, p. 72.

84. "Ideo cum talis proprietas non est possibilis naturae rei, ideo modus significandi similis illae proprietati non est possibilis dictioni rem talis naturae significanti eo quod modi signficandi dictionis debent esse compossibiles rei significatae; aliter enim posset res significari eo modo, quo ipsa non posset intelligi, quod patet esse falsum." Boethius of Dacia, *Modi significandi*, q. 56, p. 146.

When we call God just, wise, good, etc., we are, according to Thomas, signifying the same thing by means of diverse modes of understanding, and these do not correspond to diverse modes of being. The properties are not multiple in God but only in our understanding.[85] The Modist would object that "every intellect understanding a thing other than it is, is false."[86] For the Modistae, the modes of signifying and understanding must come directly from the properties of things. According to Modistic grammar, then, if theological speech is not completely grounded in the divine reality, it is meaningless.[87] What can we be signifying with such terms as 'God,' 'deity,' 'wise,' 'powerful,' if we do not have direct conceptual access to God's mode of being?

Thomas answers that the intellect does not understand things according to their modes of being but according to its own mode of being. The intellect understands material things immaterially. In a similar way, the intellect understands God who is simple according to the intellect's own composite mode of being. Our intellect even understands itself under diverse conceptions, but it knows that all these conceptions correspond to one and the same thing.[88] In speech about God, the modes of signifying are dependent upon the modes of understanding, yet the latter do not correspond to the divine reality so much as to our own mode of being. The three levels of modes in Thomas cannot be equivalent, because our signifying and our understanding fall short of the [modes of being of] divine reality. In one sense there is a diminishment of truth from being to understanding to signifying. In another sense, revelation provides language that is more true than we can understand. Hence, in answer to the question, can we signify better than we understand, Thomas would say "no and yes." The answer is not as simple as some have conceived it.[89]

---

85. Cf. ST I, q. 13, a. 4.
86. ST I, q. 13, a. 12, obj. 3.
87. ST I, q. 13, a. 2, obj. 3.
88. ST I, q. 13, a. 12 c; cf. q. 13, a. 9.
89. Cf. E. J. Ashworth, "Can I Speak More Clearly Than I Understand?" in *Studies in Medieval Linguistic Thought,* ed. K. Körner, H. J. Niederehe, and R. H. Robins (Amsterdam: John Benjamins B. V., 1980), pp. 29–39. Ashworth argues that Thomas equates the level of understanding with the accuracy of signifying, while Henry of Ghent represents the Augustinian view that we understand better than we can signify. She then opposes these two views to that shared by Scotus and Ockham, who contend that we can easily denote more accurately than we understand, just as a child may signify ac-

## 4.2 The Question of Character
### 4.2.1 The Doctrine of Divine Names

An important element in this discussion is the character of Thomas' theological language, that is, its apophatic character. It is a well-known axiom of Thomas' theology that we do not know what God is, but we know what God is not. On this point, he is influenced by Maimonides and Ps.Dionysius. Maimonides claims that any affirmation about God is better understood to be a negation of sorts. To call God "living" is really to say that God is not like an inanimate object.[90] Ps.Dionysius likewise contends that no name (or attribute) can be equal to the truth about God, yet his denial of the accuracy of such names is not absolute.[91]

According to Ps.Dionysius, Scripture itself provides a hierarchy of names that apply more or less to God. The use of creaturely metaphors, for example, is meant to prevent crude anthropomorphisms. Obviously, God is not a lion but exhibits the strength and instills fear like a lion.[92] The more distant an expression is from perfect immate-

---

curately or "denote" the sun with a word without understanding much at all about the sun.

90. Cf. ST I, q. 13, a. 2 c.

91. Unfortunately, some scholars have failed to see the important differences between Maimonides and Ps.Dionysius and have unnecessarily supposed that Thomas adopted the whole of each one's teaching on divine naming. When Thomas cites one, we should not assume that he means both.

92. Cf. Ps.Dionysius' argument in the *Divine Names:* "We must not dare to resort to words or conceptions concerning that hidden divinity . . . apart from what the sacred scriptures have divinely revealed. . . . We are raised up to the enlightening beams of sacred scriptures, and with these to illuminate us, with our beings shaped to songs of praise, we behold the divine light." *Divine Names,* ch. 1, 588A–589B, in *Pseudo-Dionysius,* trans. C. Luibheid in *Classics of Western Spirituality* (New York: Paulist Press, 1987), p. 50. Scriptural symbolism is indeed ultimately denied because the divine is not a thing to be described, but the words of Scripture are useful for training and directing one's gaze in preparation for the heavenly experience of contemplation without such symbols.

For a critical survey of the secondary literature, see J.-M. Hornus, "Les recherches récentes sur le pseudo-Denys l'Aréopagite," *Revue d'Histoire et de Philosophie Religieuses* 35 (1955): 404–48. For more recent works, see W. J. Carroll, "Pseudo-Dionysius the Areopagite—A Bibliography: 1960–1980," *Patristic and Byzantine Review* 1 (1982): 225–34.

rial being, the more easily it is seen to be metaphorical and not literal. Perfection terms such as 'good' and 'one', however, require a more sophisticated noetic. God is not named "good" as Socrates is called "good," that is, conforming to a norm other than one's own self and that can be measured more or less. Moreover, because God is simple, perfections must preexist in God as one. And yet even these perfections are, according to Ps.Dionysius, more truly denied because they are said properly not of God but of creatures.[93]

The difficulty in understanding Thomas' doctrine of divine names is determining the force of the negative critique. Is it a negation of knowing or of signifying? Must we set aside our conceptions or our speech? If Maimonides' categorical denial of the accuracy of divine names applies to all theological language, there would be no grounds for Thomas' concern, expressed on his deathbed, about his teaching on the Eucharist. In effect, any number of ways of speaking or "languages" about the Eucharist would be equidistant from the metaphysical reality, the truth of things. If, on the other hand, apophaticism is understood in noetic terms, then the use of words, especially such revealed use of terms, may provide guidance to our rational reflection. According to Thomas, the force of Ps.Dionysius' teaching pertains foremost to Scripture.[94] One may approach the ineffable divine mystery with the surety that Scripture does speak in the language of men, but it also signifies the divine reality. Revelation itself would be empty if its "language" did not in fact reveal the truth about God, i.e., "what is necessary for our salvation."[95] Scripture then teaches that God truly has such perfections. Further, one's explanation of that mystery will be more or less true as it approaches such truth. God is cause, then, not in the Plotinian sense of an emanating monad but in the Christian sense of a knowing and loving God, who causes as a willful, free Creator who is one with his being and whose being is the very definition of wisdom and goodness because substantially so.

---

93. Cf. *Divine Names*, ch. 2.
94. By using what Scripture has disclosed, "we are raised upward toward the truth of the mind's vision, a truth which is simple and one." Ps. Dionysius, *Divine Names*, ch. 1, 592C; cited by Thomas, ST I, q. 1, a. 9 ad 3.
95. Cf. ST I, q. 1, a. 1.

One not uncommon way of interpreting Thomas' apophaticism is to say that there can be no real relations between words and things in theology. In other words, if we assume that words signify concepts directly and things secondarily, the failure of comprehension is fatal to theological language. Our ignorance of divine reality, God's mode of being, prevents our words from signifying meaningfully. Theological language then can function only rhetorically—not informing the mind but simply provoking a change in the will.

In response to this kind of reading, we may point out that Thomas does not propose that our words merely signify our concepts. Rather, words signify things by means of the "mediated conception of the intellect."[96] Moreover, (and this is especially important in the context of our discussion of the possible Modistic influence on Thomas) "words do not signify things directly according to the mode of being which they have in reality, but indirectly according to the mode in which we understand them."[97] Hence, we can separate things in our mind and in our speech that are in fact united in reality. We may speak about a property such as "redness" in the abstract because we think of it abstractly, yet we are not signifying a separate thing (a being). What we signify has being only as an accident in a substance: concrete instances of "red." Moreover, one's ability to signify "red" is not dependent upon a complete conceptualization and understanding of color and the particular properties of what is seen as red in the light spectrum. The mediating conception can be more or less rich, and the significative power of the expression remains the same. This point is evident in that the power of linguistic expression is not limited to the power of the speaker's conceptualization. For example, a child on the deck of a ship may point and call out, "Whale," at which time a biologist on the ship may hear and immediately bring to mind a very sophisticated set

---

96. "Et sic patet quod voces referentur ad res significandas, mediante conceptione intellectus." ST I, q. 13, a. 1 c. Cf. Aquinas, *Expositio Libro Peryermenias* I, lect. 2; *Sententia super Metaphysicam* IV, lect. 16 (652); V, lect. 22 (1133); VI, lect. 4 (1224).

97. "[M]odus significandi vocum non consequatur immediate modum essendi rerum, sed mediante modo intelligendi." Aquinas, *Super Metaphysicam* VII, lect. 1 (1253). Cf. ST I, q. 34, a. 1 c; *De veritate*, q. 4, a. 1.

of notions regarding the probable type of whale in this part of the world, its purpose for breaching, and so forth. The child's ability to signify with the word is not limited to his simple understanding. The child may think that the whale is a big fish, that it is "playing," that it is "smiling," etc., but the child's exclamation is no less accurate in signifying. The word signifies both thing and concept, or rather, one by means of the other.[98]

Applying this example to theological language, we can see that an imperfection in conception does not necessarily negate the applicability of a term. Our understanding of the one whom we call wise and good may contain errors regarding the manner of conceiving God being wise and good, yet the names still apply. Thomas argues:

> With respect to the names that we attribute to God, there are two things to consider; namely, the perfections signified such as goodness, life and others; and [secondly] the manner of signifying. Regarding what these names signify, they literally and more properly said of God than of creatures [because] they are said of God first.[99]

Such names are not "convenient" to God in regard to the way we understand them. What is signified, however, is not our conception but things by means of our conception. Moreover, the understanding is not identical to the meaning of the word, or rather with what the word signifies. A word signifies both the concept and the thing, although one or both may be erroneous. We name such and such because we understand such and such to be something for which we have a word or words, and we wish to communicate that understanding. But if we are communicating only a concept, we are each one hopelessly trapped

---

98. If the word signified the concept, and the concept signified the thing, the child's use of the term "whale" would presumably evoke in his audience the same simple concept of "whale" as a big fish. This is clearly not the case, for his audience will have a variety of different conceptions depending upon their experience of the thing itself. Cf. J. O'Callaghan, *Thomistic Realism and the Linguistic Turn: Toward a More Perfect Form of Existence* (Notre Dame: University of Notre Dame Press, 2003) 26–29.

99. "In nominibus igitur quae Deo attribuimus, est duo considerare, scilicet, perfectiones ipsas significatas, ut bonitatem, vitam, et huiusmodi; et modum significandi. Quantum igitur ad id quod significant huiusmodi nomina, proprie competunt Deo, et magis proprie quam ipsis creaturis, et per prius dicuntur de eo." ST I, q. 13, a. 3 c.

in our own minds and each person's language is his own. God is unlike anything else we know, and therefore other conceptions are no help to us for purposes of comparison and relation.

Thomas argues, however, that names such as 'good' do signify the divine in some way. We cannot know how, but we do know that such perfections are truly said of God in the sense that they actually do signify the divine. The meaning of calling God "good" is not limited to "God is the cause of goodness" or "God is not evil" but that "what we call goodness in creatures, preexists in God."[100] God is the cause of goodness in the world precisely because God is goodness and diffuses such goodness into the world. To say that goodness is "in" God in a more excellent way or "preexists" in Him is indeed to make an affirmation about God. The name "good" applies literally and properly to God, being more truly said of Him than of creatures. God is known among creatures by God's creative diffusion and our participation. What Thomas denies of God is the way in which our minds conceptualize such goodness, i.e., in a limited and accidental way. Because we understand divine things according to the modes of created things, we must separate such modes from our understanding and our signifying.[101] Thus, on the basis of revelation, the word is more accurate than we can imagine, not less so.

### 4.2.2 Analogous Predication: More Than Grammar

In order to substantiate this point, we return now to the analogical character of theological language as Aquinas presents it. Having discussed his views on grammar, we are in a better position to understand what is at stake. Theological language is a very particular kind of analogy, yet its peculiar nature is not evident in all of Aquinas' discussions. A treatment that draws only from the *Summa contra Gentiles*, for instance, will be inadequate for defining the function of theological language as a particular use of analogy. In this work, Thomas proposes to set forth the truth of the Catholic faith through demonstration.[102] He marks a clear division in the structure of the four-part

---

100. ST I, q. 13, a. 2 c.
101. Cf. ST I, q. 39, a. 2.
102. Cf. *Summa contra Gentiles* (abbreviated ScG) I, ch. 2.

work between truths knowable by reason and truths known by revelation. Truths known by revelation are reserved for the fourth book.[103] The overtly philosophical procedure of the *contra Gentiles* has important consequences for the discussion of divine names. Arguing that theological language is not simply metaphorical, Thomas points out that "as far as what is signified by perfection names, the name is accurate."[104] The mode of the perfection signified, however, is defective in its inaccuracy. The reason is this: we know perfections in created things where such perfections are distinct from the created nature. We can only signify perfections abstractly as forms or qualities, but God is simple, without distinction between substance and quality. Because we cannot conceive or signify a perfection existing in an eminent way, we deny the term on account of the manner of signifying." Everything predicated of God is said essentially, and that is possible through the circumlocution of negation.

Our speech about God, however, cannot be simply one of equivocation. When we construct arguments from creatures to God and name God analogously, we understand something about God.[105] In the *contra Gentiles* Thomas states that a term is analogous when it is said "according to an order or a certain respect to some one thing." One use is dependent upon or made by means of the other.[106] He describes this order in two ways: (1) "being is said first of substance and then of accident both according to nature and the meaning of the name"; and (2) "what is first according to nature is posterior according to cognition."[107] These two orders describe two processes of predication, not two types of analogy. For instance, we know that medicine

---

103. That is, the doctrines of the Trinity (Bk. IV, chs. 1–26), Incarnation (27–55), sacraments (56–78), and the final end of humans (79–97).

104. "[Q]uantum ad illud ad quod significandum nomen fuit impositum." ScG I, ch. 30.

105. "Frustra aliquod nomen de aliquo praedicatum, nisi per illud nomen aliquid de eo intelligamus." ScG I, ch. 33.

106. Rather than by an ordering of two things to some third. Thomas makes this point in the other texts. Its importance will become evident shortly.

107. "[E]ns dicitur prius de substantia quam de accidente et secundum naturam et secundum nominis rationem." "[Q]uod est prius secundum naturam, est posterius secundum cognition." ScG I, ch. 34.

is healthy by its effect in the animal. As the cause, medicine is first called "healthy," but the meaning of the term refers foremost to the animal. In the same way, we know God according to effects and yet are cognizant that such perfections are first in God as cause.

What is apparent from this argument is that the nature of the medicine is not in any way known. By its positive effect in the animal, we cannot know if it is solid or liquid, its contents or anything else except that it is the cause of health in the animal. Transferring this example directly to theological language raises some questions. The effect of medicine in an animal is not a property of the medicine itself but a result of an interaction with a sick subject. Is goodness predicated of God in this way? Are we merely affirming a causal power in God to produce goodness in the world? What we have is a correlate of the proof for the existence of God, only through goodness. In that sense, we have not moved beyond the five proofs offered in ST I, q. 2, whose conclusions are "what we mean when we say 'God.'"[108]

Thomas' discussions in his commentary on the *Sentences* and in the *Summa theologiae* are more complete in this sense: they include divisions of analogous predication that are not simply causal. In the *contra Gentiles*, we find only two divisions according to the priority of the name's meaning in the first or second analogate known. In his commentary on the *Sentences* we find a threefold division of analogous predication: (1) according to intention only and not according to being; (2) according to being only and not according to intention; and (3) according to intention and according to being.[109] The first point to be noticed about this division is that the two orders found in the *contra Gentiles* are both in the third division here. The ordering of predication with regard to knowing is secondary, because in this *Summa* the discussion of analogy is an explanation of the way theological language works, not a justification for speech about God. Also, the fact that a particular term is used analogously "does not entail the assertion that the denominating form is in all or only one of the analogates."[110]

---

108. That is, we call the First Cause "God." ST I, q. 2 c.
109. Cf. *Super Sent.* I, d. 19, q. 5, a. 2.
110. McInerny, *Being and Predication*, 281.

By showing the distinctions in the broader arena of analogical predication, Thomas is able to root theological language in divine reality more directly. It is important, however, that he separates theological predication from the notion of common nature or participation. The order is of one thing to another and not to a third thing. The first and third divisions listed above are accordingly both illustrated with the example of 'health.' One can call both medicine and urine "healthy" by their order to the healthy animal, for they are either the cause of or sign of such health.[111] The order of medicine and animal with respect to health is, however, a particular instance of analogical predication. The one is ordered to the other as cause to effect, and yet the health of the animal is not essentially dependent upon medicine but simply can, when lost, be restored by medicine. When names are said of God and creatures, however, Thomas argues that the "denominating form" is in both, though the proper meaning is only in one. The theological use of analogy is not based upon an accidental or intentional order of things. It is a particular kind of analogy in which one thing is named according to an essential order to another. An animal can be healthy at some time without medicine, but a person cannot be good or even exist without God, the good to which he is ordered.

This discussion of analogy is a part of the discussion of divine names and is contextualized by the discussion of naming in general, i.e., the way in which names do and do not signify God. The mediating role of our conception in signification, the inescapably composite character of our language, as well as the accuracy of our signification with respect to what is signified but not how it is understood and signified—all these are on the table prior to the introduction of analogy. The discussion of analogy then answers the question, not of how we can speak about God, but how such speech is meaningful.

One way of understanding the use of terms for two different subjects is to see one being the cause of the property in the other. In that case, however, it is difficult to tie the proper meaning of a term to God. Healthy said of medicine indicates something about medicine's

---

111. Cf. ST I, q. 13, a. 5.

causal power only. Names are not said of God and creatures merely as "cause of" and "subject of," as in the case of health said of medicine and the animal. Good said of God is far more than a description of causal power. When we call God "good," we also mean that such perfection is in God truly.

Note in the example of 'healthy' that the proper meaning remains in the animal and not in the medicine which causes the health in the animal. "Subject of" and "cause of" are not the same in this example. In a striking way Thomas turns this very argument in ST I, q. 13, a. 5 into an objection in a. 6. He then answers the objection with the point that such predication is not said essentially. Divine names, however, are said causally and essentially of God. We are not ignorant of the nature of God in the way that we are ignorant of the medicine known only through the cured animal. The denial of accuracy in naming God serves as a reminder that we signify better than we know, better than we can understand, for the truth of the predication, the proper meaning, is in God even though it exists in a way that is beyond our comprehension.[112]

Aquinas describes the analogical nature of theological language precisely in order to affirm our ability to speak meaningfully about God. Just as "whale" in the mouth of a small child and in the mouth of the biologist is equally applicable, so the name "good" is equally applicable when I use it of God and when Jesus said it of the Father, even though the latter most certainly possessed a corresponding perfect concept of such goodness.[113] Our imperfect conception does not demand that we deny the application of the word but only our way of using it according to imperfect concepts, just as we would deny the connoted anthropomorphisms in the child's signifying of the whale.

---

112. This point is then rather different from the Augustinian apophaticism in which things are more truly than we understand and more truly understood than signified. Cf. Augustine, *De Trinitate* V, prol.

113. On another level, with regard to our self-expression, we understand better than we can signify. Just as the biologist may have trouble putting all of his experience and study of the whale into finite speech, so I will have trouble expressing what I understand about God being good. My experience of God can be richer than a finite explanation of it. Hence, theological writing is by definition incomplete and endless.

The name "good" signifies God properly even though the manner in which it signifies, as a predicate inhering in a composite individual, is improper. But one may ask whether the term so qualified actually applies, or should it in all honesty and more truly be denied? It is neither an easy nor a trivial question to ask: When Thomas calls certain terms "analogous," do they actually "hook up with" the divine reality? Or do they merely indicate certain conceptual gymnastics that really do "shatter against the divine"?

Thomas answers these concerns about the content of such predication by demonstrating the continuity of our naming in ordinary and theological speech. We name as we know, God included. To illustrate this principle, Thomas uses a rather mundane example, that of stone *(lapis)*. We impose the name by reason of our experience of its effects, i.e., hurting the foot *(laedens pedem)*.[114] We name the thing by its effects rather than by means of some insight into the essence. Or in a more technical sense,

> That by which a name is used for signifying differs from what the name is used to signify. [For example] the name *lapis* (stone) is used because it hurts the foot *(laedit)*, yet the name is not used to signify "hurting the foot" but for signifying that certain type of body that does hurt the foot. Otherwise everything that hurt one's foot would be a "stone."[115]

We know by means of a quality or effect and name the thing by means of it. Our signifying then is made with reference to the thing itself, although by means of a quality. In a similar way, our naming of God refers to the divine nature by means of the divine effects. We know God through the fact and goodness of creation and so name God "Creator" and "good." We do not signify stone with the sense of "hurt-

---

114. The etymology is perhaps stretched in this case, but the point is made all the more striking by using an example in which the very name takes its form from the effect in addition to signifying by means of it.

115. "[A]liud est quandoque a quo imponitur nomen ad significandum, et id ad quod significandum nomen imponitur, sicut hoc nomen *lapis* imponitur ab eo quod laedit, non tamen imponitur ad hoc significandum quod significet *laedens pedem*, sed ad significandam quandam speciem corporum, alioquin omne laedens pedem esset lapis." ST I, q. 13, a. 2 ad 2.

ing the foot" nor do we signify God as life in the sense of "life proceeds from this one." Just as we mean to indicate the stone itself by our naming, we intend in our naming of God "to signify the very principle of things just as life preexists in Him although in a more eminent manner than it is understood or signified."[116] Our naming of God is not radically different from our naming of things in the world. And for that reason, we can be confident that our language signifies the divine nature, even though we know that nature by means of effects.[117]

We cannot, on the other hand, know the nature of God in the way that we may come to know the nature of a stone through observation and investigation of the object itself. We cannot, for instance, know the composition of God as we know the composition of a stone, because God is not composite or available to our senses. Yet there is a sense in which the essence of the stone as such always looms in the distance. An explanation of its composition and its many effects does not attain necessarily to the truth of the stone's unity. Thus, the qualification that we cannot know God must be seen in its proper light. To say that God is good and wise, for example, is to affirm something about God essentially without any pretense of being comprehensive and final.

## 4.3 Conclusion

Reading Thomas within the tradition of speculative grammar has noticeable consequences for Thomas' theological language, especially when one moves to Thomas' more strictly theological works. If one assumes that words correspond to things numerically in their modes, the denial of accuracy in speech is a judgment that both concepts and words are cut adrift from any hold on the divine reality. When the modes of signifying are considered to be inseparable from words themselves, the denial of "linguistic immediacy" leads to a failure of speech altogether. Theological language would then conform to

---

116. "[S]ed ad significandum ipsum rerum principium, prout in eo praeexistit vita, licet eminentiori modo quam intelligatur vel significetur." ST I, q. 13, a. 2 ad 2.

117. Cf. ST I, q. 12, a. 13, ad 1.

Whorf's "social linguistics" whereby persons are merely agreeing to use a certain language in a certain way without it being in any way rooted in the truth of things. Ordinary and revealed language would both be unable to signify the truth about God because all manners of speaking would be equally inadequate. If, on the other hand, we can separate what is being signified from the modes of our signifying, then deficiencies or inaccuracies in the latter do not undermine our signifying altogether.

# 5. Naming God
## The Heart of the Matter

Granted that Thomas' characterization of theological language is not strictly tied to the being of things themselves, one might argue that it is too loosely connected. After all, as we noted in the previous chapter, Thomas is dependent upon the sometimes radical apophaticism of Maimonides and Ps.Dionysius. In fact, for many scholars, the Ps.Dionysian influence provides grounds for a rather severe apophaticism in Thomas. The assumption is that the mystical character of Dionysian symbols precludes any definite communicable meaning. Ps.Dionysius' characterization of theological symbols is often compared to Augustinian signs to highlight the negativity in the former's theology. But just as a whole is not the same as the sum of its parts, so a particular theological position is not the same as the sum of its influences. The influence of Ps.Dionysius on the theology of Thomas Aquinas is certainly no longer in dispute, but the character of that influence is not at all settled.

From Ps.Dionysius' *Divine Names*, Thomas identifies three ways of naming God: by negation, causality, and eminence.[1] On the questions of whether we can name God, or whether some name is said of

---

1. Thomas, *Super Librum Dionysii*, ch. 7, lect. 4. Cf. *Super Sent.* I, d. 3 div. textus; d. 22, q. 1, aa. 1 and 2; d. 35, q. 1, a. 1; *Summa contra Gentiles* I, chs. 14 and 30; III, ch. 49; *Super Boetium De Trinitate* q. 1, a. 2; q. 6, a. 3; *Ad Romanos* I, 6 (117); *De potentia* q. 7, a. 5 ad 2. Throughout this discussion, I will translate the Latin terms *remotio* and *ablatio* as 'negation.' As Wolfson has demonstrated, the difference between the terms is minimal and concerns their original contexts and not their use in these discussions. Cf. Wolfson, "Saint Thomas on Divine Attributes," in *Mélanges offerts à Étienne Gilson* (Toronto: PIMS, 1959), 673–700.

God properly, Ps.Dionysius is the central authority in Aquinas' first major work, his commentary on the *Sentences*.[2] When we turn to a similar discussion in his *Summa Theologiae*, however, we are met with a rather surprising discovery.[3] Thomas refers to Ps.Dionysius eight times in his discussion of divine naming, but none of the references are central to the articles themselves.[4] That is to say, nowhere in these twelve articles does Thomas make an argument based upon the *Divine Names*. Indeed, texts from Ps.Dionysius appear to function as counterparts to Thomas' own arguments, serving not as authority but as principal opponent. By way of contrast, Thomas' citation of Ps.Dionysius in the remaining 42 questions of the treatise on God is overwhelmingly in the response section, very often on par with Augustine in being used to interpret Scripture.[5]

Why did Thomas not use Ps.Dionysius as a central authority in his most focused treatment of divine naming?[6] This question becomes more striking in light of Thomas' frequent reliance upon the Areopagite's authority in virtually all of his writings.[7] Moreover, Thomas wrote a commentary on the *Divine Names* either a few years before he began the *Summa Theologiae* (in Orvieto, 1261–65) or simultaneously with the first part (in Rome, 1265–68).[8] Not only the subject matter

---

2. Also, *Super Sent.* I, d. 4, q. 2, a. 1, and d. 8, q. 4, a. 3 (citing *Divine Names*, ch. 7). Cf. also, d. 2, q. 1, a. 2; d. 8, q. 4, a. 3; d. 22, q. 1; d. 34, q. 3.

3. ST I, q. 13.

4. The sole citation in the body of an article is a definition serving only to corroborate the central authority and preceding argument. Two other citations are presented as responses to Ps.Dionysius' own text. Cf. ST I, q. 13, a. 3.

5. Of the 36 times Thomas cites Ps.Dionysius in the remaining questions of the treatise *De Deo* (ST I, qq. 1–43), he employs Ps.Dionysius as an interpretative authority 25 times, in the *sed contra*, main argument, or response sections, often to interpret Scripture itself (an honor usually reserved for Augustine). See, e.g., ST I, q. 1, a. 9; q. 4, a. 2; q. 6, a. 1,. Even this small survey of citation reveals the anomolous character of Thomas' use of Ps.Dionysius in ST I, q. 13.

6. A comparison of similar discussions in the *Sentence* commentary, for example, reveals that Thomas was quite willing to quote Ps.Dionysius throughout even several times in the course of a single argument. Cf. *Super Sent.* I, d. 22 passim; d. 34, q. 3. Also, *De potentia* q. 7, a. 5.

7. Cf. J. Durantel, *Saint Thomas et le Pseudo-Denis* (Paris, 1919), 60–207.

8. J.-P. Torrell, *Saint Thomas Aquinas*, trans. R. Royal (Washington, D.C.: The Catholic University of America Press, 1996), vol. I, 127–29, 346; J. A. Weisheipl, *Friar*

but also the timetable of Thomas' education and scholarly work would suggest that Ps.Dionysius' *Divine Names* was at the forefront of Thomas' mind at the time. Why then at the point where Ps.Dionysius' relevance is most obvious, does Thomas hold his authority at arm's length? What is Thomas doing here and why?

One possibility, of course, is that Thomas is merely repeating what others have said. It is commonly assumed that Thomas was rather unoriginal as a theologian. Much of the material Thomas uses, for example, in discussing the Trinity of Persons can be found in works by William of Auvergne and Alexander of Hales,[9] not to mention Albert the Great. His most notable contribution to theological discussions is usually seen as bringing greater clarity and concision to the discussion.[10] After all, the task of the theologian is not to be original at all. To be called original in medieval circles was one step from being summoned before an ecclesiastical court for examination. On the other hand, it is well known that Thomas stood out from the crowd with his opinion on the beatific vision.[11] His teachings were even implicated in the condemnations of 1277.[12] Further, his own

---

*Thomas d'Aquino* (Washington, D.C.: The Catholic University of America Press, 1983), 174–75, 197, 382. While neither author offers evidence for his decision, they seem to favor the Roman dating.

9. Under that name may be included the *Summa Halensis* largely written by Alexander of Hales and completed by John of La Rochelle. I. Brady, O.F.M., "The 'Summa Theologiae' of Alexander of Hales," *Archivum franciscanum historicum* 70 (1977): 437–47.

10. E.g., J. Châtillon, "Unitas, Aequalitas, Concordia," 337–80.

11. Cf. W. Hoye, *Actualitas omnium actuum: Man's Beatific Vision of God as Apprehended by Thomas Aquinas* (Meisenheim (am Glan): Hain, 1975); Chr. Trottmann, *La Vision Béatifique. Des Disputes Scolastiques à sa Définition par Benoit XII* (Ecole Française de Rome, 1995).

12. Cf. Luca Bianchi, "1277: A Turning Point in Medieval Philosophy?" in *Was ist Philosophie im Mittelalter?* ed. J. A. Aertsen and A. Speer, Miscellanea Mediaevalia, vol. 26 (Berlin: Walter de Gruyter, 1998), 90–110; R. Hissette, "L'implication de Thomas d'Aquin dans la censure parisienne de 1277," *Recherches de Théologie et Philosophie Médiévales* 64 (1997): 3–31; J. F. Wippel, "Thomas Aquinas and the Condemnation of 1277," *The Modern Schoolman* 72 (1995): 233–72. Also see J. M. M. H. Thijssen, "What Really Happened on 7 March 1277?" in *Texts and Contexts in Ancient and Medieval Science*, ed. E. Sylla and M. McVaugh (Leiden: E. J. Brill, 1997), 84–114.

teacher Albert took exception to his definition of theology.[13] Thomas was quite able to take positions differing from those of his predecessors or peers.

A second possibility is that Thomas could be distancing himself from these texts of Ps.Dionysius because of a prevailing interpretation, much as Boethius was not often invoked in the late twelfth and early thirteenth centuries as a result of the controversies surrounding Gilbert of Poitiers' well-known and highly suspect interpretation.[14] One bit of evidence for this second possibility is that Thomas refers to other positions with the enigmatic *quidam* and *alii* (i.e., "certain others").[15] His naming of Maimonides does not then exhaust the list of his opponents. At least one other theologian, most likely an interpreter of Ps.Dionysius, is implicated. Moreover, for this unnamed master's opinion to shape Thomas' use of Ps.Dionysius requires that such opinion carry great weight. If we can determine the fact and identity of such an unnamed master, we might have a better idea of Thomas' intentions and teaching in this key discussion.

## 5.1 The Thirteenth-Century Context

The authority of Ps.Dionysius in the West was not great prior to the mid-thirteenth century. His work was, of course, known and used by some in the previous four centuries, but not by the majority, nor were these works part of theological instruction. Works heavily influenced by Ps.Dionysius, such as those of Eriugena or Hugh of St. Victor, as well as Eriugena's actual translations of Ps.Dionysius, remained at the periphery of theological instruction, in the latter instance at

---

13. Cf. R. McInerny, "Albert and Thomas on Theology," in *Albert der Grosse*, ed. A. Zimmerman, Miscellanea Mediaevalia, vol. 14 (Berlin: Walter de Gruyter, 1981), 50–60; M.-D. Chenu, *La théologie comme science au XIIIe siècle*, Bibliothèque Thomiste, vol. 33 (Paris, 1957), 42–43, 97–100.

14. Cf. M. Gibson, "The *Opuscula Sacra* in the Middle Ages," in *Boethius: His Life, Thought and Influence* ed. M. Gibson (Oxford: Basil Blackwell, 1981), 214–34, esp. 227. On the conflict surrounding Gilbert's work, see N. M. Häring, "The Case of Gilbert de la Porrée, Bishop of Poitiers (1142–1154)," *Mediaeval Studies* 13 (1951): 1–40.

15. ST I, q. 13, a. 2 c.

least partly due to the obscurity of the Latin.¹⁶ With the translations by John Saracen sometime after 1167, the Ps.Dionysian texts became more accessible to the Latin audience.¹⁷ However, the centerpiece of university theological instruction, Peter the Lombard's *Sentences*, as well as early thirteenth-century *summas* of theology¹⁸ virtually ignored Ps.Dionysius.

Albert the Great was the first to interpret the works of Ps.Dionysius into scholastic theology.¹⁹ Albert was the first and only thirteenth-century theologian to comment on all the writings of Ps.Dionysius. He commented on the *Celestial Hierarchy* in 1248 in Paris, and by 1252 in Cologne he had finished his lectures on the remaining books.²⁰ What makes this fact significant is Albert's fame—it was extraordinary. Roger Bacon complained loudly in 1266 that "the whole mob at Paris refers to him as to Aristotle, or Avicenna, or Averroes and other authorities." He has "such authority in his own lifetime," Bacon says, "as no one ever had."²¹ One may easily surmise that Albert's lectures

---

16. J. Leclercq, "Influence and Noninfluence of Dionysius in the Western Middle Ages," introduction to *Pseudo-Dionysius. The Complete Works*, trans. C. Luibheid (New York: Paulist Press, 1987), 25–32.

17. The Ps.Dionysian text available in the mid-thirteenth century included translations by both Eriugena and Saracen, the letters of Ps.Dionysius and paraphrases by Thomas Gallus. Cf. H.-F. Dondaine, O.P., *Le Corpus Dionysien de l'Université de Paris au XIIIe siècle* (Rome: Edizioni di Storia e Letteratura, 1953).

18. E.g., William of Auvergne's *Magisterium divinale et sapientiale* in *Opera Omnia*, 2 vols., ed. F. Hotot (Orléans-Paris, 1674; reprinted Frankfurt, 1963). William of Auxerre, *Summa Aurea*, 4 vols. (Rome: Collegii S. Bonaventurae ad Claras Aquas, 1980).

19. Cf. M.-D. Chenu, "Le dernier avatar de la théologie orientale en Occident au XIIIe siècle," in *Mélanges Auguste-Pelzer* (Louvain, 1947), 159–81.

20. I.e., *Ecclesiastical Hierarchy, Divine Names, Mystical Theology*. Cf. J. A. Weisheipl, O.P., "The Life and Works of St. Albert the Great," in *Albertus Magnus and the Sciences*, ed. J. A. Weisheipl (Toronto: Pontifical Institute of Mediaeval Studies, 1980), 13–51.

21. Roger Bacon, *Opus tertium*, in *Opera quaedam hactenus inedita*, ed. J. S. Brewer (London: Longman, Green, Longman, and Roberts, 1859), vol. I, pp. 30–31. According to S. Easton, Bacon was not familiar with Albert's teachings. Hence, his criticisms are aimed as much at proponents of Albert's teaching as at Albert himself. It is also the more striking to realize the strength of Albert's influence (in the Theology faculty) being felt by a master of Arts. Cf. S. Easton, *Roger Bacon and His Search for a Universal Science* (New York: Russell & Russell, 1971), 210–31.

were well attended and well noted. Consequently, Albert's reading of Ps.Dionysius would have been known to many, not only because of his extensive and unique lectures but also because of his frequent use of Ps.Dionysius in his other works.[22]

We have then at least some basis for conjecturing that in the mid-thirteenth century Ps.Dionysius was understood, at least in Paris and Cologne, according to Albert's interpretation. Albert was alone in having lectured on all the Ps.Dionysian works. Albert's opinions were well known, respected, and cited even by name, a mark of respect no one else at the time enjoyed. Moreover, Thomas was certainly very familiar with Albert's interpretations, as much as anyone at that time was. He attended Albert's Parisian lectures on the *Celestial Hierarchy* and later went with Albert to Cologne, where he heard lectures on the remaining works, including those on the *Divine Names*.[23] Short of proof, we do have a basis for a working hypothesis; namely, that the authority of Ps.Dionysius was inextricably linked with Albert.

If, in fact, Thomas wished to take exception to a contemporary's interpretation, he would no doubt have an able and prominent opponent in Albert. The question is, does Thomas take exception to Albert's teaching? Do Thomas and Albert part ways on the reading of Ps.Dionysius? An affirmative answer would necessarily have implications for Thomas' use of Ps.Dionysius, even though the latter was for Thomas a major and often-cited authority.[24] To test this hypothesis,

---

22. E.g., Albert cites Ps.Dionysius frequently in his *Sentences* commentary (c. 1243–45). Cf. Weisheipl, "Life and Works," 21–23.

23. Cf. Torrell, *Saint Thomas Aquinas*, 18–35.

24. At the beginning of this century, virtually no scholar paid attention to the Platonic and Neoplatonic elements of Thomas' work. Cf. H. A. Montagne, "Notre programme," *Revue Thomiste* 17 (1909): 15. As Durantel noted in 1919, however, Thomas' overall dependence upon Ps.Dionysius as an authority is quite striking. J. Durantel, *Saint Thomas et le Pseudo-Denis* (Paris, 1919). I would have to disagree with the many scholars who cite Durantel as having demonstrated that Ps.Dionysius is the most heavily cited authority (Scripture excepted) in the *Summa theologiae*. E. g., T. C. O'Brien, "The Dionysian Corpus," Appendix 3 in vol. 14 of Blackfriars edition of the *Summa theologiae* (p. 183). In fact, both Augustine and Aristotle are cited twice as many times as Ps.Dionysius. Cf. R. Deferrari and Sr. M. Barry, *A Complete Index of The Summa Theologiae of St. Thomas Aquinas* (Washington, D. C.: Catholic University of America Press, 1956). In the whole of Thomas' works (not the *Summa* alone) Ps.Dionysius is

we must examine the texts and compare Albert's interpretation of the Areopagite's teaching with that of Thomas.

## 5.2 Interpreting Pseudo-Dionysius

### 5.2.1 Albert's Commentary on the *Divine Names*

Albert begins his commentary with an article on the particular character of the names considered in this work. Names such as One, Trinity, Cause, Wisdom, and so forth refer to God as cause such that the attributes signified are things emanating from God, and such attributes are in God "truly and absolutely as far as the thing is signified by the name, although the manner of signifying is deficient in representing what God is."[25] God remains hidden because we impose these names according to our creaturely experience, and what we know or encounter are the divine "processions" in God's actions, not God Himself. What is in God remains hidden. Our knowledge of God as cause is limited to the divine attributes and does not reach to what God is. We know only *that* God is and this indefinitely or confusedly as "an infinite sea of substance."[26] There is, of course, no striking difference between Albert and Thomas on these matters, but this last point raises some concern. While Thomas would agree that we do not know *what* God is but only *that* God is (and what God is not), he does not say that such knowledge is indefinite. Thomas would also argue that knowing what God is not provides some insight into the divine nature.[27]

---

cited 1702 times. In comparison, Aristotle is cited more than 4000 times and Augustine is cited more than 6000 times. Cf. Robert Busa, *Index Thomisticus* (Stuttgart-Bad Cannstatt : Frommann-Holzboog, 1974–1979), section II, Concordantia Altera: Aristotle, in vol. 1, pp. 529–31, and [Philosophus], in vol. 4, pp. 504–11; Augustine, in vol. 1, pp. 564–74; Ps.Dionysius, in vol. 2, pp. 301–4.

25. [V]ere et absolute, quantum ad rem significatam per nomen, quamvis modus significandi deficiat a repraesentatione eius, secundum quod est in deo." Albert, *Super Dionysium De divinis nominibus*, ed. P. Simon (Cologne, 1972) ch. 1, §3, p. 2. Cf. also, ch. 4, §3, p. 114;

26. Cf. ibid., ch. 1, §3, ad 5, p. 2. Reference to the "sea of substance" comes from John Damascene, *De fide orthodoxe* I, 1, c. 9.

27. Eg., ST I, qq. 2–11.

For Albert, the affirmative value of a divine name is equivalent to its causal import. "God is praised by way of all things caused, because God is the cause of all things."[28] For that reason, he agrees with Ps.Dionysius in naming God first "good" rather than "being" and thereby disagrees with his more famous student. Though this particular disagreement might not seem significant on the surface, Albert's reasoning here belies a greater divide. His basis for naming God by way of analogy is not, as it is for Thomas, the participation of creatures in the divine perfections. Naming by means of "processions" means for Thomas naming by means of creatures.[29] For Albert, the term is synonymous with theophanies, manifestations of the divine. Hence, he distinguishes the being of God from perfections. For that reason, Albert denies that we can have access to the being of God even in the beatific vision. What is had by the blessed is only a certain knowledge *that* God exists.[30]

Albert interprets in a rather curious way Ps.Dionysius' intention "to explain divine names by which God is named through the divine processions [or effects]."[31] For a name to be "proper" to God, it must refer to a causal property, and goodness signifies the divine essence as a "disposition of one in the act of causing."[32] God's essential properties, on the other hand, remain unknown, for Albert does not equate the being of God with the being of God in the act of causing. In other words, the absence of a "univocal, immediate, and essential effect" means that our knowledge by way of effect attains merely to the causal activity; it does not "generate knowledge of essence."[33] It seems that in

---

28. "[Q]uod convenienter laudatur deus ex rationibus omnium causatorum ab ipso, quia ipse est causa omnium." Albert, *Super Dionysium*, ch. 1, §56, p. 35. Cf. ch. 1, §46, p. 28 ("non cognoscatur nisi per suum causatum, non nominatur nisi per nomen causati sui").

29. Cf. ST I, prologues to qq. 2 and 44.

30. Cf. Albert, *Super Dionysium*, ch. 1, p. 10.

31. "[I]ntendat exponere divina nomina, quibus nominatur deus per processiones ipsius." Ibid., ch. 3, §3, p. 102.

32. "[P]rout est in dispositione causantis in actu." Ibid., ch. 4, §3, p. 115. Cf. ch. 2, §45, p. 74, and ch. 4, §9, p. 118.

33. "[C]um non cognoscamus ipsum per effectum univocum sibi et immediate et

making this point Albert makes too much of the distinction between principle and cause, thus keeping the idea of preexistent perfections effectively out of the discussion. In order to investigate this problem in Albert's theory of divine naming, we will focus on the issue of causation in three parts: (1) our knowledge of God as cause; (2) the end of such knowledge; and (3) the resulting theory of naming God: by negation, excess, and causality.

First, our knowledge of God. Being known through effects, God is rightly called "cause" in the most fundamental sense, causal of all. And yet such causal activity is unlike our causing, because it is perfect: efficient and final and essential.[34] It is most appropriate to name God causally rather than to name God something else "to which all causes are led back, . . . [for] what is not a cause through its essence but through something . . . is not a First Cause."[35] However, no cause can be known perfectly through its effects unless such causing is univocal and immediate. A truly univocal cause produces only one effect. Even the assertion that God's essence and goodness are equivalent does not, for Albert, provide any clarification. The reason is this: good is considered in a cause in two ways—either as a habit or in the action of the cause. But there can be no habit or potency in God. Therefore, we consider good in God according to the causal action of God. That is to say, "Goodness is said to be the disposition of the cause insofar as it is in act. . . . for the [divine] essence does not communicate itself but only goodness."[36] Hence, goodness is not the same as the divine

---

essentialem." Albert, *Super Dionysium*, ch. 1, §51, p. 32; ch. 5, §32, p. 322; cf. Francis Catania, "'Knowable' and 'Namable' in Albert the Great's Commentary on the *Divine Names*," in *Albert the Great*, ed. F. J. Kovach and R. W. Shahan (Norman: University of Oklahoma Press, 1980), 109.

34. Cf. Albert, *Super Dionysium*, ch. 1, §33. Cf. E. Wéber, "Négativité et causalité: leur articulation dans l'apophatisme de l'école d'Albert le Grand," in *Albertus Magnus und der Albertismus*, ed. M. Hönen and A. de Libera (Leiden: E. J. Brill, 1995), 66.

35. Albert, *Super Dionysium*, ch. 1, §41, p. 23.

36. Ibid., ch. 4, §3, p. 114. "Goodness" signifies the divine essence by means of a disposition (ad 5). One wonders then what difference is intended between the 'habit,' which Albert denies, and the 'disposition,' which he allows. Albert goes on to affirm the identity of divine action according to essence, will, wisdom, and so forth in order to support his argument "that God acts through His essence," yet we name such essence only *as* causing, not as it is, i.e., what it is.

essence; neither is it property of the essence, but it is a property of the causal act.[37]

Like Thomas, Albert argues that knowing God as cause, we can assert only *that* God is, not *what* God is. Strictly speaking, God is perfectly knowable and namable *per se,* but our capacity is severely deficient.[38] To illustrate this point, Albert uses the common scholastic example from Aristotle's *Metaphysics:* as the eyes of a bat are to the light of the sun, so our soul's intellective power is to what is by nature most manifest.[39] Albert's explanation of this metaphor, however, is not common. According to its nature, the created intellect is "not proportioned for knowing God. . . . Nevertheless, by means of the illuminations or theophanies coming from God, such proportion is made, not for seeing what God is, but only for seeing God as an object according to this or that reason."[40] And to see God "according to this or that reason" is not to know God according to this or that essential attribute, for only the existence of God is known, not the "whatness" of God or of divine wisdom, goodness, etc. Moreover, and most curiously, Albert is not referring here to the vision of God in this life but to the vision of the blessed. The blessed's vision of God without mediation attains only to illuminations, or theophanies. The illuminating subject itself is not seen, only what comes from it and surrounds it. Strictly speaking, we do not "see" the sun because the light by which we see comes from it. This point is not a simple-minded claim that a light cannot illumine or make itself evident; rather it is a statement that the primary

---

37. Ibid., ch. 5, §32, p. 322.
38. Albert, *Summa Theologiae* I, tr. 3, q. 17 ad 6–8.
39. Albert, *Super Dionysium,* ch. 1, §50, ad 5; ch. 7, §25, p. 356; *Super Mysticam Theologicam,* ed. P. Simon (Cologne, 1978), ch. 1, p. 456; ch. 5, p. 473. Cf. Aristotle, *Metaphysics,* Bk. 2, ch. 1 (993b 9–11). That is to say, just as a bat cannot see the sun because of the bat's own deficiencies, so the human intellect cannot apprehend separate substances according to their quiddities. Compare Thomas, *Sentencia super Metaphysicam,* Bk. 2, lect. 1, §284–286.
40. "[Q]uod intellectus creatus secundum naturalia sua non habet proportionem ad cognoscendum deum, secundum tamen quod iuvatur per illuminationes sive theophanies descendentes a deo, efficitur proportionatus, non quidem ad videndum, quid est deus, sed ad videndum ipsum attingendo substantiam eius, secundum quod ipse se obicit sub tali vel tali ratione." Albert, *Super Dionysium,* ch. 1, §21, p. 11. Also, Albert, *In Metaphysics,* Bk. 2, ch. 2, p. 93.

light of the universe—physical in the case of the sun and metaphysical in the case of God—is so overwhelmingly brilliant beyond our capacities that the source or cause itself remains hidden by such brilliance. Even for the angels and the blessed, God is knowable only confusedly, because they do not comprehend what God is. "Confusedly," because the effects through which God is known as cause—both in this life and in the next—are not univocal, immediate, and essential. The difference in "seeing" God in these two states is that the blessed see immediately *that* God exists, while here we may know only by faith *that* God exists.[41] The difference lies not in what is known but in one's certainty, for we can never know anything about God in Himself. In both states, "what God's goodness and wisdom may be remains hidden from us"; it is more true to negate such things, both what is signified and its mode.[42]

A simple example will make this point a little clearer. We refer to a lamp in the room as a "light." We turn on the lamp, and it produces or gives off light by which we may see things in the room. When we say to someone, "Turn the light on," we signify a light bulb without electricity. Thus, with one and the same word, we refer to a cold dark bulb and the illumination it provides when electrified. The question is whether we name God "life" or "wisdom" or "good" in the way we name a light bulb—on or off—a "light," that is, by virtue of the potential and sometimes actual illuminating effect. In that case, only the illumination provided by the electrified bulb is properly understood to be, and named, "light." On the other hand, is God more appropriately named "light" in the way we would say a flame is a light, that is, by its

---

41. Albert, *Super Dionysium*, ch. 1, §27, p. 13. Cf. Catania, "'Knowable' and 'Namable,'" 106–7.

42. "[Q]uamvis quid sit bonitas et sapientia eius, maneat nobis occultum." Albert, *Super Dionysium*, ch. 2, §55, p. 80. Thomas, on the other hand, would argue that the assertion of essential causality allows us to talk about the cause itself. ST I, q. 4, a. 2. Albert is not, for that matter, insinuating a capriciousness on the part of God, but only stating that such connections cannot be made. Looking at a well-constructed house, for example, Albert would acknowledge that it was built by someone who knew how to do carpentry, but he would not exclude the possibility that it was done by a fisherman. Looking at the same house, Thomas would argue that the quality of the work leads one to conclude that it was indeed done by a carpenter.

very nature. A flame cannot be other than illuminating, so God cannot be other than good, life, etc. The analogy of the bulb, however, reveals Albert's focus—causing goodness, being, wisdom is only something God does, not what in fact God is.[43]

Our failure to know God demands that our naming of God begin in negation. One must remove everything from such naming, because God is nothing we can understand and is beyond everything. Negation is, therefore, most proper, as it corresponds to the inadequacy of our language and knowing.[44] Albert explains the Ps.Dionysian schema of naming God in the following way:

> [First] we ascend to God from creatures by every negation, that is, by negating everything from God. [Then] by excess, we posit in God those things that are in creatures. [Finally] we affirm that God is the cause of everything in creatures, so that if one finds wisdom in a creature, I say that God is not such wisdom but is the cause of this wisdom and is the one more eminently having wisdom.[45]

In this schema, the second and third ways are not essentially distinct, because Albert does not confirm that what God has is what God is. Unlike Thomas, he does not place wisdom in God substantially but causally only. Hence, a few lines later he states that the way of excess is where the thing signified "exceeds the signification of the name." The way of excess then, according to Albert, refers to what is beyond signification *per se* and not simply beyond our mode of signification. Thus, what is signified is considered in two ways:

---

43. Cf. F. Ruello, *Les 'Noms Divins' et Leurs 'Raisons' selon Saint Albert le Grand* (Paris: J. Vrin, 1963), ch. 2.

44. "[I]ntellectus cessat, postquam pertransivit omnia ultra quae est Deus." Albert, *Super Dionysium*, ch. 1, §§50–51, pp. 31–32; ch. 5, §17, p. 312. Cf. E. Wéber, "Langage et méthode négatifs chez Albert le Grand," *Revue des sciences philosophiques et théologiques* 65 (1981): 75–99.

45. "[Q]uia ex creaturis in deum ascendimus *in ablatione omnium,* idest omnia negando ab ipso, *et* in *excessu,* idest ea quae sunt in creaturis, excedenter ponendo in ipso, *et in omnium causa,* idest ponendo eum causam omnium quae sunt in creaturis, ut si inveniam sapientiam in creaturis, dicam, quod deus non est talis sapientia, sed est causa huius sapientiae et est eminenter habens sapientiam." Albert, *Super Dionysium,* ch. 7, §28, p. 358. Cf. Albert, *Summa Theologiae* I, q. 16.

either according to what is in the effect, and this is the mode of naming by way of cause; or according to what is in the cause which is beyond this mode, and this is the way of naming through negation.⁴⁶

Divine predication then remains equivocal. The bases for naming God are simply not the same as that for creatures, and what is in God exceeds not only our mode of signification but also our very signification. When Albert refers such predication to the (divine) cause that is beyond the mode of (creaturely) effect, he proceeds by negation, not by eminence. Accordingly, Albert negates both what is signified by the name and the manner of such signification.⁴⁷ What is "in" God is beyond the very signification of any divine name. The most perfect and true knowledge of God is had through ignorance, by denying completely what is signified by a name.

Ps.Dionysius states that the truth about God is hidden by means of veils. Albert interprets these veils as figures and symbols that indicate God as cause without revealing God's nature.⁴⁸ Albert distinguishes "that to which a name is imposed" from "that by which a name is imposed," thereby distinguishing substance from quality. Regarding that "to which the name is imposed," such names as "life" or "wisdom" are more properly said of God than of creatures, inasmuch as God is the cause of such things in creation. With regard to the quality or mode "by which the name is imposed," it is more proper to things. However, we understand such perfections as they are in inferior things and as inhering in a substance accidentally, both that "to which a name is imposed" and that "by which a name is imposed."⁴⁹ Albert calls names figurative or mystical in their mode of signifying

---

46. "[V]el secundum quod ist in effectu, et sic est modus, qui est per causam, aut secundum quod est in causa, quae est extra istum modum, et sic est modus per omnium ablationem." Albert, *Super Dionysium*, ch. 7, §29, p. 358. Cf. Wéber, "Négativité et Causalité," 58f.

47. "[Q]uod, *divinissima*, idest perfectissima et verissima, *dei cognitio est per ignorantium*, idest per omnium ablationem, quia simpliciter verum est, secundum quod significatur per nomen." Albert, *Super Dionysium*, ch. 7, §30, p. 359.

48. Albert, *Super Dionysium*, ch. 1, §43, p. 25.

49. There is then a diversity of *rationes significandi* in God and creatures that prevents us from naming God properly.

and symbolic in reference to what is signified; that is, first in God as cause and posterior in creatures through similitude. Note that these two categories are of the same words, only in different respects. Names such as 'intellect,' 'life,' 'light,' 'substance,' then, name God mystically insofar as they are known only in creatures and creaturely modes. These terms function symbolically insofar as the things known as divine effects are attributed to the cause by a certain similitude.

With this interpretation, it appears that Albert has blurred the lines between two different works of Ps.Dionysius: the *Divine Names* and another work (the *Symbolic Theology*) that we know only through Ps.Dionysius' own references and description within his four extant works.[50] For Ps.Dionysius, there is a distinction between those similitudes that are prior in God and in creatures only by participation (life, wisdom) and those similitudes that are prior in creatures and merely transferred to God (rock, lion). It seems that Albert is unwilling to admit that names apply to that in which creatures participate, namely, the goodness or wisdom that is caused by God in creatures yet is also one with the divine essence. What is missing is a theory of analogous predication, the consequence of which is an elision of the distinction between things said of God properly (i.e., "substantially") and things said symbolically or metaphorically. The only difference left is the kind of name, not degree of applicability. Perfection names are intelligible and abstract. Other names are sensible. Yet neither class of names is proper to God in Himself but only to God in the act of causing.

Albert's argument suggests that an inability to know perfectly means an inability to name properly. To name God then is merely to indicate that God exists. For example, naming God "wisdom" is equivalent to saying "God exists."[51] Our ignorance then is a necessary corollary of the divine simplicity. This doctrine, according to Albert, dictates that knowledge of God's being would entail knowledge of God's

---

50. Cf. Ps.Dionysius, *Divine Names*, chs. 2–4.

51. Cf. Albert, *Super Dionysium*, ch. 2, §56, p. 81. "Participation," according to Albert, does not involved intelligibility but only an awareness of existence. There is no similitude of divine goodness, thus our participation merely convinces us of a reality beyond our knowing. Also, ibid., ch. 4, §5, p. 116.

goodness and even God's self-knowledge.⁵² Our ignorance of the most fundamental aspect, being, implies our ignorance of all else. In short, because God is unique and simple, God is known perfectly or not at all. But knowing that God exists and that only confusedly is not much. And far from comprehending God as object, the mind seems not to attain to God at all; the ontological distance is simply infinite and unbridgeable.

For Albert the heart of Ps.Dionysius' teaching is the *Mystical Theology*. Albert uses the complete negation of (conceptual) knowing and language presented in that text as a guide in reading the other works. Thus, his reading of the *Divine Names* is entirely mystical, and by this I mean fundamentally negative. From the beginning, Albert denies any real possibility of knowing and naming God *per se*.⁵³ In a mystical sense, God is eminent in all things and consequently named by all things. As cause, God is named Being, Good, Wisdom, and so forth; but what God is according to the divine nature remains a [complete] mystery wrapped in darkness.⁵⁴ For this reason Albert sees theology not as a speculative science but as a practical one, simply ordered to piety.

### 5.2.2 Thomas' Commentary on the *Divine Names*

According to Thomas' commentary, the subject matter of Ps.Dionysius' *Divine Names* is the treatment of the intelligible names of God.⁵⁵ The work concerns those similitudes found in creatures con-

---

52. Such knowledge would also require the knowing human mind to be greater than the known divine subject, and this cannot be. Ibid., ch. 1, §21, p. 10.

53. Confirming texts in Albert, *Super Dionysium*, ch. 1, §21, p. 11; §30, p. 15; ch. 2, §55, p. 80; ch. 4, §1, p. 113; ch. 5, §32, p. 322; ch. 7, §11, p. 345; §29, p. 358; and Albert, *Summa Theologiae* I, q. 13, c. 5, pp. 48–49.

54. This is not to say that theology is mere grammar for Albert. "[S]i enim fides nostra consiteret tantum verbis, vana esset (If our faith consisted only in words, it would be in vain)." Albert, *Super Dionysium*, ch. 2, §18, p. 56. Theology is for Albert, however, ordered not to speculative knowledge but to piety. See his *Summa Theologiae* I, q. 3.

55. Cf. Thomas, *Super Librum Dionysii*, proemium, ch. 4, lect. 4 (§322). For a current bibliography on Dionysius and Aquinas, consult F. O'Rourke, *Pseudo-Dionysius and the Metaphysics of Aquinas*. Studien und Texte zur Geistesgeschichte des Mittelalters, Bd. 32 (Leiden: E. J. Brill, 1992).

sidered to be derived from God and thus said of God prior and properly, such as 'being,' 'good,' 'life,' 'wisdom' and so forth. Thomas distinguishes the *Divine Names* from Ps.Dionysius' other works by its concentration on those names that are taken from intelligible likenesses as opposed to those names we predicate of God by way of metaphor.[56] If one "diligently searches through Scripture, one will find the names of God distinguished ... according to the procession of perfections."[57] That is, through the divine names found in Scripture, we may have knowledge of God as principle and as cause.[58] The *Divine Names* is an examination of the way in which these names refer to God: the basis for their use and their mode of predication.

First, in our knowledge and naming of God we are dependent upon and even constricted by revelation. The reason is this: something known only by one cannot be signified or thought except insofar as it is manifested by that knowing one.[59] Because God alone knows the divine nature perfectly, no one else is able to speak about or think about God except insofar as such truth is revealed by God. However, we cannot know the natures of immaterial substances either by reason or by revelation, because our understanding is through sensible things.

Although through revelation we are elevated for knowing something of which we would otherwise be ignorant, such revelation does not elevate us to know in a way other than through sensible things. Just as Ps.Dionysius says in the *Celestial Hierarchy*, "it is impossible for the divine light to illumine us unless it be covered in a variety of holy veils."[60]

---

56. Thomas, *Super Librum Dionysii*, ch. 1, lect. 3 (§104); ch. 4, lect. 4 (§322); ch. 13, lect. 4 (§999). On the issue of intelligibility, cf. J. A. Weisheipl, "The Axiom *Opus naturae est opus intelligentiae* and Its Origins," in *Albertus Magnus Doctor Universalis: 1280/1980*, ed. G. Meyer and A. Zimmerman (Mainz, 1980), 441–63.

57. "[I]nvenies, si diligenter in Scripturis scruteris, *dividentem*, idest distinquentem, ... idest secundum processus perfectionum." Thomas, *Super Librum Dionysii*, ch. 1, lect. 2 (§53).

58. Ibid., ch. 1, lect. 2 (§45).

59. Ibid., ch. 1, lect. 1 (§§13–15).

60. "Unde quamvis per revelationem elevemur ad aliquid cognoscendum quod alias esset nobis ignotum, non tamen ad hoc quod alio modo cognoscamus nisi per sensibilia; unde dicit Dionysius in I c. Caelestis hierarchiae quod impossibile est nobis superlucere divinum radium nisi circumvelatum varietate sacrorum velaminum." Thomas, *Super Boetium de Trinitate*, q. 6, a. 3 c.

The fact that revelation is proportioned to our understanding is no solution to the problem, for such revelation is veiled in sensible and material forms.[61] Our understanding is through sensible things in either case. Is revelation then given in vain? It seems that we must remain forever ignorant of God. Certainly, God cannot be comprehended perfectly by a finite mind, and this no one denies. And yet there are many promises in Scripture regarding our knowledge and vision of God.[62] For that reason, Thomas insists that there must be a way for the finite human mind to know God.

Indeed, we must know at least in some confused way what we are seeking before we can determine its existence. We begin at least with some awareness of God's existence. Further, by knowing what God is not, by noting that God is not a body, not finite, not composite, for example, we are able to come to a less vague assertion. This way of negation also proceeds according to a certain order. Saying that God is not a body is far less informative than saying that God is not good, that is, as we are sometimes good.[63] Negation leads somewhere, and it is not, according to Thomas, a denial of the possibility of our knowing and naming God at all.

The way of negation is a way of defining the inadequacy and deficiency in our naming of God.[64] We say that God is wisdom because wisdom comes from God. We also say that God is not wisdom because wisdom does not pertain to God in the way it pertains to creatures. Yet Aquinas differs from Albert in the following way: he does not go on to

---

61. Cf. Ps.Dionysius, *Celestial Hierarchy*, ch. 1; *Divine Names*, ch. 1.

62. E.g., 1 John 3:2; Job 19:26; Eph. 1:17; and John 17:3.

63. For that reason, Thomas normally contrasts comprehension of God (what we do not have) not with a confused awareness of existence but rather with knowing what God is not. Thomas, *Super Librum Dionysii*, ch. 1, lect. 2 §68. As will become evident below, this point is one of the subtle but important differences between Thomas and Albert.

64. Thomas, *Super Librum Dionysii*, ch. 2, lect. 4. Cf. Thomas, *De potentia*, q. 7, a. 5 ad 2. Thomas argued that the way of negation in its mystical form (i.e., in the *Mystical Theology*) is the last and highest. The mystical union is one in which the operation of the intellect "rests." Thomas, *Super Librum Dionysii*, prologue and ch. 1, lect. 3 (§83). Such union points to a fulfillment of intellect rather than its emptying. As motion is to rest, so reasoning is to this mystical union.

deny wisdom of God as a significative name, but argues that wisdom must be in God in virtue of God's simplicity and perfect causation. Since everything acts according to its nature, such actions are telling of the nature. For that reason, Thomas says, we can know that perfections preexist in God, although their mode of being in God is beyond us.[65] Ps.Dionysius' pagan predecessors, on the other hands, distinguished the first principles from the secondary. They applied the negative predicates to the One, the First Principle, and the affirmative predicates to the secondary principles coming from the One. On the basis of Scripture, Ps.Dionysius "transformed" this dichotomy by collapsing these principles into one and thereby declared that God possessed all the characteristics affirmed.[66] Consequently, divine names signify the divine nature as well as what comes from God.[67] Thomas seizes upon this notion to say "through certain divine names in Scripture, we have some cognition about God . . . namely . . . that God is known as Principle and Cause."[68] Knowing God as Principle and Cause is not equivalent to knowing God *in se*, but such knowing is beyond affirming that the First Cause simply is.[69] And this point is meaningful because we participate in what proceeds from God.

Participation then, according to Thomas, is a way of knowing. He defines participation by way of a contrast with abstraction.

---

65. Thomas, *Super Librum Dionysii*, ch. 5, lect. 3, §§664–666. Cf. ST I, q. 4, a. 2. Cf. L. Sweeney, "Metaphysics and God: Plotinus and Aquinas," in *Die Metaphysik im Mittelalter*, ed. P. Wilpert, Miscellanea Mediaevalia, vol. 2 (Berlin: Walter de Gruyter, 1963), 232–39.

66. Cf. S. Gersh, "Ideas and Energies in Pseudo-Dionysius the Areopagite," in E. A. Livingstone, ed., *Studia Patristica* 15/1 (Berlin: Akademie Verlag, 1984), 298.

67. V. Lossky argues that the distinction between the inaccessible divine nature and the communication of divine energies is found in Ps.Dionysius. Lossky, *The Mystical Theology of the Eastern Church* (London, 1957), 71ff. S. Gersh is not persuaded and replies that the pagan sources of Ps.Dionysius have not been well understood by Lossky. S. Gersh, *From Iamblichus to Eriugena: An Investigation of the Prehistory and Evolution of the Pseudo-Dionysian Tradition* (Leiden : Brill, 1978), 156–67.

68. "[Q]uod ex divinis nominbus praedictam cognitionem de Deo capiamus . . . scilicet quod per divina nomina Deus cognoscatur ut Principium et Causa." Thomas, *Super Librum Dionysii*, ch. I, lect. 2, §53; also, ch. 7, lect. 1, §708.

69. Ibid., ch. 1, lect. 2, §45.

Knowable things that are below our intellect have a more simple being in our intellect than in themselves. [For example,] we know all material things by abstraction. Divine things, however, are more simple and perfect in themselves than in our intellect, so the knowledge of divine things is not through abstraction but through participation; and this in two ways. First, our intellects participate in the intellectual power and light of divine Wisdom. Secondly, things present to our intellect participate in divine things; that is, all things are good insofar as they participate in divine goodness.[70]

The difference is the location of the greater simplicity—in the knowing mind or in the thing itself. By abstraction, the being of the thing in the knowing mind is more simple than its being in itself (concrete reality). But concerning those intelligible realities above and more simple than our intellect, we understand them less simply than they are. In both cases, the Ps.Dionysian precept remains valid: namely, "everything is received in the manner of the receiver."[71] Moreover, as Thomas points out, Ps.Dionysius' distinction between a thing's mode of being in the intellect and its mode of being in itself emphasizes the continuity in our ways of knowing things "below" and "above" our intellect. This distinction provides an account of how we can know and name things that do not exist according to our mode of being. Thus, far from undermining our naming of God, this important distinction actually validates our naming of God even as the accuracy of our

---

70. "Sunt autem quaedam cognoscibilia, quae sunt infra intellectum nostrum, quae quidem habent simplicius esse in intellectu nostro, quam in seipsis, sicut sunt omnes res corporales, unde huiusmodi res dicuntur cognosci a nobis per abstractionem. Divina autem simplicia et perfectiora sunt in seipsis quam in intellectu nostro . . . unde divinorum cognitio dicitur fieri non per abstractionem, sed per participationem. Sed haec participatio est duplex: una . . . intellectus noster participat intellectualem virtutem et diviniae Sapientiae lumen; alia vero, secundum quod divina participantur in rebus quae se intellectui nostro offerunt, inquantum scilicet per participationem divinae Bonitatis, omnia sunt bona." Thomas, *Super Librum Dionysii*, ch. 2, lect. 4 §§176–177; also, ch. 1, lect. 2, §67.

71. Ps.Dionysius, *Divine Names*, ch. 1, 588B; ch. 2, 645A–B, etc. On the importance of Ps.Dionysius for Thomas' epistemology, see Thomas, *Super sent.* II, d. 14, q. 1, a. 2 c. Cf. D. Black, "The Influence of the *De Divinis Nominibus* on the Epistemology of St. Thomas Aquinas," *Patristic, Mediaeval and Renaissance Conference Proceedings* 10 (1985): 45.

mode of understanding and signifying is denied. Consequently, Thomas can say that our naming goes beyond our understanding. When we name God "good" or "wise" or other such names, we do not mean thereby that God has such qualities but that such perfections come from God and yet are one principle in the divine nature.[72]

Thomas goes on to explain that our way of knowing and naming God is threefold: by negation, causality, and transcendence. Although Thomas presents several variations on this order, nowhere does he offer an account that ends in naming by way of causality.[73] Knowing God by way of creatures is the more obvious but less perfect means for knowing God. It is the way of the philosopher and is part of Thomas' famous "five ways."[74] Understandably, Thomas tends to begin with the way of causality in most of his discussions, yet he goes on to make use of what revelation provides: namely, a portrait of God's perfect actuality, which means that God is whatever God has.[75]

This type of negation is little more than the assertion of transcendence, the first word of revelation according to Ps.Dionysius.[76] We deny our access to that One rather than deny the possibility of knowing that One, for through revelation that One has deigned to communicate with us. It is not without reason that Thomas returns to this theme numerous times in the first chapter of his commentary. Indeed, Ps.Dionysius himself notes it no fewer than six times, saying that we

---

72. Thomas, *Super Librum Dionysii*, ch. 2, lect. 4 (§180). Cf. ch. 1, lect. 2, §54; ch. 5, lect. 3, §666.

73. Ibid., ch. 7, lect. 3 and 4; cf. *Super Boetium* q. 6, a. 3; *De potentia* q. 7, a. 5. Cf. M. Ewbank, "Diverse Orderings of Dionysius's *Triplex via* by Thomas Aquinas," *Mediaeval Studies* 52 (1990): 82–109. The oft-cited counterexample from *Super Librum Dionysii*, ch. 7, lect. 4, §729, should be seen only as Thomas' attention to the sequence of topics in the text and not as the order of his own argument.

74. ST I, q. 2, a. 3.

75. E.g., Thomas, *Super Sent.* I, d. 3; *Summa contra Gentiles* I, ch. 30; III, ch. 49; *Super epistolam Ad Romanos* I.6; ST I, q. 12, a. 12; q. 13, aa. 1, 10. Cf. Ewbank, "Diverse Orderings," 109; Sweeney, "Metaphysics and God," 235–36.

76. Ps.Dionysius. *Divine Names*, ch. 1: "In the scriptures the Deity has benevolently taught us that understanding and direct contemplation of itself is [sic] inaccessible to beings, since it actually surpasses being."

must not dare to resort to any words or conceptions "apart from what the sacred Scriptures have divinely revealed."[77] By an observation of God's effects, one may indeed have a conception of the existence of some transcendent cause, but it is only by revelation that we can know anything about that cause.[78] What Scripture reveals is that God is both cause and principle "according to what is represented in the perfections of creatures."[79] For Thomas, the character of theology grows out of this conviction that Scripture guides and informs us in a positive way. To say that the light and content of revelation is proportioned to our capacities is not to say that revelation does not contain the truth about God but that it does not contain the full truth about God. Just as a great scientist might grossly simplify and condense his speech in order to teach a small child, so God has proportioned His communication to us. And the better the scientist is in choosing words that capture his meaning yet move the child's mind, the better the child will learn and be drawn up little by little into the world of the scientist. What is communicated is meant to draw us up to things beyond our present grasp. With respect to things below the level of intellect, the "drawing up" is a movement toward comprehension. With respect to things above the level of our intellect, such "drawing up" is a movement toward greater participation, a greater understanding by way of greater likeness in being.

### 5.3 Thomas' Argument in ST I, q. 13, a. 2

Returning to the *Summa theologiae*, we find Thomas' theory of divine naming in the first three articles of question 13. These articles concern respectively (1) the suitability of names for God *(conveniunt)*; (2) the object of such names: divine essence or some external procession; and (3) whether names are said properly of God. We will focus on only one of these articles, the second. The text of one of the objections is as follows: "Dionysius says, 'You will find a chorus of theolo-

---

77. Ps.Dionysius, *Divine Names*, ch. 1.
78. E.g., Thomas, *Super Librum Dionysii*, ch. 1, lect. 3, §§85–88.
79. ST I, q. 13, a. 2 ad 3.

gians seeking to distinguish clearly and laudably the divine processions in the naming of God.' This means that the names which theologians use in praising God are distinguished according to the different effects. However, to speak of the causal activity of a thing is not to speak of its essence, hence such words are not said of God substantially."[80] In other words, to refer to a cause as cause is not the same as referring to the essence or nature of a thing.

Aquinas notes that there are several opinions on names said absolutely and affirmatively of God. Certain theologians have said that such names more accurately remove something from our conception of God. For example, when we call God "living," we are actually saying that God is not an inanimate object. To say that God is "good" is to assert that God is not evil. Such is the teaching of Maimonides. "Others," Thomas says, contend that these names signify a habit or relation of God to creatures. To say that God is "good" is then to signify that God is the cause of goodness in the world. From what we have seen in Albert's commentary, it appears that this opinion is his. If this is true, one may expect that Thomas would directly address Albert's arguments—and it seems that he does.

First, Thomas offers three reasons why the aforementioned opinions of Maimonides (and possibly of Albert) are unacceptable. (1) In neither of these positions could one affirm one name over another. By simple negation or causal naming, there is no qualitative difference between saying that God is "good" and that God is "body." One simply means that God is cause of goodness and bodies or that God is not evil and not a being in potency. The implication here is that it is easily recognized that calling God "good" is preferable to and more meaningful than calling God "body." (2) It would follow from these two positions that everything is said of God *per posterius,* i.e., first and prop-

---

80. "[D]icit Dionysius, 1 cap. *De div. nom.: Omnem sanctorem theologorum hymnum inveniris, ad bonos thearchiae processus, manifestative et laudative Dei nominationes dividentem:* et est sensus, quod nomina quae in divinam laudem sancti doctores assumunt, secundum processus ipsius Dei distinguuntur. Sed quod significat processum alicuius rei, nihil significat ad eius essentiam pertinens. Ergo nomina dicta de Deo, non dicuntur de ipso substantialiter." ST I, q. 13, a. 2 ob. 2.

erly of creatures and only secondly of God. Just as "health" is said of medicine only by its effect in the patient, and therefore attributed properly only to the patient, so "being" and "wisdom" are said of God only by the effect in creatures. The implication is that such naming does not allow us to determine whether God is in fact willfully good, but only that coming into contact with God has a beneficial effect on us. Moreover, we might add, the experience of suffering would lead one to name God accordingly as its cause. (3) The two positions are also unable to account for our intentions in speech. When we call God "living," we do indeed mean more with such affirmation than that God is not an inanimate body or that God is the cause of life.

An adequate explanation of divine naming, then, must meet these requirements. For Thomas, we name things as we understand them. Therefore, we signify God according to what we know, and we know God from creatures. This means that we understand immaterial and simple things through sensible and composite things. So far Albert would agree. However, because the *ratio* or basis for our naming is that found in creatures and not in God, Albert would at this point introduce the principle of negation to say that such naming does not apply to God Himself. Thomas, on the other hand, introduces the following proposition: God possesses preeminently all perfections of creatures. First, because the more perfect the cause, the more preeminent will be the perfections of effects in the cause. Second, God is perfect, subsistent being and must contain all perfections of being. Thus, "in the cause of all, everything must preexist," that is, those things of which it is said to be is better than not to be.[81]

Creatures do not represent God simply and equally. Creatures represent God insofar as they possess some perfection and are accordingly similar to God. This is not to say that God is in a genus or one being among many, yet more perfect. Creatures possess some likeness to their cause only insofar as that cause is essential and perfect act and

---

81. "[P]rima causa effectiva rerum, oportet omnium rerum perfectiones praeexistere in Deo." Thomas, ST I, q. 4, a. 2 c. For our purposes, it is also important that the preceding argument in ST I, q. 4, a. 2 is based upon chapter five of the *Divine Names* and cites it four times.

insofar as creatures participate in such perfections. For that reason the affirmative and absolute divine names do in fact signify the divine substance. Admittedly, they are deficient in representation, but such names are predicated of God substantially, as cause and as principle. What we call "good" in creatures preexists in God in a more eminent manner. Using a common rule from logic, namely, "everything acts according to itself," Thomas argues that to name a cause by means of its effect is to identify something of the cause in the effect and affirm it of the cause itself.[82] To say that God is good is to signify that God is cause of goodness in creatures and is goodness preeminently. Or as Augustine says, "in so far as God is good, we exist."[83]

Ps.Dionysius' apophatic critique of theological language is for Thomas a qualification pointing not to the impossibility of naming God but to the impossibility of knowing and naming God perfectly. He can make this argument because he sees creation as an adequate vehicle for divine communication. And this is due not so much to the perfective quality of creatures but to the perfection of God's causal act as well as the sure guidance of Scripture in naming God.

Thus, in answer to the initial objection around which this study is built, Thomas points out that we commonly name things by their qualities or effects. In everyday speech, we fully intend to signify actual things by means of their effects, understanding without confusion the thing itself to be indicated through the named effects. We know and name a stone, for instance, by its effect of hurting our feet, yet we do not signify the effect of the stone with the name "hard" but the stone itself when we refer to it with a name. Consequently, to say that we name God by means of effects is in itself a false problem, for our

---

82. ST I, q. 4, a. 3 c: "Cum enim omne agens agat sibi simile in quantum est agens, agit autem unumquodque secundum suam formam, necesse est quod in effectu sit similitudo formae agentis." Cf. Thomas, *Super Librum Dionysii*, ch. 1, lect. 3, §§89–90: "Omnis autem causa intantum potest nominari ex nomine sui effectus, inquantum habet in se similitudinem eius . . . quia similitudo omnium rerum praeexistit in divina essentia non per eamdem rationem, sed eminentius; *convenit laudare ex omnibus causatis;* non tamen univoce sed supereminenter." Cf. also ch. 7, lect. 2, §708.

83. "[I]nquantum [Deus] bonus est, sumus." Augustine, *De doctrina Christiana*, I.32, quoted in Thomas, ST I, q. 13, a. 2 c.

way of naming creatures functions with this distinction in mind. Thus, Aquinas admits:

> We impose divine names from the effects of God, that is, according to diverse processions of perfections. Creatures, [therefore] represent God although imperfectly.... Nevertheless these names are not imposed for signifying these processions or effects such that to say "God is living" means "life proceeds from God." They are imposed for signifying the very principle of things, just as life preexists in God, although in a manner more eminent that we can understand or signify.[84]

The three ways of naming—by negation, by causality, and by eminence—are not alternatives but three steps in one process. Accordingly, Thomas always refers to them together.[85]

## 5.4 Conclusion

The most fundamental questions of theology are not whether "Son" signifies a relation of origin or a procession, or whether "Word" is a personal name. Our ability to deal with these questions depends on our answers to more basic questions, those that are at the center of the whirlwind of modern debates on theological language. We must ask ourselves, what do we think we are doing when we speak about God. In what way are we naming God?

The most fundamental principles of Thomas Aquinas' theory of divine naming are: (1) we do not know what God is, only what God is not; and (2) we name as we know. It appears, on the other hand, that we use many affirmative terms in our theological discourse. We name God "Being," "Good," and "Wisdom." We also name God "Father, Son,

---

84. "[D]ivina nomina imponuntur quidem a processibus deitatis; sicut enim secundum diversos processus perfectionum, creaturae Deum repraesentant, licet imperfecte... Sed tamen haec nomina non imponit ad significandum ipsos processus, ut cum dicitur *Deus est vivens*, sit sensus, *ab eo procedit vita*: sed ad significandum ipsum rerum principium, prout in eo praeexistit vita, licet eminentiori modo quam intelligatur vel significatur." Thomas, ST I, q. 13, a. 2 ad 2.

85. Cf. Wéber, "Négativité et Causalité," 55. These three ways are ordered differently according to different contexts, but they are always together. In any case, the conclusion is always the same: a balance of affirmation and negation in knowing and naming God.

and Holy Spirit." We mean by these terms more than that God is the cause of our being, our wisdom. We also mean more than that the Father is not the Son and the Son is not the other two. As Ps.Dionysius says in the *Divine Names*, our best explanation falls short of what these names actually mean. We must ascribe to God our power to use them well.[86] If we are to understand Aquinas' theological project, we must take account of his apophaticism, learning to balance the affirmative terminology with the negative strains of his theological discourse. And yet this negativity is not absolute, for therein we find not a denial of theological insight but a guide as we progress from faith to understanding.

## 5.5 Epilogue

Denys of Ryckel, a Carthusian monk, writing in the late fifteenth century, called Albert "the most skilled" in Peripatetic philosophy and the true interpreter of the "Prince of theologians," Ps.Dionysius.[87] However, after briefly summarizing the two positions we have just presented above,[88] he expresses some concern. "It seems," he says, "that this [second] opinion agrees with what Albert wrote . . . ; namely, that God has nothing in common with creatures either as in a species or genus or as the principle of analogy. . . . It does not seem then that we can make any true predication of God. And these words sound inept."[89] Denys goes on to argue unequivocally "that perfections of

---

86. Dionysius, *Divine Names*, ch. 13 (981C).

87. Cf. K. Emery, Jr., "The Matter and Order of Philosophy according to Denys the Carthusian," in *Was ist Philosophie im Mittelalter*, ed. J. A. Aertsen and A. Speer, Miscellanea Mediaevalia, vol. 26 (Berlin: Walter de Gruyter, 1998), 669–70. Emery notes that Denys enjoyed an advantage of perspective as none before him and was said to have "put the entire medieval tradition on the balance scale." Cf. E. A. Synan, "Cardinal Virtues in the Cosmos of Saint Bonaventure," *S. Bonaventura 1274–1974* (Grottaferrata, 1974), vol. 3, p. 21.

88. In discussing whether the perfections of creatures are properly said of God, Denys follows Thomas' argument from the *Summa* almost point by point. That is surely not accidental.

89. "Verumtamen huic opinioni concordare videtur, quod super Mysticam theologiam scribit Albertus: Deus non habet aliquod commune quod sit in ipso et creaturis, neque ut species, neque ut genus, neque ut analogiae principium; . . . Propter quod

creatures are in God preeminently . . . [and] this is the teaching of the saints, Ps.Dionysius, Anselm, and many others, chiefly, Thomas, Alexander, Bonaventure, . . . and many who follow."[90]

---

etiam non est aliquae apud nos praedicatio vera de Deo. Quae verba inepte sonare censentur." Denys the Carthusian, "Difficultatum praecipuarum," in *Opera Omnia*, vol. 16, p. 486. It would seem then that Gersh's argument for a fourteenth-century Byzantine origin to the Christian distinction between the unknowable divine essence and the evident processions may be in need of correction. Cf. S. Gersh, *From Iamblichus to Eriugena*, p. 167, n. 184.

90. "[Q]uod perfectiones creaturarum sunt in Deo praeeminter . . . Haec est doctrina sanctorum Dionysii et Anselmi, ac plurium aliorum: quam doctores praecipui, Thomas, Alexander, Bonaventura . . . et alii multi sequuntur." Denys the Carthusian, "Difficultatum praecipuarum," in *Opera Omnia*, vol. 16, p. 487.

# Conclusion

The trajectory of this work has not been a linear one. As we have attempted to highlight the nature of Thomas' theological method and especially his theory of Trinitarian appropriations, we have traversed a wide field of topics. What began as an account of order in presentation ended in an examination of divine naming theory. Overall, this study can be understood as a narrowing of focus from the outer contours of the *Summa Theologiae* to the painstaking analysis of a single article. The difficulty in understanding Thomas' theological method is partly due to the complexity of his intellectual context. The variety of opinions on fundamental issues as well as the rapidity of development in theological method and instruction makes historical concerns inescapable. Many scholars have noted that the medieval period enjoyed perhaps the most unified vision of the world. Yet on the question of our knowledge and naming of God, one can find significant diversity. It is precisely that diversity we have attempted to demonstrate, not for the sake of diversity but for the sake of accuracy. We were concerned first with reading Thomas as a theologian in his own right, distinct from his predecessors and peers in his theological method. We saw that his *Summa theologiae* is a well-ordered and careful presentation with pedagogical concerns at the forefront. Moreover, his teaching is not subject to the modern critique of the "Latin tradition" because his presentation does not conform to the presumed pattern.

We then went on to detail this very structure, demonstrating the development of presentation and doctrine. We showed that Thomas' Trinitarian language is not a rational demonstration but a logical presentation and investigation of doctrine. His account of the Trinity of

Persons and the coherence of language about those Persons is an expression of "faith seeking understanding." This point is most readily seen in the development of terminology from the early questions to the later ones (e.g. q. 3 and q. 39). Terms such as 'essence' and 'person' are not defined absolutely but in accordance with the context of revelation and the investigation of its various aspects. Such terms are ultimately defined in relation to one another as the discourse of theology builds upon itself.

We pursued a further delineation of Thomas' theological method by contrasting it with certain twelfth- and thirteenth-century presentations, particularly with respect to his discussion of appropriations. We came to see that Thomas' work did not follow the molds of his predecessors, because of his view of the relation between nature and grace. According to Thomas, there is a continuity of human existence in its natural state and in a state of grace. The functioning of the soul does not change radically with the infusion of grace but attains to its natural *telos*. Thus, Thomas' assertion for continuity between our natural existence and graced existence provides him with grounds for being much more exacting in his analysis of our naming of God.

Many scholars, however, have seen an entirely too positivist view of theological language in Thomas. Many have seen his analysis of theological language as an example of the "speculative grammar" pursued by certain Arts masters in the thirteenth century. This method of grammatical speculation on the being of things in the world assumes a virtual correspondence between our speech and reality. On the contrary, Thomas argues that our language is in some measure conventional and that it reveals as much about our thought as about external reality. We can, for instance, consider concrete, composite things in an abstract manner. We also use composite language to talk about what is not composite, e.g., God. For that reason, this awareness of the character of our thought and language can be a source of great insight into divine revelation as we differentiate the thing signified from our modes of understanding and signifying.

It is at this point that a reading of the apophaticism in Thomas' theology becomes crucial. If we can do no more than say that theological terms have miraculous new meanings, then all we shall be able to achieve is the arrangement of more or less coherent verbal patterns, without having the remotest idea what we are actually talking about. We are indeed limited to the terms of revelation, for "one can find no created similitude of what pertains to the unity of divine essence and to the distinction of [divine] Persons . . . [because] this mystery exceeds the power of natural reason."[1] Yet Thomas insists that there is a continuity between truths naturally known and those revealed.[2] By revelation we know that God is radically distinct from the world, and not its highest member. Revealed language conforms to our way of knowing and naming, yet such language pertains to God *in se*, although it falls short of the infinity and perfection of divine nature.

Consequently, in the last chapter, we examined the accuracy of theological language with a comparison of Thomas and Albert. The question is not so much whether we are signifying the divine substance but whether we are doing it in a meaningful way. Albert, for instance, agrees that God is signified in theological discourse, but he denies that such language means anything other than "God exists." His vision of theology is for that reason practical rather than speculative. Thomas, on the other hand, argues strongly for conceptual naming. As imperfect and incomplete as our naming may be, it does indeed refer to God properly.

Thus, to say that "we name God as we know God" and that "we do not know what God is but only what God is not" should not be understood as eliminating the possibility of coherent speech about God. Admittedly, Thomas says that there is a sense in which "God does not have a name . . . because his essence is beyond that which we understand about God and signify with words."[3] Yet our common naming of things in the world is itself not based upon a perfect knowledge of

---

1. "[E]a de Deo quae unitatem divinae essentiae et distinctionem personarum pertinent. . . . sufficiens similitudo in rebus creatis non invenitur, sed hoc mysterium omnem naturalis rationis facultatem." Thomas, *Super Librum Dionysii*, proemium, p. 1.

2. Indeed, what is revealed is communicated by means of higher and more excellent effects. Cf. Thomas, ST I, q. 12, a. 12 ad 1.

3. ST I, q. 13, a. 1 ad 1.

essences. We do not perfectly know the essence of God or the essence of a fly. Our naming of things in both cases proceeds by way of effects in some way. Thus, when we say that God is good or wise, we do in fact, according to Thomas, signify the divine substance, even though we do not know the divine substance directly or perfectly.[4]

Thomas' theological method is a consideration of various sources and an attempt to reconcile differences within the tradition. Yet Thomas is quite unlike his predecessors in several important ways: (1) the selection of authorities is not a mere compilation as in Abelard's *Sic et Non* or even in Peter the Lombard's *Sentences;* and (2) the ordering of topics is integral to the solution of questions. Also, in his *Catena Aurea,* for example, Thomas sets aside as needed the letter of his quotations in favor of the "sense."

The underlying question in his work is not "what can we say about this issue?" but "what is the truth of the matter?" The aim is not grammatical but metaphysical. The biblical witness, for example, is highly privileged not only because it is the best way of speaking. It is also privileged because it reveals the truth about God and creatures, what is necessary for our salvation.[5]

Further, Thomas follows the Augustinian model of "faith seeking understanding" rather than the Anselmian one. Thomas embraced the guidance of revelation in philosophical reflection and did not try to separate the two as Anselm proposed to do. Thomas' work was successful in this endeavor because he so carefully respected the power, role, and limit of human reason. Unlike Abelard in the twelfth century and William of Auvergne in the thirteenth century, Thomas did not think that theological truths could in most cases be demonstrated. Yet rational reflection guided by faith can attain to a great deal of understanding. Philosophy is, therefore, more obviously a handmaid in Thomas' theology and less an approach to theology.

The manifestation of the doctrine of the Trinity through the theory of appropriations must be understood in this light, i.e., according

---

4. Cf. ST I, q. 13, a. 2 c.
5. Cf. ST I, q. 32, a. 1 ad 3.

to Thomas' theological method. On the surface, it seems that Thomas' discussion of appropriation breaks his own rules of theological argument. His discussion of the three Persons as unity, equality, and concord, or as power, wisdom, and goodness, may appear to be an effort to demonstrate the Trinity. In that case, expressions found to be less acceptable would be set aside in favor of more suitable and accurate expressions. Yet Thomas does not choose one set of appropriations over another. He is careful to delineate the way each triad is to be interpreted. More importantly, the discussion of appropriated terms is dependent on the preceding theological presentation of the Trinity. Revelation dictates rules about what can and cannot be said (and understood) about these three Persons. Just as metaphorical or symbolic language about God is dependent upon more proper language, so appropriations are dependent upon the proper names. Trinitarian language then is not some vague symbolism but pertains to the truth about God. When we name God "Father, Son, and Holy Spirit," or "wisdom," "truth," "good," we refer to God better than we know, not less, because God has revealed Himself in so many ways. And the better the teacher, the better the teaching . . .

# Bibliography

Abelard. *Dialectica*. Edited by de Rijk. Assen: Van Gorcum, 1956.
_____. *Introductio ad Theologia*. Patrologia Latina, 178. Paris: Garnier, 1885.
_____. *Theologia Christiana*. Patrologia Latina, 178. Paris: Garnier, 1885.
Albert the Great. *Metaphysica*. Edited by B. Geyer. *Opera Omnia*, vol. 16. Cologne, 1964.
_____. *Summa Theologiae*. Edited by D. Siedler. *Opera Omnia*, vol. 34. Cologne, 1978.
_____. *Super Dionysium De divinis nominibus*. Edited by P. Simon. *Opera Omnia*, vol. 37/1. Cologne, 1972
_____. *Super Mysticam Theologicam*. Edited by P. Simon. *Opera Omnia* vol. 37/2. Cologne, 1978.
Anderson, R. "Medieval Speculative Grammar: A Study of the Modistae." Dissertation. Notre Dame, 1989.
Anselm. *Anselm of Canterbury*. 4 vols. Edited and translated by J. Hopkins and H. Richardson. Toronto: Edwin Mellen Press, 1974.
Aristotle. *Aristotle: On Interpretation. Commentary by St. Thomas and Cajetan*. Translated by Jean T. Oesterle. Milwaukee: Marquette University Press, 1962.
_____. *Aristotle's Posterior Analytics*. Translated by H. Apostle. Oxford: Clarendon Press, 1963.
_____. *Metaphysics*. Translated by W. D. Ross. In *The Basic Works of Aristotle*, edited by R. McKeon. New York: Random House, 1941.
Ashworth, E. J. *The Tradition of Medieval Logic and Speculative Grammar from Anselm to the End of the Seventeenth Century: A Bibliography from 1836 Onwards*. Toronto: Pontifical Institute of Mediaeval Studies, 1978.
_____. "Can I Speak More Clearly Than I Understand?" In *Studies in Medieval Linguistic Thought*, edited by K. Körner, H. J. Niederehe, and R. H. Robins, pp. 29–39. Amsterdam: John Benjamins B. V., 1980.
_____. "Signification and Modes of Signifying in Thirteenth-Century Logic: A Preface to Aquinas on Analogy." *Medieval Philosophy and Theology* 1 (1991): 39–67.
Augustine. *De Trinitate*. Edited by W. J. Mountain. Turnhout, 1968.
_____. *The Trinity*. Translated by Edmund Hill, O.P. The Works of St. Augustine, I.5. Brooklyn: New City Press, 1991.

Bailleux, E. "Le personnalisme de saint Thomas en théologie trinitaire." *Revue Thomiste* 61 (1961): 25–42.

_____. "La création, oeuvre de la Trinité, selon saint Thomas." *Revue Thomiste* 62 (1962): 27–50.

_____. "Le Christ et son Esprit." *Revue Thomiste* 73 (1973): 373–400.

Bantle, F. X. "Person und Personbegriff in der Trinitätslehre Karl Rahners." *Münchener Theologische Zeitschrift* 30 (1979): 11–24.

Bardy, G. "Sur les sources patristiques greques de S. Thomas dans la 1ère partie de la Somme théologique." *Revue des sciences philosophiques et théologiques* 12 (1923): 493–502.

Barnes, M. R. "Augustine in Contemporary Trinitarian Theology." *Theological Studies* 56 (1995): 237–50.

_____. "De Régnon Reconsidered." *Augustinian Studies* 26 (1995): 51–79.

Barth, K. *Church Dogmatics*. Translated by G. Bromiley. Edinburgh: T & T Clark, 1957.

Bianchi, L. "1277: A Turning Point in Medieval Philosophy?" In *Was ist Philosophie im Mittelalter?* edited by J. A. Aertsen and A. Speer, pp. 90–110. Miscellanea Mediaevalia, vol. 26. Berlin: Walter de Gruyter, 1998.

Billot, Ludovico Cardinal, S.J. *De Deo uno et trino. Commentarius in primam partem S. Thomae*. Rome, 1935.

Black, D. "The Influence of the *De Divinis Nominibus* on the Epistemology of St. Thomas Aquinas." *Patristic, Mediaeval and Renaissance Conference Proceedings* 10 (1985): 41–52.

Bloomfield, M. W. Book review of Bursill-Hall's *Speculative Grammars of the Middle Ages*. *Speculum* 49 (1974): 102–5.

Boethius. *The Consolation of Philosophy*. Translated by R. Green. New York: MacMillan, 1962.

Boethius of Dacia. *Modi signficiandi sive Quaestiones super Priscianum majorem*. Edited by J. Pinborg, H. Roos, and S. Jensen. Copenhagen, 1969.

Bonaventure. *Doctoris Seraphici S. Bonaventurae opera omnia*. 10 vols. Quaracchi: Collegium S. Bonaventurae, 1882–1902.

_____. *Disputed Questions on the Mystery of the Trinity*. Edited and translated by Zachary Hayes. St. Bonaventure, New York: The Franciscan Institute, 1979.

Bourassa, F. "Personne et conscience en theologie trinitaire." *Gregorianum* 50 (1974): 471–93, 677–720.

_____. "Sur le Traité de la Trinité." *Gregorianum* 47 (1966): 254–85.

Brady, I., O.F.M. "The '*Summa Theologiae*' of Alexander of Hales." *Archivum franciscanum historicum* 70 (1977): 437–47.

Buersmeyer, K. "Verb and Existence." *New Scholasticism* 60 (1986): 152–55.

_____. "Aquinas on the '*Modi significandi*.'" *The Modern Schoolman* 54 (1987): 73–95.

Burrell, D., C.S.C. "Indwelling: Presence and Dialogue." *Theological Studies* 22 (1961): 1–17.

_____. *Aquinas: God and Action.* Notre Dame: University of Notre Dame Press, 1979.
_____. *Knowing the Unknowable God.* Notre Dame: University of Notre Dame Press, 1986.
_____. *Freedom and Creation in Three Traditions.* Notre Dame: University of Notre Dame Press, 1993.
Bursill-Hall, G. L. *Speculative Grammars of the Middle Ages.* The Hague: Mouton, 1971.
_____. "Toward a History of Linguistics in the Middle Ages, 1100–1450." In *Studies in the History of Linguistics,* edited by D. Hayes, pp. 77–92. Bloomington: Indiana University Press, 1974.
_____. "The Modistae Revisited." In *L'Héritage des grammariens latins de l'antiquité aux lumière,* edited by I. Rosier, pp. 215–32. Louvain: Peters, 1988.
Busa, R. *Index Thomisticus.* Stuttgart-Bad Cannstatt: Frommann-Holzboog, 1974–79.
Buytaert, E. M. "Abaelard's Trinitarian Doctrine." In *Peter Abaelard. The Man and his Work.* Mediaevalia Lovaniensia, ser. 1/2, pp. 127–52. Louvain, 1973.
Cajetan. *In Summa Theologiae.* Rome: Leonine Commission, 1882.
*The Cambridge History of Later Medieval Philosophy.* Edited by Norman Kretzmann, Anthony Kenny, Jan Pinborg. Cambridge: Cambridge University Press, 1982.
Carroll, W. J. "Pseudo-Dionysius the Areopagite—A Bibliography: 1960–1980." *The Patristic and Byzantine Review* I (1982): 225–34.
Cary, P. "On Behalf of Classical Trinitarianism: A Critique of Rahner on the Trinity." *The Thomist* (1992): 365–405.
Catania, F. J. "'Knowable' and 'Namable' in Albert the Great's Commentary on the *Divine Names.*" In *Albert the Great,* edited by F. J. Kovach and R. W. Shahan, pp. 97–128. Norman: University of Oklahoma Press, 1980.
Cavadini, J. "Augustine's De Trinitate." *Augustinian Studies* 23 (1992): 103–23.
Chambat, L. *Présence et union: Les missions des personnes de la Trinité selon Thomas d'Aquin.* Fontenelle, 1945.
Châtillon, J. "Unitas, Aequalitas, Concordia vel Connexio. Recherches sur les Origines de la Théorie Thomiste des Appropriations S.T. 1, 39, 7–8." In *St. Thomas Aquinas 1274–1974* Commemorative Studies (Symposium) I, edited by A. A. Maurer pp. 337–80. Toronto: PIMS, 1974.
Chenu, M.-D., O.P. "Maître Thomas est-il une 'autorité'?" *Revue Thomiste* 30 (1925): 187–94.
_____. "Grammaire et Théologie aux XIIe et XIIIe siècles." *Archives D'Histoire Doctrinale et Littéraire du moyen âge* 10 (1935): 1–28.
_____. "Le plan de la Somme théologique de Saint Thomas." *Revue Thomiste* 45 (1939): 93–107.
_____. *Introduction à l'étude de S. Thomas d'Aquin.* Paris, 1950.
_____. *La théologie au douzieme siècle.* Paris: J. Vrin, 1957.

_____. *La théologie comme science au XIIIe siècle*. Bibliothèque Thomiste 33. Paris, 1957.
_____. *Das Werk des hl. Thomas von Aquin*. Heidelberg-Graz, 1960.
_____. *Towards Understanding Saint Thomas*. Translated by S. Landry, O.P., and D. Hughes, O.P. Chicago: Henry Regnery Company, 1964.
Colish, M. *Peter Lombard*. 2 vols. Leiden: E. J. Brill, 1994.
Congar, Y. "Bio-bibliographie de Cajétan." *Revue Thomiste* 17 (1934): 3–49.
_____. "Vision de l'Église chez S. Thomas d'Aquin." *Revue des sciences philosophiques et theologiques* 62 (1978): 523–42.
_____. *I Believe in the Holy Spirit*. Translated by David Smith. 3 vols. New York: Seabury Press, 1983.
Corbin, M. *La Trinité ou l'Excès de Dieu* (Paris: Editions du Cerf, 1997).
Cottiaux, J. "La conception de la théologie chez Abélard." *Revue d'histoire ecclésiastique* 28 (1932): 247–95.
Courth, F. *Trinität in der Scholastik*. Handbuch der Dogmengeschichte, vol. 11, fasc. Ib, edited by M. Schmaus. Freiburg-Basel-Wien, 1985.
Cunningham, F., O.P. *The Indwelling of the Trinity: A Historico-Doctrinal Study of the Theory of St. Thomas Aquinas*. Dubuque, Iowa: Priory Press, 1955.
Cunningham, F. A., S.J. "Speculative Grammar in St. Thomas Aquinas." *Laval théologique et philosophique* 17 (1961): 76–86.
Daffara, M., O.P. *De Deo Uno et Trino*. Marietti, 1945.
Dalmau, J. "De Deo Uno et Trino." In *Sacrae Theologiae Summa*, vol. 2. Matriti, 1953.
Daly, M. *Beyond God the Father. Towards a Philosophy of Women's Liberation*. Boston: Beacon Press, 1973.
Deferrari, R., and Sr. M. Barry. *A Complete Index of The Summa Theologiae of St. Thomas Aquinas*. Washington, D.C.: Catholic University of America Press, 1956.
Denzinger, H. *Enchiridion Symbolorum*. Barcelona: Herder, 1963.
de Régnon, T. *Études de théologie positive sur la sainte Trinité*. 4 vols. Paris: Victor Retaux, 1892–98.
de Rijk, L. M. *Logica Modernorum: A Contribution to the History of Early Terminist Logic*. 2 vols. Assen: Van Gorcum, 1962–67.
[Pseudo]-Dionysius the Areopagite. *Pseudo-Dionysius. The Complete Works*. Edited and translated by Colm Luibheid. Classics of Western Spirituality. New York: Paulist Press, 1987.
Dionysius (Denys) the Carthusian. *Opera omnia*. Montreuil-sur-Mer, 1896–1935.
Dondaine, A. *Ecrits de la "Petite École" Porretaine*. Paris-Montréal, 1962.
Dondaine, H.-F., O.P. "'Alia lectura fratris Thome' (Super I Sent.)." *Mediaeval Studies* 42 (1980): 308–36.
_____. *La Trinité*. Paris, 1962.
_____. *Le Corpus Dionysien de l'Université de Paris au XIIIe siècle*. Rome: Edizioni de Storia e Letteratura, 1953.

Duquesne, M. "Personne et existence." *Revue des sciences philosophiques et théologiques* 36 (1952): 626–55.
Durantel, F. *Saint Thomas et le Pseudo-Denis.* Paris, 1919.
Easton, S. *Roger Bacon and His Search for a Universal Science.* New York: Russell & Russell, 1971.
Egan, J. M. "Naming in St. Thomas' Theology of the Trinity." In *From An Abundant Spring* (New York: P. J. Kennedy & Sons, 1952), pp. 152–71.
Elders, L. "Structure et fonction de l'argument 'sed contra' dans la Somme Théologique de Saint Thomas." *Divus Thomas* 80 (1977): 245–46.
———. "Les citations de Saint Augustin dans la 'Somme Theologique' de Saint Thomas d'Aquin." *Doctor Communis* 40 (1987): 115–67.
———. *The Philosophical Theology of St. Thomas Aquinas.* Leiden: E. J. Brill, 1990.
———. *The Metaphysics of Being of St. Thomas Aquinas in a Historical Perspective.* Leiden: E. J. Brill, 1993.
Elswijk, H. C. van. *Gilbert Porreta. Sa vie, son oeuvre, sa pensie.* Louvain, 1966.
Emery, G. *La Trinité créatrice: Trinité et création dans les commentaires aux Sentences de Thomas d'Aquin et de ses précurseurs Albert le Grand et Bonaventure.* Paris: J. Vrin, 1995.
———. "Essentialisme ou personalisme dans le traité de Dieu chez saint Thomas d'Aquin?" *Revue Thomiste* 98 (1998): 5–38.
Emery, K., Jr. "The Matter and Order of Philosophy according to Denys the Carthusian." In *Was ist Philosophie im Mittelalter?* edited by J. A. Aertsen and A. Speer, pp. 667–79. Miscellanea Mediaevalia, vol. 26. Berlin: Walter de Gruyter, 1998.
———. "Twofold Wisdom and Contemplation in Denys of Ryckel (Dionysius Cartusiensis, 1402–1471)." *Journal of Medieval and Renaissance Studies* 18 (1988): 99–134.
Entrich, M., O.P. *Albertus Magnus.* Cologne: Verlag Styria, 1982.
Ewbank, M. "Diverse Orderings of Dionysius's *Triplex via* by Thomas Aquinas." *Mediaeval Studies* 52 (1990): 82–109.
Farrell, W. *A Companion to the Summa.* New York: Sheed & Ward, 1941.
Forte, B. *The Trinity as History.* New York: Alba House, 1989.
Fortmann, E. J. *The Triune God: A Historical Study of the Doctrine of the Trinity.* Philadelphia: Westminster, 1972.
Fredborg, K. M. "The Dependence of Petrus Helias' *Summa super Priscianum* on William of Conches' *Glose super Priscianum.*" *Cahiers de L'Institut du Moyen-Age Grec et Latin* 11 (1973): 1–57.
———. "Some Notes on the Grammar of William of Conches." *Cahiers de L'Institut du Moyen-Age Grec et Latin* 37 (1981): 21–28.
Frisch, Rev. J. C. "The Use of Grammar in the Trinitarian Theology of Saint Thomas Aquinas." Unpublished dissertation. L'Institut Catholique, Paris, 1970.
Gabriel, A. L. "Metaphysics in the Curriculum of Studies of the Mediaeval Univer-

sities." In *2: Die Metaphysik im Mittelalter*, edited by P. Wilpert, pp. 92–102. Miscellanea Mediaevalia, vol. 2. Berlin: Walter de Gruyter, 1963.

Garrigou-Lagrange, R. "L'habitation de la Sainte Trinité et l'expérience mystique." *Revue Thomiste* 33 (1928): 449–74.

———. *The Trinity and God the Creator: A Commentary on St. Thomas' Theological Summa Ia, aa. 27–119*. Translated by F. C. Eckhoff. London: B. Herder, 1952.

Geiger, L.-B. *Le probléme de l'amour chez S. Thomas d'Aquin*. Montréal-Paris, 1958.

Gersh, S. "Anselm of Cantebury." In *A History of Twelfth-Century Western Philosophy*, edited by Peter Dronke, pp. 255–78. Cambridge: Cambridge University Press, 1988.

———. "Ideas and Energies in Pseudo-Dionysius the Areopagite." In *Studia Patristica* 15/1, edited by E. A. Livingstone, pp. 297–301. Berlin: Akademie Verlag, 1984.

———. *From Iamblichus to Eriugena: An Investigation of the Prehistory and Evolution of the Pseudo-Dionysian Tradition*. Leiden: Brill, 1978.

Ghellinck, J. de. "Histoire de persona et hypostasis dans un écrit anonyme porretain du XIIe siécle." *Revue neoscolastique de philosophie* (1934): 111–28.

Gibson, M. *Boethius: His Life, Thought and Influence*. Oxford: Basil Blackwell, 1981.

Gilson, E. *Being and Some Philosophers*. Toronto: Pontifical Institute of Mediaeval Studies, 1952.

———. *Le Thomisme: Introduction à la philosophie de saint Thomas d'Aquin*. 6th ed. Paris, 1965.

———. *The Christian Philosophy of St. Thomas Aquinas*. Translated by L. K. Shook. New York: Random House, 1955.

Gonzales, O. *Misterio trinitario y existencia humana: Estudio histórico teologico entorno a San Buenaventura*. Biblioteca de teología 6. Madrid, 1966.

Gorch, M. M., O.P. "Le Problème des Trois Sommes: Alexander de Hales, Thomas d'Aquin, Albert le Grand." *Revue Thomiste* 39 (1931): 293–301.

Gössmann, E. *Glaube und Gotteserkenntnis im Mittelalter*. Handbuch der Dogmengeschichte 1: Das Dasein im Glauben, edited by M. Schmaus, A. Grillmeier, and L. Scheffczyk. Freiburg: Herder, 1971.

———. "Die Methode der Trinitätslehre in der *Summa Halensis*." *Münchner Theologische Zeitschrift* 6 (1955): 253–62.

———. *Metaphysik und Heilsgeschichte. Eine theologische Untersuchung der Summa halensis*. Munich, 1964.

Grabmann, M. "De Thoma Erfordiensi Auctore Grammaticae Quae Ioanni Duns Scoto Adscribitur." *Archivum Franciscanum Historicum* 15 (1922): 273–77.

———. *Mittelalterliches Geistesleben*. 2 vols. Munich, 1926.

———. "Die Stellung des Kardinal Cajetan in der Geschichte des Thomismus." *Angelicum* 2 (1934): 547–60.

———. "De theologie ut scientia argumentativa secundum S. Albertum Magnum et S. Thomam Aquinatem." *Angelicum* 14 (1937): 39–60.

———. *Thomas von Erfurt und die Sprachlogik dees mittelalterlichen Aristotelismus.* Sitzungsberichte der Bayerischen Akademie der Wissenschaften, Philosophisch-historische Abteilung. Bd. 2. Munich, 1943.

———. *Die theologische Erkenntnis- und Einleitungslehre des Heiligen Thomas von Aquin auf Grund seiner Schrift in Boethium de Trinitate.* Thomistische Studien 4. Freiburg, 1948.

Greshake, G. *Der Dreieine Gott.* Freiburg im Breisgau, 1997.

Gunton, C. *The Promise of Trinitarian Theology.* Edinburgh: T&T Clark, 1991.

Hackett, J. M. G. "The Attitude of Roger Bacon on the *Scientia* of Albertus Magnus." In *Albertus Magnus and the Sciences,* edited by J. A. Weisheipl, O.P., pp. 53–72. Toronto: Pontifical Institute of Mediaeval Studies, 1980.

Hankey, W. "The *De Trinitate* of St. Boethius and the Structure of the *Summa theologicae* of St. Thomas Aquinas." In *Congresso internazionale di studi boeziani* (Pavia, 5–8 October, 1980), pp. 367–75. Rome: L. Obertello, 1981.

———. "The Place of the Psychological Image of the Trinity in the Arguments of Augustine's *De Trinite,* Anselm's *Monologion* and Aquinas' *Summa Theologiae.*" *Dionysius* 3 (1979): 99–110.

Häring, N. M. "The Case of Gilbert de la Porrée, Bishop of Poitiers (1142–1154)." *Mediaeval Studies* 13 (1951): 1–40.

———. "Sprachlogische und philosophische Voraussetzungen zum Verständnis der Christologie Gilberts von Poitiers." *Scholastik* 32 (1957): 373–97.

———. "Petrus Lombardus und die Sprachlogik in der Trinitätslehre der Porretanerschule." In *Miscellanea Lombardiana,* pp. 113–27. Novara, 1957.

———. "A Treatise on the Trinity by Gilbert of Poitiers," *Recherches de théologie ancienne et médiévale* 39 (1972): 14–50.

Hayes, Z., O.F.M. *Saint Bonaventure's Disputed Questions on the Mystery of the Trinity.* New York: The Franciscan Institute, 1979.

Heinzmann, R. "Der Plan der *Summa theologiae* in der Tradition der frühscholastischen Systembildung." In *Thomas von Aquino,* edited by W. P. Eckert, pp. 455–69. Mainz, 1974.

Henniger, M. *Relations: Medieval Theories 1250–1325.* Oxford: Clarendon, 1989.

Hill, E., O.P. *The Mystery of the Trinity.* London: Geoffrey Chapman, 1985.

Hill, W. *The Three-Personed God. The Trinity as a Mystery of Salvation.* Washington, D.C.: The Catholic University of America Press, 1983.

Hissette, R. *Enquête sur les 219 articles condamnés à Paris le 7 mars 1277.* Paris, 1977.

———. "L'implication de Thomas d'Aquin dans la censure parisienne de 1277." *Recherches de théologie et philosophie médiévales* 64 (1997): 3–31.

Hödl, L. *Von der Wirklichkeit und Wirksamkeit des dreieinen Gottes nach der appropriativen Trinitätstheologie des 12. Jahrhunderts.* Munich, 1965.

———. "Die philosophische Gotteslehre des Thomas von Aquin OP in der Diskussion der Schulen um die Wende des 13. zum 14. Jahrhundert." *Revista de filosofia neoscolastica* 70 (1978): 113–34.

Hornus, J. M. "Les recherches récentes sur le pseudo-Denys l'Aréopagite." *Revue d'Histoire et de Philosophie Religieuses* 35 (1955): 404–48.

Horst, U. "Beiträge vom Einfluß Abaelards auf Robert von Melun." *Recherches de Théologie ancienne et médiévale* 26 (1959): 311–26.

———. "Über die Frage einer Heilsekonomischen Theologie bei Thomas von Aquin." *Münchener theologische Zeitschrift* 12 (1961): 97–111.

———. *Die Trinitäts- und Gotteslehre des Robert von Melun*. Mainz, 1964.

Hoye, W. *Actualitas omnium actuum: Man's Beatific Vision of God as Apprehended by Thomas Aquinas*. Meisenheim (am Glan): Hain, 1975.

Hugh of St. Victor. "*Tractatus de trinitate et de reparatione hominis* du MS. Douai 365." Edited by R. Baron. *Mélanges de science religieuse* 18 (1961): 111–12.

Hunt, R. W. "Studies on Priscian in the Eleventh and Twelfth Centuries." *Mediaeval and Renaissance Studies* 2 (1950): 39–51.

———. "*Absoluta*. The Summa of Petrus Hispanus on Priscianus Minor." *Historiographia linguistica* 2 (1975): 1–23.

Imle, F. "Die essentiellen Grundlagen des trinitarischen Innenlebens nach Alexander von Hales." In *Aus der Geisteswelt des Mittelalters* (Festschrift M. Grabmann). Beiträge zur Geschichte her Philosophie des Mittelalters, Suppl. III/1, 545–53. Munich, 1935.

Inciarte, F. "Zur Rolle der Praedikation in der Theologie des Thomas von Aquin am Beispiel der Trinitätslehre." *Miscellanea Mediaevalia* 13 (1983): 256–69.

Jenkins, J., C.S.C. *Knowledge and Faith in Thomas Aquinas*. Cambridge: Cambridge University Press, 1997.

John of Dacia. *Johannis Daci Opera*. 2 vols. Edited by A. Otto and H. Roos. Copenhagen: G.E.C. Gad, 1955.

John of St. Thomas. *Cursus theologicus*. Paris: Ludovicus Vives, 1883.

Johnson, E. A. *She Who Is*. New York: Crossroad, 1996.

Johnson, M. "'Alia lectura fratris Thome,' A List of the New Texts of St. Thomas Aquinas found in Lincoln College, Oxford, MS. Lat. 95." *Recherches de théologie ancienne et médiévale* 57 (1990): 34–61.

Jolivet, J. "Comparaison des théories du langage chez Abélard et chez les Nominalistes du XIVe siècle." In *Peter Abelard*, edited by E. M. Buytaert, pp. 163–78. Leuven, 1974.

———. "Rhétorique et théologie dans une page de Gilbert de Poitiers." In *Gilbert de Poitiers et ses Contemporains*, edited by J. Jolivet and A. de Libera, pp. 183–98. Naples: Bibliopolis, 1987.

Jordan, M. "Modes of Discourse in Aquinas' Metaphysics." *New Scholasticism* 54 (1980): 401–46.

———. *Ordering Wisdom*. Notre Dame: University of Notre Dame Press, 1986.

———. "The Competition of Authoritative Languages and Aquinas' Theological Rhetoric." *Medieval Philosophy and Theology* 4 (1994): 71–90.

Jorissen, H. "Zur Struktur des Traktates 'De Deo' in der *Summa theologiae* des Thomas von Aquin." In *Im Gespräch mit dem Dreieinen Gott. Elemente einer trinitarischen Ontologie* (Festschrift W. Breuning), edited by M. Böhnke and H. P. Heinz, pp. 231–57. Düsseldorf, 1985.

Jungel, E. *The Doctrine of the Trinity: God's Being Is in Becoming.* Grand Rapids, Mich.: Eerdman's, 1976.
_____. *God as the Mystery of the World.* Grand Rapids, Mich.: Eerdmans, 1983.
Kasper, W. *The God of Jesus Christ.* Translated by M. J. O'Connell. New York: Crossroad, 1984.
Kearney, E. F. "Master Peter Abelard, Expositor of Sacred Scripture: An Analysis of Abelard's Approach to Biblical Exposition in Selected Writings on Scripture." Dissertation. Marquette, 1980.
Kelly, L. G. "God and Speculative Grammar." In *L'Héritage des grammariens latins de l'antiquité aux lumière,* edited by I. Rosier, pp. 205–13. Louvain: Peters, 1988.
Kenan, O. B. *The History of Franciscan Theology.* New York: The Franciscan Institute, 1994.
King, A. H. *The Question of 'Person' and 'Subject' in Trinitarian Theology: Moltmann's Challenge to Rahner and its Implications.* Dissertation. Fordham University, 1987.
Knoch, W. "'Deus unus est trinus.' Beobachtungen zur frühscholastischen Gotteslehre." In *Im Gespräch mit dem Dreieinen Gott. Elemente einer trinitarischen Ontologie* (Festschrift W. Breuning), edited by M. Bohnke and H. P. Heinz, pp. 209–30. Düsseldorf, 1985.
_____. A. Krause, *Zur Analogie bei Cajetan und Thomas von Aquin.* Halle/Saale: Hallescher Verlag, 1999.
Krempel, A. *La doctrine de la relation chez Saint Thomas. Exposé historique et systématique.* Paris, 1952.
Kung, H., and J. Moltmann, eds. *Concilium: Conflicts About the Holy Spirit.* New York: Seabury Press, 1979.
LaCugna, C. "Re-Conceiving the Trinity as the Mystery of Salvation." *Scottish Journal of Theology* 38 (1985): 1–23.
_____. "The Relational God: Aquinas and Beyond." *Theological Studies* 46 (1985): 647–63.
_____. *God For Us: The Trinity and Christian Life.* San Francisco: Harper Collins, 1991.
_____, and K. McDonnell. "Returning from 'The Far Country': Theses for a Contemporary Trinitarian Theology." *Scottish Journal of Theology* 41 (1988): 191–215.
Lafont, G. *Structures et méthode dans la Somme théologique de saint Thomas d'Aquin.* Paris-Bruges, 1961.
Lampe, G. W. H. *God as Spirit.* Oxford: Clarendon Press, 1977.
Lash, N. "Considering the Trinity." *Modern Theology* (1986) 183–96.
Lavalette, H. *La notion d'appropriation dans la théologie trinitaire de S. Thomas d'Aquin.* Rome, 1959.
Leclercq, J. "Influence and Noninfluence of Dionysius in the Western Middle Ages." In *Pseudo-Dionysius. The Complete Works,* edited and translated by C. Luibheid, pp. 25–32. New York: Paulist Press, 1987.

Liske, M. "Die sprachliche Richtigkeit bei Thomas von Aquin." *Freiburger Zeitschrift für Philosophie und Theologie* 32 (1985): 373–90.
Lonergan, B. *Divinarum Personum conceptio analogica*. Rome, 1959.
———. *De Deo trino. II: Pars systematica*. Rome: Gregorian University, 1964.
———. *Verbum. Word and Idea in Aquinas*. Edited by David B. Burrell, C.S.C. Notre Dame: University of Notre Dame Press, 1967.
Lossky, V. *The Mystical Theology of the Eastern Church*. London, 1957.
Lucy, J. A., and James V. Wertsch. "Vygotsky and Whorf: A Comparative Analysis." In *Social and Functional Approaches to Language and Thought*, edited by Maya Hickman, pp. 67–85. Orlando: Academic Press, 1987.
Mackey, J. P. *The Christian Experience of God as Trinity*. London, 1983.
Malet, A. *Personne et amour dans la théologie trinitaire de Saint Thomas d'Aquin*. Bibliothèque Thomiste 32. Paris: J. Vrin, 1956.
Mandonnet, P. F. "Cajétan." In *Dictionnaire de théologie catholique*, II: 1313–29. Paris: J. Vrin, 1923.
———. "Leben und Schriften des M. Thomas in einem kurzen Abriß." In *Thomas von Aquin*, edited by K. Bernath, I:11–23. Darmstadt, 1978.
Marenbon, J. *The Philosophy of Peter Abelard*. Cambridge: University Press, 1997.
Margerie, B. de. *La Trinité chrétienne dans l'histoire*. Théologie historique 3. Paris, 1975.
Maritain, J. *Degrees of Knowledge*. Translated by G. B. Phelan. London: Geoffrey Bles, 1959.
Martelet, G. "Theologie und Heilsökonomie in der Christologie der 'Tertia.'" In *Gott in Welt* (Festschrift Karl Rahner), edited by J. B. Metz, II:8–10. Freiburg: Herder, 1964.
Martin of Dacia. *Martini de Dacia Opera*. Edited by Heinrich Roos. Copenhagen: G. E. C. Gad, 1961.
Martineau, R. "Le plan de la *Summa Aurea* de Guillaume d'Auxerre." *Études et Recherches* 2 (1937): 79–114.
McCallum, J. R. *Abelard's Christian Theology*. Oxford: Blackwell, 1948.
McFague, S. *Models of God. Theology for an Ecological, Nuclear Age*. Philadelphia: Fortress Press, 1987.
McInerny, R. *St. Thomas Aquinas*. Notre Dame: University of Notre Dame Press, 1977.
———. "Albert and Thomas on Theology." In *Albert der Grosse*, edited by Albert Zimmerman, pp. 50–60. Miscellanea Mediaevalia, vol. 14. Berlin: Walter de Gruyter, 1981.
———. *Being and Predication: Thomistic Interpretations*. Studies in Philosophy and the History of Philosophy, vol. 16. Washington, D.C.: The Catholic University of America Press, 1986.
———. *Aquinas and Analogy*. Washington, D.C.: The Catholic University of America Press, 1996.
Meersseman, O., O.P. *Introductio in Opera Omnia Alberti Magni*. Bruges, 1931.
Merriell, J. *To the Image of the Trinity: A Study in the Development of Aquinas'*

Teaching. Studies and Texts, 96. Toronto: Pontifical Institute of Mediaeval Studies, 1990.
Metz, J. B. *Christliche Anthropozentrik. Über die Denkform des Thomas von Aquin.* Munich 1962.
Meyer, H. *Thomas von Aquin; sein System und seine geistesgeschichtliche Stellung.* Paderborn, 1961.
Michel, A. "L'Évolution du concept de 'personne' dans la philosophie chrétienne." *Revue philosophique de Louvain* 26 (1919): 351–83.
Moltmann, J. *The Crucified God: The Cross of Christ as the Foundation and Criticism of Christian Theology.* Translated by R. A. Wilson and John Bowden. New York: Harper and Row, 1974.
———. *The Trinity and the Kingdom of God.* Translated by Margaret Kohl. San Francisco: Harper & Row, 1981.
———. "Die Einheit des dreieinigen Gottes: Bemerkungen zur heilsgeschichtlichen Begrundung und zur Begrifflichkeit der Trinitätslehre." In *Trinität. Aktuelle Perspektiven der Theologie,* edited by W. Breuning, pp. 97–113. Freiburg, 1984.
———. *History and the Triune God.* Translated by John Bowden. New York: Crossroad, 1992.
Montagne, H. A. "Notre programme." *Revue Thomiste* 17 (1909): 15.
Mühlen, H. "Person und Appropriation. Zum Verständnis des Axioms: *In Deo omnia sunt unum, ubi non obviat relationis oppositio.*" *Münchener theologische Zeitschrift* 16 (1965): 37–57.
Müller, E. "Real Relations and the Divine: Issues in Thomas' Understanding of God's Relation to the World." *Theological Studies* 56 (1995): 673–95.
Newman, John Henry Cardinal. *Essay on the Development of Christian Doctrine.* London: J. Toovey, 1846.
O'Brien, T. C. "The Dionysian Corpus." In *Summa Theologiae,* vol. 14, pp. 182–93. London: Blackfriars, 1975.
O'Callaghan, J. *Thomistic Realism and the Linguistic Turn: Toward a More Perfect Form of Existence.* Notre Dame: University of Notre Dame Press, 2003.
O'Donnell, J. "The Trinity in Contemporary German Theology." *Heythrop Journal* 23 (1982): 153–67.
O'Mahoney, B. E. "A Medieval Semantic: The Scholastic *Tractatus de modis Significandi.*" *Laurentium* 5 (1964): 448–86.
O'Rourke, F. *Pseudo-Dionysius and the Metaphysics of Aquinas.* Studien und Texte zur Geistesgeschichte des Mittelalters 32. Leiden: E. J. Brill, 1992.
Otto of Freising. *Gesta Frederici.* Monumentis Germaniae Historicis 46. Hannover, 1912.
Paetow, L. J. *The Arts Course at Medieval Universities with Special Reference to Grammar and Rhetoric.* Champaign, Ill., 1910.
———. *The Battle of the Seven Arts.* Berkeley, 1914.
Paissac, H., O.P. *Théologie du Verb. S. Augustin et S. Thomas.* Paris: Éditions du Cerf, 1951.

Pannenberg, W. "Die Subjektivität Gottes und die Trinitätslehre." *Grundfragen systematischer Theologie* 2, pp. 96–111. Gottingen, 1980.
Park, S.-C. *Die Rezeption der Mittelalterlichen Sprachphilosophie in der Theologie des Thomas von Aquin*. Leiden: Brill, 1999.
Patfoort, A. "L'unité de la *Ia Pars* et le mouvement interne de la *Somme théologique* de S. Thomas d'Aquin." *Revue des sciences philosophiques et théologiques* 47 (1963): 513–44.
———. "Missions divines et expérience des Personnes divines selon S. Thomas." *Angelicum* 63 (1986): 545–59.
Pelikan, J. "The Doctrine of the Filioque in Thomas Aquinas and Its Patristic Antecedents." In *St. Thomas Aquinas 1274–1974, Commemorative Studies*, edited by A. A. Maurer (Symposium) I, 315–36. Toronto: PIMS, 1974.
Persson, P. E. "Le plan de la Somme théologique et le rapport 'Ratio-Revelatio.'" *Revue philosophique de Louvain* 56 (1958): 545–75.
Pesch, O. H. *The God Question in Thomas Aquinas and Martin Luther*. Translated by Gottfried G. Krodel. Philadelphia: Fortress Press, 1972.
———. "Um den Plan der Summa Theologiae des hl. Thomas von Aquin. Zu Max Secklers neuem Deutungsversuch." In *Thomas von Aquin*, edited by K. Bernath, I:411–37. Düsseldorf, 1978.
———. *Thomas von Aquin: Grenze und Grosse mittelalterlicher Theologie: eine Einfuhrung*. Mainz: Matthias-Grunewald, 1988.
Peter Helias. *Summa super Priscianum*. 2 vols. Edited by L. Reilly, C.S.B. Studies and Texts 113. Toronto: Pontifical Institute of Mediaeval Studies, 1993.
Peter Lombard. *Libri IV Sententiarum*. Florence: Collegi S. Bonaventurae, 1916.
Pieper, J. *Guide to Thomas Aquinas*. Notre Dame: University of Notre Dame Press, 1987.
———. *Problems of Modern Faith*. Chicago: Franciscan Herald Press, 1985.
———. *Tradition als Herausforderung*. Munich: Kösel Verlag, 1963.
———. *Über den Begriff der Tradition*. Cologne: Opladen, 1958.
Pinborg, J. *Die Entwicklung der Sprachtheorie im Mittelalter*. Beiträge zur Geschichte der Philosophie und Theologie des Mittelalters. Bd. 42, Heft 2. Copenhagen: Verlag Arne Frost-Hansen, 1967.
———. *Logik und Semantik im Mittelalter: Ein Überblick*. Stuttgart: Friedrich Frommann Verlag, 1972.
———. "Some Syntactical Concepts in Medieval Grammar." *Classica et Mediaevalia Dissertationes* 9 (1973): 501–33.
Porter, L. "On Keeping Persons in the Trinity: A Linguistic Approach to Trinitarian Thought." *Theological Studies* 41 (1980): 530–48.
Prestige, G. L. *God in Patristic Thought*. London: SPCK, 1952.
Rahner, K. "Bemerkungen zum dogmatischen Traktat 'De Trinitate.'" *Schriften*, vol. 4, pp. 103–33. Einsiedeln, 1960.
———. "Über die Unbegreiflichkeit Gottes bei Thomas von Aquin." In *Thomas von Aquin 1274/1974*, edited by L. Öing-Hanhoff, pp. 33–45. Munich, 1974.

———. *The Trinity*. Translated by Joseph Donceel. New York: Herder and Herder, 1970.
Ratzinger, J. "Concerning the Notion of Person in Theology." *Communio* 17 (1990): 439–54.
Richard, R. L., S.J. *The Problem of an Apologetical Perspective in the Trinitarian Theology of St. Thomas Aquinas*. Analecta Gregoriana 131. Rome, 1963.
———. "The Development of *Suppositio naturalis* in Medieval Logic." *Vivarium* (1971): 71–107.
———. "Introduction" to Peter Hispanus, *Tractatus* (Assen: Van Gorcum, 1972).
Robins, R. H. *Ancient and Mediaeval Grammatical Theory in Europe*. Port Washington, N.Y.: Kennikat Press, 1971.
Rocca, G., O.P. "The Distinction between *res significata* and *modus significandi* in Aquinas' Theological Epistemology." *The Thomist* 55 (1991): 173–98.
Roger Bacon. *Opera quaedam hactenus inedita*. Edited by J. S. Brewer. London: Longman, Green, and Roberts, 1859.
Roos, H., S.J. *Die 'Modi significandi' des Martinus de Dacia*. Beiträge zur Geschichte der Philosophie und Theologie des Mittelalters. Bd. 37/2. Münster, 1952.
Rorem, P. *Pseudo-Dionysius*. New York: Oxford University Press, 1993.
———. "The Place of the *Mystical Theology* in the Pseudo-Dionysian Corpus." *Dionysius* 4 (1980): 87–98.
Rosier, I. *La grammaire spéculative des Modistes*. Lille: Presses de Lille, 1983.
———. "*Res significata* et *modus significandi*: Les implications d'une distinction médiévale." In *Sprachtheorien in Spätantike und Mittelalter*, edited by S. Ebbesen, pp. 135–68. Tübingen: Gunter Narr Verlag, 1995.
Roy, O. du. *L'intelligence de la foi en la Trinité selon S. Augustin. Genése de sa théologie trinitaire jusqu'en 391*. Paris, 1966.
Ruello, F. "Saint Thomas et Pierre Lombard. Les relations trinitaires et la structure du Commentaire des *Sentences* de Saint Thomas d'Aquin." *Studi Tomistici* 1 (1974): 176–209.
———. *Les 'Noms Divins' et Leurs 'Raisons' selon Saint Albert le Grand*. Paris: J. Vrin, 1963.
———. "Une source probable de la théologie trinitaire de saint Thomas." *Recherches de science religieuse* 43 (1955): 104–28.
Ruether, R. R. *Sexism and God-Talk*. Boston: Beacon Press, 1983.
Schafer, P. O., O.F.M. *Bibliographia de vita, operibus, et doctrina Joannis Duns Scoti*. 2 vols. Rome, 1955.
Scheffczyk, L. "Die Trinitätslehre des Thomas von Aquin im Spiegel gegenwärtiger Kritik." *Studi Tomistici* 59 (1995): 163–90.
Scherer, G. "Die Unbegreiflichkeit Gottes und die Trinität bei Thomas von Aquin." In *Im Gespräch mit dem Dreieinen Gott. Elemente einer trinitarischen Ontologie* (Festschrift W. Breuning), edited by M. Böhnke and H. P. Heinz, pp. 258–75. Düsseldorf, 1985.
Schillebeeckx, E. *De sacramentele Heilseconomie*. Anvers, 1952.

Schmaus, Michael. *Der* Liber Propugnatorius *des Thomas Anglicus und die Lehruntershiede zwischen Thomas von Aquin und Duns Scotus.* 2 vols. Münster, 1930.

———. "Das Fortwirken der augustinischen Trinitätspsychologie bis zur karolingischen Zeit." In *Vitae et Veritati* (Festgabe K. Adam), pp. 44–56. Düsseldorf, 1956.

———. "Die trinitarische Gottesebenbildlichkeit nach dem Sentenzenkommentar Alberts des Großen." In *Virtus politica* (Festschrift A. Hufnagel), edited by J. Möller, pp. 273–306. Stuttgart: Friedrich Frommann Verlag, 1974.

———. "Bonaventura und Thomas von Aquin. Ein Vergleich." In *Aktualität der Scholastik?* edited by J. Ratzinger, pp. 53–77. Regensburg, 1975.

———. "Die Einheit des trinitarischen Wirkens in der Ost- und Westkirche." In *Renovatio et Reformatio* (Festschrift L. Hödl), edited by M. Gerwing and G. Ruppert, pp. 71–79. Munich, 1984.

Schmidbaur, H. C. *Personarum Trinitas. Dei trinitarische Gotteslehre des heiligen Thomas von Aquin.* St. Ottilien: EOS Verlag, 1992.

Schmidt, M. A. *Gottheit und Trinität nach dem Kommentar des Gilbert Porreta zu Boethius' 'De Trinitate.'* Basel, 1956.

Schoonenberg, P. "Trinity—the Consummated Covenant. Theses on the Doctrine of the Trinitarian God." *Studies in Religion* 5 (1975–76): 111–16.

Schoot, Henk J. M. *Christ the 'Name' of God. Thomas Aquinas on Naming Christ.* Louvain: Peeters, 1993.

———. "Aquinas and Supposition: the Possibilities and Limitations of Logic in Divinis." *Vivarium* 31/2 (1993): 193–225.

Seckler, M. *Das Heil in der Geschichte. Geschichtstheologisches Denken bei Thomas von Aquin.* Munich: Kösel Verlag, 1964.

Siger of Courtrai. *Zeger van Kortrijk Commentator van Perihermeneias.* Edited by P. Verhaak. Brussels, 1964.

Sikes, J. G. *Peter Abailard.* Cambridge, 1932.

Simonis, W. "Über das 'Werden' Gottes. Gedanken zum Begriff der ökonomischen Trinität." *Münchener Theologischen Zeitschrift* 33 (1982): 133–39.

Sokolowski, R. *The God of Faith and Reason.* Notre Dame: University of Notre Dame Press, 1982.

Stohr, A. *Die Trinitätslehre des hl. Bonaventure.* Münster, 1923.

Sträter, C. "Le point de départ du traité thomiste de la Trinité." *Sciences ecclésiastique* 14 (1962): 71–87.

*Summa halensis.* 4 vols. Quarrachi, 1924–48.

Sweeney, L. "Metaphysics and God: Plotinus and Aquinas." In *Die Metaphysik im Mittelalter,* edited by P. Wilpert, pp. 232–39. Miscellanea Mediaevalia, vol. 2. Berlin: Walter de Gruyter, 1963.

Synan, E. A. "Cardinal Virtues in the Cosmos of Saint Bonaventure." In *S. Bonaventura 1274–1974,* edited by J. G. Bougerol, vol. 3, pp. 5–31. Grottaferrata: Collegio San Bonaventura, 1974.

Thijssen, J. M. M. H. "What Really Happened on 7 March 1277?" In *Texts and Con-*

*texts in Ancient and Medieval Science,* edited by E. Sylla and M. McVaugh, pp. 84–114. New York, 1987.

———. "1277 Revisited: A New Interpretation of the Doctrinal Investigations of Thomas Aquinas and Giles of Rome." *Vivarium* 35 (1997): 72–101.

Thomas Aquinas. *Expositio super librum Boethii De Trinitate.* Edited by B. Decker. Leiden: Brill, 1955; reprint with corrections, 1965.

———. *Sentencia Libri De anima.* Edited by A. M. Pierotta. Turin: Marietti, 1959.

———. *Super Librum Dionysii De divinis nominibus.* Edited by C. Pera. Turin: Marietti, 1950.

———. *Sententia super Metaphysicam.* Edited by R. M. Spiazzi. Turin: Marietti, 1950.

———. *Opusculum De Ente et Essentia.* Edited by I. Sestili. Turin: Marietti, 1957.

———. *Quaestiones Disputatae.* 2 vols. Edited by Spiazzi, Pession, Calcaterr, Centi, Bazzi. Turin: Marietti, 1949.

———. *Quaestiones Quodlibetales.* Edited by Spiazzi. Turin: Marietti, 1949.

———. *Summa contra Gentiles.* Rome: Marietti, 1946.

———. *Summa Theologiae.* Ottawa: Garden City Press, 1941.

———. *Scriptum super libros Sententiarum Magistri Petri Lombardi.* Edited by Mandonnet and Moos. 4 vols. Paris: Lethielleux, 1929.

Thomas of Erfurt. *Grammatica Speculativa of Thomas of Erfurt.* Edited and translated by G. L. Bursill-Hall. London: Longman, 1972.

Thompson, J. *Modern Trinitarian Perspectives.* New York: Oxford University Press, 1994.

Thurot, C. *Notices et extraits de divers manuscrits latins pour servir à l'histoire des doctrines grammaticales au moyen âge.* Paris, 1868.

Torrell, J.-P. *Saint Thomas Aquinas, vol. 1: The Person and His Work.* Translated by Robert Royal. Washington, D.C.: The Catholic University of America Press, 1996.

———. "La vision de Dieu *per essentiam* selon saint Thomas d'Aquin." *Micrologus* 5 (1997): 43–68.

Trottmann, C. *La Vision béatifique: des disputes scolastiques à sa définition par Benoit XII.* École Française de Rome, 1995.

Vagaggini, C. "La hantise des *rationes necessariae* de saint Anselme dans la théologie des processiones trinitaires de saint Thomas." In *Spicilegium Beccense,* vol. 1, pp. 103–39. Paris: J. Vrin, 1959.

Vanier, P. *Théologie trinitaire chez Saint Thomas d'Aquin. Evolution du concept d'action notionelle.* Paris-Montréal, 1953.

Van Steenberghen, F. *Aristotle in the West.* Translated by L. Johnston. Louvain: E. Nauwelaerts, 1955.

Verhaak, P. *Zeger van Kortrijk commentator van Perihermeneias.* Brussels, 1964.

Wainwright, A. W. *Trinity in the New Testament.* London: SPCK, 1962.

Wéber, E. "Négativité et causalité: leur articulation dans l'apophatisme de l'école d'Albert le Grand." In *Albertus Magnus und der Albertismus,* edited by M. Hönen and A. de Libera, pp. 51–90. Leiden: E. J. Brill, 1995.

———. "Langage et méthode négatifs chez Albert le Grand." *Revue des sciences philosophiques et théologiques* 65 (1981): 75–99.
Weinandy, T. *Does God Change? The Word Becoming the Incarnation.* Petersham, Mass.: St. Bede's Publications, 1985.
———. "The Immanent and Economic Trinity." *The Thomist* 57 (1993): 655–66.
Weisheipl, J. A., O.P. "The Meaning of Sacra Doctrina in Summa Theologiae 1, q.l." *The Thomist* 38 (1974): 49–80.
———. "The Axiom *Opus naturae est opus intelligentiae* and Its Origins." In *Albertus Magnus Doctor Universalis: 1280/1980,* edited by G. Meyer and A. Zimmerman, pp. 441–63. Mainz, 1980.
———. *Albertus Magnus and the Sciences.* Toronto: Pontifical Institute of Mediaeval Studies, 1980.
———. *Friar Thomas d'Aquino: His Life, Thought and Works.* Washington, D.C.: The Catholic University of America Press, 1983.
———. *Thomas d'Aquino and Albert, His Teacher.* Pontifical Institute of Mediaeval Studies: The Etienne Gilson Series 2. Toronto, 1980.
White, V., O.P. *Holy Teaching: The Idea of Theology according to St. Thomas Aquinas.* London: Blackfriars, 1958.
Whorf, B. *Language, Thought, and Reality: Selected Writings.* Cambridge: Technology Press of Massachusetts Institute of Technology, 1956.
Wiles, M. *Faith and the Mystery of God.* Philadelphia: Fortress Press, 1982.
———. *Working Papers in Doctrine.* London, 1976.
William of Auvergne. *Opera omnia.* Paris, 1674; repr. Frankfurt, 1963.
William of Auxerre (Altissiodorensis). *Summa Aurea,* 4 vols. Rome: Collegii S. Bonaventurae ad Claras Aquas, 1980.
William of Shyreswood. *Introductiones in Logicam.* Translation and commentary by H. Brands and C. Kann. Hamburg: Felix Meiner, 1995.
Williams, M. E. *The Teaching of Gilbert Porreta on the Trinity as Found in His Commentaries on Boethius.* Analecta Gregoriana 56. Rome: Gregorian University, 1951.
Willis, W., Jr. *Theism, Atheism and the Doctrine of the Trinity.* Atlanta: Scholars Press, 1987.
Wilson-Kastner, P. *Faith, Feminism and the Mutual Relation.* Washington, D.C.: University Press of America, 1981.
Wippel, J. F. "Thomas Aquinas and the Condemnation of 1277." *The Modern Schoolman* 72 (1995): 233–72.
———. *The Metaphysical Thought of Thomas Aquinas.* Washington, D.C.: The Catholic University of America Press, 2000.
Wolfson, H. "Saint Thomas on Divine Attributes." In *Mélanges offerts à Étienne Gilson,* pp. 673–700. Toronto: PIMS, 1959.
Wolters, G. "Die Lehre der Modisten." In *Sprachphilosophie. Ein internationales Handbuch zeitgenössischer Forschung,* edited by M. Dascal, K. Gerhardus, K. Lorenz, and G. Meggle, pp. 596–600. New York: Walter de Gruyter, 1992.

# Index of Names

Aristotle, 39, 165, 167, 181, 208–10, 213
Athanasius, 8
Augustine, x, 1, 4–7, 10, 23, 35, 59–60, 68–70, 74–75, 91, 95–96, 101, 104–6, 111–37, 142, 200, 205, 209–10, 227

Barnes, M. R., 5, 7
Barth, K., 6, 8–9, 99–100
Bernard of Clairveaux, 43, 56–57, 126, 179–81, 186
Bianchi, L., 206
Billot, L., 37–39
Black, D., 222
Boethius, 27, 69, 75, 91, 93–94, 98, 137
Boethius of Dacia, 162, 165–72, 177, 181, 185, 189–90
Bonaventure, x, 4–5, 181, 230
Bourassa, F., 15
Brady, I., 206
Buersmeyer, K., 141, 167
Burrell, D., 19, 76, 143
Bursill-Hall, G. L., 161, 166–67, 174–78, 185
Busa, R., 210

Cajetan, 37–46, 48, 67, 76
Carroll, W. J., 192
Catania, F. J., 212, 214
Cavadini, J., 35, 70, 123
Châtillon, J., 111–16, 206
Chenu, M.-D., 13–23, 118, 178–81, 207–8
Colish, M., 71
Congar, I., 7, 23, 39
Corbin, M., 74
Cunningham, F. A., 161, 174

Daffara, M., 38
Dalmau, J., 38
Daly, M., 9
Deferrari, R., 209
Denzinger, H., 51, 110
de Régnon, T., 4–8
de Rijk, L. M., 177–78, 181–82, 185
[Pseudo]-Dionysius the Areopagite, xi, 4, 52, 163, 192–93, 204–30
Dionysius (Denys) the Carthusian, 229–30
Dondaine, H.-F., 208
Durantel, F., 205, 209

Easton, S., 208
Elders, L., 68
Emery, G., 27, 59, 74
Emery, K., Jr., 229
Entrich, M., 181
Ewbank, M., 223

Farrell, W. A., 38
Fortmann, E. J., 75
Fredborg, K. M., 176, 184

Garrigou-Lagrange, R., 37, 39
Gersh, S., 116, 125, 221, 230
Gibson, M., 207
Gilbert of Poitiers, 42, 55–57, 91, 93, 127–28, 131, 158, 180, 207
Gilson, E., 43, 188
Grabmann, M., 39, 164–65, 173–76
Gregory the Great, 126
Gunton, C., 8, 114

Häring, N. M., 127, 131, 207
Hayes, Z., 4–5, 174
Henniger, M., 92
Hill, E., 114, 120–24
Hissette, R., 206
Hornus, J. M., 192
Horst, U., 15–16, 57
Hoye, W., 79, 206
Hugh of St. Victor, 75, 207
Hunt, R. W., 176, 182

Joachim of Fiore, 51
John Chrysostom, 53
John of Damascus, 52
John of St. Thomas, 37
Jolivet, J., 166
Jordan, M., 141, 163, 172, 183
Jorissen, H., 7, 22, 25, 54, 57–59
Jungel, E., 8–9

Kasper, W., 7–8, 23, 100
Kearney, E. F., 129
Kelly, L. G., 175–76
Krempel, A., 89

LaCugna, C., 8–9, 23
Lafont, G., 7, 15–16, 23
Lampe, G. W. H., 8, 19
Leclercq, J., 208
Lonergan, B., 76, 114
Lossky, V., 221
Lucy, J. A., 183

Malet, A., 7, 15, 23, 26
Marenbon, J., 125
Maritain, J., 37, 39
Martelet, G., 13
Martin of Dacia, 165, 169, 174–75, 181
McCallum, J. R., 127
McFague, S., 9
McInerny, R., 32–33, 37, 39, 43, 115, 143–44, 188, 198, 207
Metz, J. B., 13
Meyer, H., 89
Michel of Marbais, 165
Moltmann, J., 7–9, 23, 100
Montagne, H. A., 209
Müller, J., 164

Newman, J. H. C., 117

O'Brien, T. C., 209
O'Callaghan, J., 195
O'Rourke, F., 218
Otto of Freising, 126

Paetow, L. J., 168, 176
Paissac, H., 71
Park, S.-C., 161, 173–74
Patfoort, A., 14–15, 39
Pesch, O. H., 14–18, 23, 38, 120
Peter Helias, 166–69, 176, 178, 182
Peter Lombard, x, 4, 12, 34, 56–57, 71, 158, 208, 234
Pieper, J., 19
Pinborg, J., 162, 164–65, 171, 176–80, 185
Prestige, G. L., 117–19

Rahner, K., 1–2, 5–8, 13, 23, 58, 99–100, 110
Richard of St. Victor, 4, 74
Richard, R., 72
Robert Kilwardby, 175–76
Robins, R. H., 167, 175, 185, 191
Rocca, G., 141–42, 157
Roger Bacon, 176, 208
Roos, H., 162, 166, 169–70, 174–75
Rosier, I., 167, 175
Ruello, F., 215
Ruether, R., 9

Sabellius, 83–84, 158
Schafer, P. O., 174
Schillebeeckx, H., 15
Schmaus, M., 4–5, 74
Schmidbaur, H. C., 8, 26, 57, 59, 67, 69, 79, 93
Schoonenberg, P., 8
Schoot, H. J. M., 161–62
Seckler, M., 15–18
Siger of Courtrai, 165, 167, 181
Sikes, J. G., 125, 127
Simonis, W., 7
Sokolowski, R., 148
Sträter, C., 15, 24–25, 38–39
Sweeney, L., 221, 223
Synan, E. A., 229

# Index of Names

Thijssen, J. M. M. H., 206
Thomas of Erfurt, 165–68, 172–73, 180, 185
Thompson, J., 114
Thurot, C., 175
Torrell, J.-P., 51, 205, 209
Trottmann, C., 52–53, 60, 206

Vagaggini, C., 72
Vanier, P., 26
Verhaak, P., 181

Wainwright, A., 117
Wéber, E., 212, 215–16, 228

Weisheipl, J., 181, 205, 208–9, 219
White, V., 37
Whorf, B., 160, 183–84, 203
Wiles, M., 19
William of Auvergne, 206, 208, 234
William of Auxerre, x, 208
William of Syreswood, 174
Williams, M. E., 93, 128
Willis, W., Jr., 23
Wilson-Kastner, P., 9
Wippel, J., 206
Wolfson, H., 204
Wolters, G., 165

# Index of Topics

Abstraction, 24, 45–46, 58–59, 141, 172, 221–22
Accidents, 45, 66, 86, 91–94, 127, 137, 152–53, 158, 194
Albigensian, 51
Analogy, 35–36, 39, 85, 89, 142, 162, 196–99, 211, 215, 229
Angels, 17, 52, 60, 121, 214
Apophatic, 52, 114, 130, 160, 163, 189, 192–94, 200, 204, 227–29, 232
Appropriation, 29, 36, 58, 68, 75, 101, 109, 110–19, 122, 127, 132–36, 231–32, 234–35
Articles of faith, 19, 34–35, 71, 103
Athanasian creed, 55
Attributes, 23, 28–29, 31–37, 52, 56–58, 73–74, 101, 109–16, 119, 122–24, 128, 132–37, 143–45, 173, 210
Authority, 22, 32–35, 55–56, 71, 120, 205–9

Beatific vision, 24, 50–52, 60, 206, 211
Beatitude, 26, 28, 50
Body, 12, 36, 65, 145, 201, 220, 225–26

Cappadocians, 4, 8
Cause, 13, 23, 26–28, 30–32, 41, 44–45, 50, 59, 80, 84, 90, 108, 128, 144–48, 151, 162, 165, 168–72, 177–78, 182, 190; defining the term, 83, 145; divine, 13, 27–28, 31, 59; knowing God as, 20, 30, 50, 53–54, 73, 77, 142, 212–14, 221, 224; naming God as, 144–46, 152, 193, 196–98, 200, 210, 212–19, 225–29
Charity, 52
Christ, ix–xi, 1, 6, 15, 17–19, 51, 77, 118, 120, 129

Commentary: on Aristotle's works, 181; on Ps.Dionysius' *Divine Names*, 210–12, 225 (Albert's), 205, 218, 223 (Thomas'); on Lombard's *Sentences*, 52–53, 198, 205; on *Summa theologiae*, 38–39, 46 (Cajetan's)
Composition, 36, 56, 61–62, 65, 97, 127, 141, 152, 179, 186, 202
Concept, 202, 224–25, 233
Condemnation, 52, 125, 206
Contemplation, xi, 192, 223
Creation, 9, 11–13, 16–20, 26–31, 46, 53, 59, 70, 73, 77, 83–84, 89, 100, 108, 110, 112–14, 118, 124, 128–30, 140, 150, 159, 201, 216, 227

Distinction: between God and creatures, 11, 86, 135, 148; of persons, x, 3, 9, 21–22, 24, 29–30, 32, 36, 39, 47–49, 51, 55, 66, 73, 75, 79, 81, 88, 104–5, 109, 111–13, 118–19, 122, 129–32, 134, 139, 151, 158, 233; of reason, 25, 42–43, 55, 57, 59; of relations, 87, 90; virtual, 44–46. *See also* modes.
Divine essence, 1, 5, 13–15, 21–25, 29–30, 37, 40–41, 45–65, 78, 81, 87, 91–93, 110, 127, 131–40, 147–51, 156–58, 163, 211–12, 217, 224, 230, 233
Divine freedom, 9, 19–20, 26–27, 31, 118, 130
Divine missions, 4, 68–69, 78, 104, 109, 130
Divine names, xi, 141, 188, 192–97, 199–200, 211, 219, 221, 227–28
Divine nature, 23–24, 31, 65–68, 80, 83–85, 90, 98, 106, 127–29, 145–51, 201–2, 210, 218–19, 221, 233; with respect to Persons, 27–30, 39–46, 61, 101–3, 110, 128, 140; unity of, 27, 65, 109, 113, 123, 137, 147–49, 158

# Index of Topics

Divine persons. *See* person.
Divine relations, 87, 90–93, 138

Emanation, 14, 16–18, 20, 22, 82, 84
Epistemology, xii, 78, 180, 222
Equivocation, 44, 144–45, 162, 184, 197, 216

Faith, ix–xi, 1, 3, 9, 19, 22, 24, 31–40, 70–72, 74–75, 103, 116–17, 120–21, 124, 130–32, 148, 196, 214, 218, 229, 232–34
Father, ix–xi, 3, 5, 9, 17, 25–28, 38, 42, 47, 51–59, 62, 65–69, 75–76, 83, 86–90, 92, 95, 100–110, 113, 118–19, 121–59, 200, 228–29, 235

Godhead, 30, 46–47, 61. *See also* Attributes and Person.
Grace, 17, 19, 52, 54, 77, 108, 121, 135, 137, 232
Grammar, 8–9, 19, 61–62, 67, 75, 99, 118, 133, 137–41, 157, 161–96, 202, 218, 232

Holy Spirit, x–xi, 3, 7, 26–29, 35, 38, 42, 47, 51, 55–59, 62, 66, 69, 73, 75–76, 83–88, 95, 98, 100–113, 118, 122–26, 129–37, 140, 147–55, 159, 229, 235
Human nature, 20, 30, 43–45, 62, 96, 140, 149

Image of God. *See* man.
Incarnation, 8–9, 14–18, 30, 33, 51, 58, 71, 96, 100, 110, 117, 121, 197
Intellect, 26, 31, 44, 49–52, 74, 78–90, 106, 135, 145, 170, 167–72, 178, 186–91, 194, 213, 217, 220–24

Light of glory, 33–34, 51–53, 60, 78
Logic, 33, 125–27, 162, 165, 175–77, 181–88, 227

Man: image of God, 36, 120; knowledge of God, 24, 30–32, 54, 58, 72–73, 77–78, 115, 139–43, 210–12, 216–17, 219. *See also* intellect.
Mathematics, 45, 167, 187
Metaphysics, 8, 39, 45, 62, 99, 165, 186–87
Modalism, 8, 100
Modes (manners): of being, 8, 79, 112, 137, 142–44, 152–55, 162–71, 179, 187–91, 194, 221–22; of signifying, 94, 112, 140–41, 150, 162, 165–91, 202, 216; of understanding, 136, 155, 166–72, 180, 186, 189–91, 223, 232
Monopersonalism, 25, 42
Mystery, ix, 1, 3–5, 9, 18–19, 29, 35–37, 59, 70, 74–76, 112–13, 120, 124, 126, 132, 136–37, 157, 180, 193, 218, 233

Negation, 10, 54, 82, 101–2, 107, 130, 142, 156, 187, 192–93, 197, 204, 212, 215–20, 223–28
Neoplatonic, 9, 14, 17, 209
Neoscholastic, 23–25, 37–39

Order of things, 12–16, 22, 199

Participation, 52, 155, 196, 199, 211, 217, 221–24
Pedagogy, 20, 101, 231
Person: definition of, 69, 96–99; divine, x, 1–4, 15, 19, 22, 25–31, 35–36, 40–43, 48–62, 67–76, 83, 86–87, 90, 100–104, 108–13, 122, 128–36, 143, 147, 150–58, 188, 233; human, 35, 65, 149
Personality, 64, 96, 165
Preambles to the faith, 32–34
Procession: within God, 2, 26–31, 35, 59, 68–69, 75–76, 79–90, 94, 98–108, 118, 135, 210–11, 219, 225, 230; of creatures, 9, 17, 21, 59, 83–84, 228

Revelation, x–xi, 1, 5–21, 29, 32–37, 40, 50–54, 71, 75–81, 85, 102–4, 114–22, 128–36, 139–40, 150–51, 157–59, 188, 191, 196–97, 219–24, 232–35

Salvation history, 2, 4–5, 8, 13, 15–19, 100, 118–19, 139, 158
Scripture, xi, 5, 10–11, 35, 79–80, 95–96, 117, 120–21, 125–26, 129, 139, 144, 156, 163, 192–93, 205, 209, 219–25. *See also* revelation.
Signification. *See* modes.
Sin, 18, 35
Son, x, 3, 26–28, 38, 42, 47, 51–59, 62, 66–69, 73–76, 81–90, 95, 98, 100–111, 118–37, 140, 147–48, 150–59, 228–29, 235
Soteriology, 16, 18, 30
Soul, 36, 52, 65, 86, 123, 169, 171, 213, 232

Subsistence, 25, 35–36, 40, 42, 45–46, 49, 58, 89, 97–101, 105, 108

Supposit, 38, 41–46, 61, 66, 133

Unity, 183, 196, 202; of the *Summa*, 21–22; divine, x, 3–9, 21, 27–31, 36–37, 40–50, 56–65, 73–75, 81, 84–86, 90, 93, 100–113, 119, 122, 129, 134, 137–40, 147–50, 156, 158–60, 233–35

University of Paris, 164, 181

Virtue, 32, 156

Wisdom, ix–xi, 34–36, 66, 73, 83, 101, 109–11, 122–26, 129, 132–35, 143–47, 152, 154–57, 193, 210, 212–22, 226–29, 235

Word, 6, 19, 30, 73, 80–81, 87, 100, 107–8, 134, 148, 228

*Thomas Aquinas' Trinitarian Theology: A Study in Theological Method* was designed and composed in Minion by Kachergis Book Design of Pittboro, North Carolina. It was printed on sixty-pound Sebago 2000 Eggshell paper and bound by The Maple-Vail Book Manufacturing Group of Binghamton, New York.

www.ingramcontent.com/pod-product-compliance
Lightning Source LLC
Chambersburg PA
CBHW031238290426
44109CB00012B/351